T0326524

Refusal to License Intellectual Property Rights
as Abuse of Dominance

Political Economics
Competition
and Regulation

Edited by
Udo Müller, Oliver Budzinski, Yücel Calbay, Jörg Jasper
und Torsten Sundmacher

Volume 11

PETER LANG

Frankfurt am Main · Berlin · Bern · Bruxelles · New York · Oxford · Wien

Claudia Schmidt

Refusal to License Intellectual Property Rights as Abuse of Dominance

PETER LANG
Internationaler Verlag der Wissenschaften

Bibliographic Information published by the Deutsche Nationalbibliothek
The Deutsche Nationalbibliothek lists this publication in the Deutsche Nationalbibliografie; detailed bibliographic data is available in the internet at http://dnb.d-nb.de.

Zugl.: Marburg, Univ., Diss., 2010

Cover Design:
Olaf Gloeckler, Atelier Platen, Friedberg

D 4
ISSN 1439-7528
ISBN 978-3-631-61001-5

© Peter Lang GmbH
Internationaler Verlag der Wissenschaften
Frankfurt am Main 2010
All rights reserved.

www.peterlang.de

Acknowledgements

This book is a slightly modified version of my dissertation thesis which I wrote during my time as a research assistant at the economic faculty of the Philipps-University Marburg.

I am most grateful to my supervisor Professor Dr. Wolfgang Kerber for the lively discussions and his thoughtful comments. His enduring support and encouragement were decisive for the VIIsuccess of the thesis. Furthermore, I would like to thank my second advisor Professor Dr. Michael Stephan for helpful remarks. VII

I am also indebted to Professor Dr. Josef Drexl (Max-Planck Institute for Intellectual Property Rights, Competition and Tax Law, Munich) and to Professor Harry First (New York University School of Law) for their support and valuable comments. Particular thanks go to Professor Dr. Oliver Budzinski (University of Southern Denmark) and Dr. Gisela Linge for the meaningful feedback and encouragement they provided me during the last years. For proof reading this thesis I am grateful to Amanda Wassermuhl.

In addition, I would like to thank the Max-Planck Institute und the Global Hauser Program of the New York University School of Law for facilitating my research stays. I am indebted to the German Academic Exchange Service (DAAD) and the "FAZIT Stiftung" for their financial support.

Abschließend möchte ich meinen Freunden und meiner Familie für ihre unermüdliche Ermutigung danken. Gewidmet ist diese Arbeit meinen Eltern Dorothee und Heinrich Schmidt, als Dank für ihre langjährige und vielfältige Unterstützung.

Claudia Schmidt
Berlin, August 2010

Contents

Table of Abbreviations..XIII

1 Introduction 1

2 The Situation to Date 5

  2.1 Abuse of Dominance and Article 102 TFEU.................................. 6

    2.1.1 Brief Introduction to Article 102 TFEU................................ 6

    2.1.2 Reform of Article 102 TFEU... 8

      2.1.2.1 The More Economic Approach 8

      2.1.2.2 Framework for Assessing Abusive Conduct...................... 9

  2.2 An Overview of Article 102 TFEU Intellectual Property Cases............. 11

  2.3 Comparison with American Caselaw 20

    2.3.1 An Overview of Abuse of Intellectual Property Rights Cases....... 20

    2.3.2 Are There Systematic Differences Between U.S. and EU

        Decisions?.. 24

  2.4 The European *Microsoft* Case: Introduction of the Incentives Balance

    Test? 27

    2.4.1 The Decision of the Commission 28

    2.4.2 The Judgment of the CFI 32

    2.4.3 Discussion of the Microsoft Decision 35

      2.4.3.1 The Requirement of Indispensability 35

      2.4.3.2 Elimination of Competition..................................... 36

      2.4.3.3 The New Product Requirement 37

      2.4.3.4 Objective Justification and the Incentive Balance Test..... 38

  2.5 Criteria for Refusal to License in the Article 102 TFEU Guidance

    Paper.. 42

2.6 The Incentives Balance Test as a New Instrument in Competition
      Policy? 45

**3 Do Competition Policy and Intellectual Property Rights Stand in
  Conflict With Each Other?** 47

3.1 Interface between Competition Law and Intellectual Property Law 47

      3.1.1 Conflict Theory 48

      3.1.2 Theory of Complementarity 51

3.2 Innovation as a Common Objective 53

      3.2.1 Justification of Intellectual Property Rights 53

      3.2.2 Economic Goals of Competition Policy 56

      3.2.3 Interface of Competition Policy and Intellectual Property Law
            from an Economic Perspective 59

      3.2.4 Tension between European Competition Rules and Intellectual
            Property Rights 60

3.3 Interplay of Competition Law and Intellectual Property Rights as a
      Means of Fostering Innovation 63

      3.3.1 Under Which Circumstances Should Competition Law
            Interfere with Intellectual Property Rights? 63

      3.3.3 The Incentives Balance Test as a Means to Redefine
            Intellectual Property Rights 66

3.4 Conclusion: What We Have Learned So Far 68

**4 The Appropriation of Innovation: How Can We Assess the Necessity
  of Intellectual Property Rights?** 71

4.1 The Optimal Design of Intellectual Property Rights in Law and
      Economics 72

      4.1.1 Patents 72

4.1.1.1 Optimal Length 73

4.1.1.2 Optimal Breadth 76

4.1.1.3 Optimal Combination of Length and Breadth for Single

Innovations 79

4.1.1.4 Optimal Combination of Length and Breadth for

Cumulative Innovation 81

4.1.1.4.1 Limits of Patents with Cumulative Innovation ... 81

4.1.1.4.2 Licensing Agreements as Solution 83

4.1.2 Copyrights 86

4.1.2.1 Theoretical Approach to Optimal Design 87

4.1.2.2 Empirical Assessment of Optimal Copyright Scope 88

4.1.3 Intermediate Result: Necessity of Case-by-Case Design of

Intellectual Property Rights 90

4.2 Innovation Research: What Do We Know about the Appropriability

Conditions for New Knowledge? 92

4.2.1 Preconditions for Successful Innovation and Imitation 93

4.2.1.1 Influence of Different Knowledge (Sources) and

Routines 93

4.2.1.2 Spillovers, Absorptive Capacity, and Path Dependence ... 96

4.2.2. Empirical Results 99

4.2.2.1 Effectiveness of Intellectual Property Rights in

Protecting R&D 99

4.2.2.2 Why Firms Do or Do Not Patent 103

4.2.3 Alternative Strategies to Appropriate R&D Returns 106

4.2.3.1 Secrecy 106

4.2.3.2 Lead Time 109

4.2.3.3 Complementary Assets and Technologies 111

4.2.3.4 Other Appropriation Strategies 114

4.2.4 Intermediate Result: Limited Relevance of Intellectual
Property Rights for Appropriation of R&D Returns 115

4.3 Innovation in Markets with Network Effects 118

4.3.1 Theoretical Digression on Innovation and Market Structure 118

4.3.2 Markets with Network Effects 122

4.3.2.1 Characteristics of Network Industries 122

4.3.2.2 Competition, Innovation, and Intellectual Property
Rights in Networks and Standards 125

4.3.3 Intermediate Result: Considering Differences between Market
Structure, Industry Features, and Innovation 128

4.4 Conclusion: Redefining Misallocated Intellectual Property Rights
with Competition Policy 129

4.4.1 Summary of the Previous Results 129

4.4.2 Limited Practicability of the Incentives Balance Test 132

**5 Towards a New Test to Assess Refusal to License Intellectual
Property Rights Cases** 135

5.1 Experiences from Previous Caselaw: Discussion of the Criteria for
Abusive Conduct 136

5.1.2 Indispensability Criterion and Elimination of Competition 136

5.1.3 Defining Harm to Consumers: Prevention of a New Product
or Impediment to Innovation 141

5.1.4 Objective Justification 144

5.2 General Standards to Assess Exclusionary Conduct 145

5.2.1 No Economic Sense Test and Profit Sacrifice Test 145

5.2.2 Equally Efficient Competitor Test 148

5.2.3 Consumer Welfare Test and Disproportionality Test 150

5.3 Introduction of the Innovation Effects and Appropriability Test 153

5.3.1 Basic Idea.. 153

5.3.2 Design and Structure of the Test in Detail 155

    5.3.2.1 Detecting the Anti-Competitive Effects 155

        5.3.2.1.1 Indispensability for Competition in a

        Secondary Market 155

        5.3.2.1.2 Harm to Consumers... 158

    5.3.2.2 Are Intellectual Property Rights Necessary to Protect

    the Innovation? 160

        5.3.2.2.1 Methodological Approach................................. 160

        5.3.2.2.2 The Criteria in Detail 163

    5.3.2.3 Imposing the Remedy 166

        5.3.2.3.1 Choosing the Right Remedy 167

        5.3.2.3.2 Enforcement and Supervision 171

5.4 Critical Acclaim 173

    5.4.1 Analysis of the Anti-Competitive Effects 173

        5.4.1.1 Indispensability Criterion and Elimination of

        Competition 173

        5.4.1.2 Consumer Harm.. 174

    5.4.2 Objective Justification 176

        5.4.2.1 Incentives Balancing v. Appropriability Test.................. 176

        5.4.2.2 Efficiency Defense v. Appropriability Test..................... 179

    5.4.3 Problems related to the Innovation Effects and

    Appropriability Test 181

5.5 Intermediate Result 183

6 Lessons Learned and Open Questions 187

6.1 Summary of the Results... 187

6.2 Fields of Further Research... 190

6.2.1 Implementing a Dynamic Perspective 190

6.2.2 Differentiation between the Various Types of Intellectual
       Property Rights (One Size Cannot Fit All) 192

6.3 Conclusion 193

Bibliography 195

Table of Abbreviations

CFI	Court of First Instance
DoJ	U.S. Department of Justice
EC	Treaty establishing the European Community
ECJ	European Court of Justice
E.C.R.	European Court Reports
EEC	Treaty establishing the European Economic Community
FTC	Federal Trade Commission
IP	Intellectual property
IPR	Intellectual property right
ISOs	Independent service organizations
O.J.	Official Journal of the European Commission
TFEU	Treaty on the Functioning of the European Union
R&D	Research and development
TRIPS	Agreement on Trade-Related Aspects of Intellectual Property Rights
ToL	Treaty of Lisbon
UCLA	University of California, Los Angeles
WGS	Working group server

1 Introduction

Article 102 TFEU (ex Article 82 EC) prohibits the abuse of dominance. Basically, this implies that firms with market power shall not abuse their strength to impede competition or to leverage their market power to another market. In contrast, intellectual property rights allow their right holders to exclude competitors from the usage of the protected item. If exercised by a dominant firm, conflicts with Article 102 TFEU may occur. In refusal to license cases, for instance, the intellectual property right of the dominant firm protects a good or service which is deemed necessary for competition on a related market. Thus, although the intellectual property right entitles the right holder to exclude others, a refusal to license by a dominant firm may hamper or even prohibit competition on a related market and may enable the dominant firm to leverage its market power to this market. That is to say, a refusal to license intellectual property rights can constitute an abuse of dominance according to Article 102 TFEU. In this context competition authorities such as the European Commission have to solve the question whether such a refusal to license is just a legal exploitation of intellectual property rights or an attempt to extend the own market strength with anti-competitive means.1

One of the most discussed cases in the last decade is the 2004 European *Microsoft* case. Subject to Article 102 TFEU, the European Commission scrutinized whether Microsoft's refusal to disclose interface information to competitors constituted an abuse of dominance. While Microsoft justified its conduct with the possession of intellectual property rights, the Commission rejected this argument and undertook inter alia an assessment of the effects on dynamic efficiency evoked by the refusal, the so-called Incentives Balance Test. In detail, the Commission analysed the impact of the refusal to license on the overall innovation incentives, that is, the incentives of both Microsoft and its competitors, and compared the result with the supposed innovation incentives in a hypothetical situation in which Microsoft did license the interface information. The Commission concluded that if Microsoft licensed the interface information, more innovation incentives would result than otherwise. Hence, the Commission took this result as further proof that Microsoft's conduct was anti-competitive. This proceeding can also be used to explain the term "dynamic efficiency." In economic terms, dynamic efficiency comprises the steady necessity of development processes, that is, the development of new products and services, quality improvement, process optimization, and so on. By considering in which situation more innovation incentives would occur, the Commission asked under what conditions dynamic efficiency could be better improved.

In the *Microsoft* case, the Commission entered uncharted waters. According to my knowledge, in no other refusal to license intellectual property rights case has the focus been so clearly on the effects on innovation. However, focusing on dynamic efficiency is a convincing approach as the promotion of innovation is at the centre of competition law and intellectual property law as well. Nonetheless, the Commission did not only earn credit for its decision – it has also been heavily criticized. Critics argue that the Commission did not act in accordance with previous caselaw and did not use solid economic criteria. In fact, it seems as if the Commission based its decision that the refusal to license would be detrimental to innovation mainly on the assumption that low firm concentration spurs innovation more than a concentrated market structure. That is to say, it did not base its decision on traceable economic theories. Despite these criticisms, the Commission incorporated the criteria applied in the *Microsoft* case in the new guidance paper to Article 102 TFEU. As such, these criteria are likely to be used for prospective cases of refusal to license intellectual property rights – although an economic foundation for such a proceeding is missing at present.

Against this background and considering the importance of intellectual property rights for the protection of innovation, it is necessary to further consider this issue, that is, the interference of competition policy with intellectual property rights in refusal to license cases. In order to maintain innovation incentives in the long run, it is essential to analyse in-depth whether such interference undermines dynamic efficiency or whether, on the contrary, interference is desirable since it spurs dynamic efficiency. At this point, the Commission does not provide a satisfying approach; instead, the *Microsoft* case and the criteria in the guidance paper leave more questions open than they answer. It appears as though a clear approach for all kind of cases is not possible. Instead, it has to be differentiated under which conditions an intervention would be welfare-enhancing in that it promotes innovation and under which conditions competition policy should abstain from intervention.

Consequently, this thesis pursues five main goals. First, it analyses which criteria were applied before the *Microsoft* case to assess refusals to license intellectual property rights. This allows an analysis of whether these criteria employed economic theories and in what respects the Commission departs from these "old" criteria. Second, against the background that intellectual property rights indeed entitle the right holder to exclude others from the usage, the relationship between competition policy and intellectual property law is scrutinized from an economic perspective. The leading question is whether competition law is authorized to restrict intellectual property rights or whether an intervention can be interpreted as a fundamental attack on intellectual property law. Third, provided that competition law may interfere in certain cases, what are the general economic criteria that can be applied to analyse the exercise of intellectual property rights (and their effectiveness)? Related to this question is the fourth research topic that analyses whether instruments exist that can take over the function of intellectual property rights, defined as the protection of innovation for the generation of profits. Finally, the fifth goal is the development of a test –

incorporating all the results yielded in the course of this thesis – that is capable of striking the balance between maintaining competition and upholding sufficient innovation incentives for (dominant) firms. Thus, it is the overall goal of this thesis to develop an economic-founded test that can be used for the prospective assessment of refusal to license intellectual property rights cases.

For this purpose, the thesis is structured as followed: Chapter 2 gives an overview on cases concerning refusal to license intellectual property rights in Europe and the U.S. This survey analyses whether competition authorities and courts have specified criteria they apply in the examination of anticompetitive behaviour. Special attention is paid to the European *Microsoft* case, as in this case the Commission balances the effects of a refusal to license on innovation against the effects of a license on innovation. This proceeding is known as the Incentives Balance Test. The chapter concludes with a brief introduction of the Commission's guidance paper to exclusionary behaviour in regards to refusal to deal cases. This step is important, as it clarifies how the Commission intends to proceed in future cases. Throughout this thesis, I analyse whether both the criteria of previous caselaw and the criteria laid out in the guidance paper are based on sound economic principles or whether we should aim for new criteria.

Having described cases in which dominant firms abused or were accused of abusing their intellectual property rights, the next chapter clarifies whether competition law is entitled to interfere with intellectual property rights at all. Specifically, Chapter 3 analyses the relationship between competition law and intellectual property law. Based on these results, I provide an economic explanation under which circumstances competition policy ought to interfere with intellectual property rights. The chapter concludes with an economic interpretation of the Incentives Balance Test that shall serve as a starting point for the further analysis.

Chapter 4 focuses on the question of which theories can be used to assess whether a refusal to supply curtails dynamic efficiency. In detail, the focus switches to the question of how an optimal, that is, welfare-enhancing intellectual property right should be designed and what influences such optimal design. Further, broader innovation economics, in particular evolutionary economic theories and theories from the resourced-based view of the firm, are reviewed in order to analyse whether these theories provide us with insights regarding a firm's possibility to innovate and to appropriate the resulting returns *without* intellectual property rights. Eventually, the chapter examines how markets with network effects can influence innovation and competition.

Finally, the findings of the previous chapters are framed together. After discussing the requirements for abusive conduct, the *Innovation Effects and Appropriability Test* is developed that counters anti-competitive conduct but also maintains the goal of promoting innovation. In detail, the test analyses the availability of alternative appropriability mechanisms besides intellectual property rights. The refusal to license is only anti-competitive when it can be shown that the dominant firm does not depend on intellectual property rights to protect its innovation. While the Incentives Balance Test of the Commission seems to be rather random and lacks an economic foundation, the Innovation Effects and Appropriability Test closes this gap and refers to the economic theories outlined in the course of this thesis. At the same time, the new test aims at the maintenance of the initial idea behind the Incentives Balance Test, that is, the promotion of innovation and, thereby, dynamic efficiency. In general, the Innovation Effects and Appropriabilty Test is advantageous in that, first, it is based on sound economic theories and, second, firms can predict the outcome of any analysis by competition authorities. The thesis concludes with a brief summary and an outlook for further research.

2 The Situation to Date

Intellectual property rights are generally assigned to promote innovation. Nevertheless, in a few cases, dominant companies might use them unlawfully to extend their market power. Throughout this thesis, we will focus on refusal to license intellectual property rights cases. In these cases, dominant firms refuse to license their intellectual property to competitors who consider the refused item to be essential for their own products. Since competition authorities are concerned that such refusals to supply are motivated by the desire of the dominant firm to foreclose its market power, in these cases, competition authorities may be forced to interfere in the enforcement of the intellectual property rights to guarantee free competition. These interventions are controversial, to say the least, as they restrict the rights of dominant firms and, so far, there are no distinct criteria by which to analyse those cases. Consequently, it is the goal of this thesis to determine what criteria can be applied in analysing such abuse cases and how we can apply these criteria.

After a brief introduction to Article 102 TFEU, this chapter presents an overview of those cases in which dominant firms have abused or were alleged to have abused intellectual property rights. This survey aims at a first detection of criteria that had been applied in previous caselaw and a determination of whether there is consistency in the application of these cases. We then turn to American caselaw in order to analyse whether it differs significantly from European caselaw and whether we can draw any conclusions from the American decisions. Based on these insights, we move on to the European *Microsoft* case. This case is one of the most discussed and controversial cases, since the European Commission introduced the so-called Incentives Balance Test in this case as a new instrument in competition policy. This test is the first standard in European refusal to license cases that explicitly focuses on innovation effects. Therewith, the *Microsoft* case parts from previous caselaw. However, since innovation can be seen as the core of intellectual property rights,[1] the Incentives Balance Test may constitute a basis for more considerations of how to deal with abuse of intellectual property rights. Nevertheless, the opinions diverge as to whether the test is an appropriate instrument. Since the Commission released its guidance paper for Article 102 TFEU cases in December 2008,[2] this chapter will

---

1   *Compare* section 3.2.1.
2   After issuing the Guidance in December 2008, it was published in the Official Journal in February 2009. *See* Communication from the Commission – Guidance on the Commission's Enforcement Priorities in Applying Article 82 EC Treaty to Abusive Exclusionary Conduct by Dominant Undertakings [hereinafter European Commission 2009], OJ C 2009/45/2. Please note that all references to Article 82 EC should be understood as references to the current Article 102 of the Treaty on the Functioning of the European

close with a brief analysis of what the Commission suggests for prospective refusal to license intellectual property rights cases and to what extent these criteria
depart from or correspond to the previous caselaw. Of course, special attention
will be paid to the question of whether the Commission will remain committed
to the Incentives Balance Test introduced in the *Microsoft* case.

2.1 Abuse of Dominance and Article 102 TFEU

2.1.1   Brief Introduction to Article 102 TFEU

European competition policy is based mainly on three components: the merger
control regulation (Council Regulation (EC) No. 139/2004); Article 101 TFEU
(ex Article 81 EC), which is the prohibition of cartels and other anticompetitive
agreements; and Article 102 TFEU (ex Article 82 EC), which I will focus on in
my thesis.

In general, Article 102 TFEU forbids the abuse of a dominant position
within the Common Market in so far as it may impede trade between the Member States. Article 102 TFEU does not further clarify the notion of dominance.
As such, in *United Brands*,[3] the European Court clarified the legal understanding of the concept of dominance. Accordingly, a company has a dominant position if it has the economic strength that enables it to prevent effective competition on the relevant market and that allows it to act to a large extent independently from its competitors and customers (*United Brands*: para. 2). To establish
that a firm is dominant, competition authorities and courts have to define the
relevant market. Generally, market shares are a first indicator as to whether a
firm inhabits a dominant position. There may also be other factors influencing
the economic strength of a firm; for instance, when a firm possesses relevant
resources (Goyder 2003: 273). As established by caselaw, holding a dominant
position itself is not illegal. Still, the dominant firm has a responsibility not to
use its market strength to impede competition.[4] Similar to the concept of dominance, Article 102 does not provide a clear definition of abuse. Instead, it gives
a number of examples:

> a) directly or indirectly imposing unfair purchase or selling prices or other un-
> fair trading conditions;
>
> b) limiting production, markets or technical development to the prejudice of
> consumers;

Union (as renamed by the Treaty of Lisbon, which entered into force on 1 December
2009).

3   United Brands Company and United Brands Continentaal BV v Commission of the Eu-
      ropean Communities, Case 27/76 (1978), E.C.R. 207 [hereinafter: *United Brands*].
4   This implies that an otherwise normal business behaviour might be prohibited for a do-
      minant firm if that particular conduct is capable of distorting competition (Loewenthal
      2005: 458).

c) applying dissimilar conditions to equivalent transactions with other trading parties, thereby placing them at a competitive disadvantage;

d) making the conclusion of contracts subject to acceptance by the other parties of supplementary obligations which, by their nature or according to commercial usage, have no connection with the subject of such contracts.

A more general definition of the concept of abuse stems from the Hoffmann-La Roche case.5 In that case, the European Court defines "abuse" as follows:

"The concept of abuse is an objective concept relating to the behaviour of an undertaking in a dominant position which is as to influence the structure of a market where, as a result of the very presence of the undertaking in question, the degree of competition is weakened and which, through recourse to methods different from those which condition normal competition in products or services on the basis of the transactions of commercial operators, has the effect of hindering the maintenance of the degree of competition still existing in the market or the growth of that competition." (*Hoffmann-La Roche*: para. 91)

In practice, exclusionary and exploitative abuses are often differentiated. Exploitative abuses are those that directly harm consumers; for instance, by imposing excessive prices or selling with unreasonable conditions (Goyder 2003: 283). In contrast, exclusionary actions aim at changing the market structure by impeding rivals and limiting competition (Loewenthal 2005: 457). Examples for different types of exclusionary abuse are predatory pricing, tying and bundling, exclusive dealing, and refusals to deal.[6] Simply put, the exclusionary conduct consists of impeding rivals and the exploitative action consists of abusive conduct that has a negative effect on the consumer.[7] The difficulty in determining abusive conduct, especially exclusionary conduct, is that it is often hard to differentiate whether a certain action is competitive or whether it is an anti-competitive strategy aimed at impeding rivals. For example, does a dominant firm lower its prices as a response to the competitive prices on the market or as a means of forcing a weaker competitor out of the market so it can raise the prices afterwards (Motta 2004: 411)? In regards to refusal to license cases, caselaw has established criteria that give guidance as to how to assess whether a refusal to supply is a normal business practice or whether it aims at the exclusion of rivals. In the following sections, we will reconstruct the development of these criteria, thereby focusing on refusal to license intellectual property rights cases. Throughout this thesis, we will also analyse whether these criteria can be justi-

---

5   Hoffmann-La Roche & Co. AG v Commission of the European Communities, Case 85/76 (1979), E.C.R. 461 [hereinafter: *Hoffmann-La Roche*].

6   For an overview on the different case groups, compare exemplarily to Goyder 2003, Korah 2007, and Motta 2004.

7   However, as Loewenthal (2005) stresses, this distinction between exploitative abuse and exclusionary abuse is not precise since most exclusionary conduct at least indirectly harms consumers (ibid.: 457).

fied from an economic point of view or whether they must be modified. However, before doing so, we will briefly analyse the principles laid out by the Commission in the newly introduced guidance paper to Article 102 TFEU.[8] I will start with a short discussion of how the guidance paper has been embedded in recent reform processes.

2.1.2   Reform of Article 102 TFEU

2.1.2.1   The More Economic Approach

Recent reform processes in European competition policy have been inspired by the so-called "more economic approach." Even though no clear definition exists of what the more economic approach is exactly, it generally can be understood as a new orientation of competition policy. Reverting to industrial economic models and quantitative methods in case analysis aims at making European competition policy more efficient and avoiding mistakes in decision making (Röller 2005, Schmidt/Voigt 2006). The focal point of this approach is the effort to enforce more fairness in each case (Einzelfallgerechtigkeit) by analysing the different economic facts at hand. This focus on individual cases implies a strengthening of the rule of reason and, at the same time, a weakening of per se rules (Schmidt/Voigt 2006). In contrast to a per se rule, which deems a behaviour to be anti-competitive without undertaking any further investigation when certain conditions are on hand, a rule of reason is open-ended. In other words, under a rule of reason, a competition authority has to conduct a full-market analysis and consider every argument made by the involved parties (Christiansen/Kerber 2006). Generally, a shift from per se rules towards rule of reason enhances legal uncertainty for companies. It is more difficult for companies to predict the outcome of the Commission's investigation process under the rule of reason, whereas per se rules lead to more transparency (Schmidt/Voigt 2005). The more the Commission has to be geared to per se rules, the less latitude it has, making the influence of different stakeholders marginal (ibid.). Nevertheless, deciding on a rule of reason basis is advantageous in that it is possible to consider the specific circumstances of a case and, therefore, to promote more justice in individual cases. As such, the employment of economic models and quantitative methods aims at a minimization of wrong decisions and at the protection of consumer welfare (Albers 2006: 1-2). Thus, under the more economic approach and the rule of reason decision it is in principle possible to allow an otherwise anticompetitive conduct if the positive effects for the consumers overweigh.

---

8   Since this thesis focuses on refusal to license cases, I abstain from discussing the criteria for the other case groups. Instead, I will only refer to the principles that apply to all kinds of exclusionary abuse.

Having completed the reform of Article 101 TFEU and the European Merger Control on December 3, 2008, the Commission published its guidance paper on exclusionary conduct under Article 102 TFEU. The goal of this guidance paper is to ensure that Article 102 TFEU only intervenes when a distortion of competition can be determined (Kroes 2005: 2). The guidance paper was preceded by a discussion paper in 2005 by the Directorate General for Competition (DG Competition)[9] and by the recommendations of the European Advisory Group for Competition Policy (EAGCP).[10] The long reviewing phase had given reason to fear that the Commission would never come out with its guidance paper, so it was welcome when published. According to the guidance paper, the Commission seems to follow an approach that focuses on consumer harm, although, as we will see, not always stringent. Regarding the more economic approach and the tendency to follow the rule of reason, the guidance paper contains both elements of per se rules and rule of reason analysis. In the following section, I will give a brief overview of the most important criteria.

2.1.2.2 Framework for Assessing Abusive Conduct

Within the new guidance paper to Article 102 TFEU, the Commission differentiates between four types of exclusionary conduct: exclusive dealing, tying and bundling, predation, and refusal to supply. While I will concentrate only on the refusal to supply cases throughout this thesis, I will begin by introducing some general principles laid out in the guidelines, which are valid for all kinds of exclusionary conduct; that is, the standard applied, the assessment of market power, and objective justification and efficiencies.[11]

First, the Commission notes that it will concentrate on abusive conduct that is most harmful for consumers (European Commission 2009: p. 5). That is to say, the Commission will refer to the consumer welfare standard.[12] However, this is not the only standard the Commission will apply. In paragraph six of its guidance paper, the Commission further mentions that emphasis will be placed on safeguarding the competitive process and on ensuring that dominant companies do not exclude their rivals via any other means than competition on the merits. While the guidelines the Commission always comes back to the importance of consumers and the criterion of consumer harm throughout its guidelines, it is not clear exactly how the concept of harm to the competitive process

---

9   *See* DG Competition discussion paper on the application of Article 82 EC to exclusionary abuses, Brussels, December 2005 [hereinafter Discussion Paper 2005].

10 *See* EAGCP 2005.

11 For a more general discussion of the new guidance, *compare* Botteman/Ewing 2009; Gutermuth 2009; Janssens 2009; Katsoulacos 2009; Killick/Komninos 2009; Lowe 2009; Motta 2009; Niels 2009; Sher 2009; Verheyden/Desmedt 2009 and Zhios 2009.

12 *Compare* also *to* section 3.2.2.

and the concept of harm to consumers are related and which concept will be preferred (Katsoulacos 2009: 5).

Another criterion depicted by the Commission is the notion of "anticompetitive foreclosure." As introduced by the guidelines, this requirement has two aspects: first, the foreclosure, that is, the dominant company impedes competitors from being active in the market and reserves the market for itself; second, the harm to consumers due to the foreclosure (European Commission 2009: para. 19). The Commission later lists factors that might promote exclusionary conduct, like the position of the dominant company and the conditions of the market (European Commission 2009: para. 20).[13] However, as Katsoulacos points out, the Commission does not clarify the relation between consumer harm and exclusionary conduct. In other words, it is unclear how the Commission will assess consumer harm when exclusionary conduct is on hand (Katsoulacos 2009: 5). Thus, even though the Commission tries to put the emphasis on consumer harm, it fails to formulate an unambiguous standard and therefore creates uncertainty for (dominant) companies.

Regarding the assessment of whether a company has market power, the Commission's guidance paper does not differ extensively from previous case-law. In general, there will be a safe haven below a market share of 40 per cent, although, in some cases, the Commission might investigate below that market share. For instance, when competitors are not able to put effective constraints on the dominant company despite the low market share (European Commission 2009: para. 14). For companies with a market share above 40 per cent, the Commission holds that the higher the market share and the longer the period this market share already lasts, the more likely is the existence of market power. Using the market share as an indicator of dominance, the Commission will still examine other factors like entry possibilities or countervailing buyer power before making a conclusion (European Commission 2009: para. 15).

The biggest change found in the Article 102 TFEU guidance paper is the introduction of an efficiency defence. The Commission acknowledges that a dominant firm may have an objective justification for its otherwise anticompetitive conduct. Accordingly, the conduct might be objectively necessary when it produces efficiencies that outweigh the negative effects on consumers (European Commission 2009: para. 28). To prove an efficiency defence, four condi-

---

13   One of the criteria for anticompetitive foreclosure worth mentioning is the "direct evidence of any exclusionary strategy." (European Commission 2009: 20) In other words, the Commission will consider the intent of the dominant company and consequently analyze internal documents in regards to any plans to exclude rivals (ibid.). According to Killick/Komninos (2009), this approach is mistaken as competition driven by the intention to win over or eliminate competitors. Instead, the Commission should focus on the effects on consumers (ibid.: 7).

tions, imported from Article 101(3) TFEU, have to be cumulatively fulfilled: 1) the efficiencies are a result of the conduct; 2) the conduct is indispensable for the realisation of the efficiencies, no less harmful alternative exits; 3) the likely efficiencies outweigh the negative effects of the conduct; and 4) the conduct does not eliminate effective competition (European Commission 2009: para. 29). The last requirement is an important one – even though conduct might evoke socially desirable efficiencies, it will still be prohibited because the dominant company maintains or strengthens its market position (Killick/ Komninos 2009: 6). Generally, we can assume that an efficiency defence will rarely succeed. As Katsoulacos puts it, the Commission treats potential efficiencies asymmetric to potential negative effects. Whereas the guidelines focus heavily on the harmful, anticompetitive aspects of particular conduct, they give much less attention to the efficiencies (Katsoulacos 2009: 6, 8). However, as the guidelines were not yet in place for the following cases, I will discuss the latter cases without referring to the new guidance paper. Nevertheless, the guidance paper also lists specific requirements for refusal to supply cases. Since caselaw has a significant influence on the development of the criteria for refusal to license cases laid out in the guidance paper, I will discuss them only at the end of the chapter.

2.2 An Overview of Article 102 TFEU Intellectual Property Cases

To date, the application of Article 102 TFEU to refusal to license intellectual property cases cannot rely on a long and developed tradition in legal practice. These cases are relatively rare, but recent caselaw shows that they are of growing importance. I will therefore give a very brief chronological overview of the present legal practice and illustrate the development of the different assessment criteria.[14]

One of the earliest cases in which the European Court of Justice (ECJ) established that a refusal to supply an input can constitute an abuse of dominance

---

14 With the commencement of the Treaty on Lisbon on December 1, 2009, the Treaty of the European Community (EC) is renamed in the Treaty of the Functioning of the European Union (TFEU). Due to the amendments Article 82 EC is renumbered in Article 102 TFEU (*compare to* the *Treaty of Lisbon amending the Treaty on European Union and the Treaty establishing the European Community, signed at Lisbon, 13 December 2007*, O.J. C 306/01 (7.12.2007) and *to* the *Consolidated Version of the Treaty on the Functioning of the European Union*, O.J. C 115/47 (9.8.2008). However, the cases described above had been decided under Article 82 EC or respectively under Article 86 EEC. Since the article did not change with regards to content, I will only refer to Article 102 TFEU in order to create uniformity.

was Commercial Solvents15 in 1974. Even though this decision did not involve intellectual property rights, it was groundbreaking for later judgments. The background of this case was that the dominant firm stopped supplying a raw input to compete with its customer in the downstream market for the final product. As the dominant firm was the only supplier of this input, the refusal to supply would have reserved the market for the final product for itself by eliminating the competition through its customer (Commercial Solvents: para. 7). Thus, the ECJ recognized that,

> "an undertaking which has a dominant position in the market in raw materials and which, with the object of reserving such a raw material for manufacturing its own derivatives, refuses to supply a customer, which is itself a manufacturer of these derivatives, and therefore risks eliminating all competition on the part of this customer, is abusing its dominant position within the meaning of Article 86 [now Article 102 TFEU; my remark]." (*Commercial Solvents*: para. 25)

This judgment was confirmed in the *Telemarketing* case.[16] This case concerned a dominant television company in the Belgian market that reserved the market for television advertising for a company belonging to the same company group as the dominant one. Thus, the television company refused to allow the telemarketing activities of third parties. While referring to the *Commercial Solvents* judgment, the court states that this behaviour is abusive as it does not result from technical restrictions and implies the possibility of eliminating competition (*Telemarketing*: para. 26-27).

In *Volvo/Veng*,[17] the ECJ firstly recognized that a refusal to license an intellectual property right may constitute an abusive behaviour. Volvo owned the intellectual property rights for the design of front wing panels for the Volvo 200 Series in the UK. Without permission, Veng imported into the UK imitations of these front wing panels from other member states of the European Union. In order to stop this import, Volvo refused to license to Veng. Thus, Veng accused Volvo of abusing its rights (Dolmans et al. 2007: 118). In a preliminary ruling, the ECJ rejected Veng's accusation. Even though the court could not establish anticompetitive behaviour in this case, the ECJ recognized that, theoretically, a conflict between competition law and intellectual property rights is indeed possible. According to the court, the refusal to license would have constituted abusive conduct only if Volvo had refused to supply spare parts to independent re-

---

15   Istituto Chemioterapico Italiano S.P.A. and Commercial Solvents Corporation v Commission (joined cases C 6/73 and 7/73), 1974, E.C.R. 223 [hereinafter Commercial Solvents].

16   See Centre belge d'études de marché - Télémarketing (CBEM) v SA Compagnie luxembourgeoise de télédiffusion (CLT) and Information publicité Benelux (IPB) (C 311/84), 1985, E.C.R. 3261 [hereinafter Telemarketing].

17   See AB *Volvo* v. Erik Veng (UK) Ltd. (C-238/87), 1988 E.C.R. 6211 [hereinafter *Volvo/Veng*].

pairers, demanded unfair prices for these spare parts, or stopped the production of particular parts even though there was still a demand for them (*Volvo/Veng*: para. 9). In other words, a downstream market has to be affected.

Nevertheless, such conduct was not evident in the *Volvo* case; therefore, Volvo's refusal to supply was not abusive conduct. Rather, the court highlighted that the purpose of intellectual property rights is to prevent others from manufacturing and selling the protected property (*Volvo/Veng*: para. 8-10).[18] As such, in the *Volvo* case, the court did not set up any criteria as to how to define abuse of intellectual property rights in the sense of Article 102 TFEU, but, as explained above, it listed some examples of what might constitute an abuse (Derclaye 2003: 688).

The *Magill* case[19] was the first case in which the court defined any specific criteria to assess the abuse of intellectual property rights. In this case, three television companies refused to license their copyright-protected program information to Magill, which wanted to offer a comprehensive weekly television guide in the UK and Ireland. Up to that point, the individual television companies had offered solely weekly guides for their own programs. Only daily listings of all programs were available in the newspapers. Thus, in April 1988, Magill filed a complaint at the European Commission that the three television companies were abusing their dominant position by not licensing their program information to Magill. The Commission established that the companies had infringed Article 102 TFEU and obliged them to disclose the information. As the appeal before the Court of First Instance (CFI) was rejected, the companies filed for the reversal of these judgments before the ECJ.

The ECJ confirmed the decisions of both the Commission and the CFI that the refusal to license these listings was abusive as it prevented the emergence of a new and well-needed product. Without a comprehensive weekly television guide, consumers had to buy three different television guides to decide which programs they would like to follow. Thus, the refusal to license the program information impeded the supply of a product that was not offered by the dominant firms. While the television companies argued that the very essence of copyrighting was to prevent others from using the protected items, the court confirmed the

---

18 A similar statement has already been made in the *Hoffman-La Roche* case in the context of trademarks. In that case, the court stated that "[i]t is sufficient to observe that to the extent to which the exercise of a trade-mark right is lawful in accordance with the provisions of Article 36 of the Treaty, such exercise is not contrary to Article 86 of the Treaty on the sole ground that is the act of an undertaking occupying a dominant position on the market if the trade-mark right has not been used as an instrument for the abuse of such a position." *Hoffmann-La Roche & Co. AG v Centrafarm Vertriebsgesellschaft Pharmazeutischer Erzeugnisse mbH (Case 102/77)*, 1978, E.C.R. 1139, para. 16.

19 See *RTE and ITP v. European Commission ("Magill")* (C-241/91 P & C-242/91 P), 1995, E.C.R. I-743 [hereinafter *Magill*].

decision of the CFI stating that the refusal to license goes far beyond of what is necessary for the essential function of copyright law, and, therefore, an objective justification was not on hand (Magill: para 55). Moreover, the refusal would enable the television companies to leverage their market power in broadcasting activities to a secondary market, namely the market for television guides. By concealing the essential information, the companies eliminated all competition in that particular market (*Magill*: para. 56).

Thus, in the Magill case, the ECJ found that under exceptional circumstances the use of intellectual property rights might be abusive. The court also established criteria to identify these exceptional circumstances (Magill, para. 50 et seqq.). If these criteria are met, the exercise of the intellectual property right infringes upon Article 102 TFEU (Thyri 2005, p. 389). According to these criteria, refusal to license intellectual property is abusive when:[20]

> 1. it prevents the appearance of a new product for which a consumer demand exists,
> 2. no objective justification for the refusal exists and
> 3. when with this conduct the owners of the rights reserve a secondary market to themselves by excluding all competition on that market (*Magill*, para. 54-56).

As an alternative to the new product criterion, the CFI introduced in the *Tiercé Ladbroke* case[21] the requirement of an essential facility function[22] to infringe Article 102 TFEU. In general, a product or service is an essential facility when the access to or the use of it is indispensable to be active in a certain market (Byrne 2006:1). Tiercé Ladbroke, a Belgian company bookmaker on horse races abroad, required a license to show pictures and sounds of French horse races. PMU und PMI, the owners of these intellectual property rights, rejected to license the pictures and sounds. In consequence, Ladbroke accused PMU and PMI of infringing Article 102 TFEU, because they abused their dominant position in the French market and impeded the introduction of a new product to the prejudice of Belgium customers (*Ladbroke*: para. 13). In its decision, the CFI established that the refusal to license an intellectual property-protected service may constitute an abuse if,

---

20 I will refer to these criteria as the *Magill* Test.
21 See Tiercé Ladbroke SA v. European Commission (Case T 540/93), 1997, E.C.R. II-923 [hereinafter Ladbroke].
22 The essential facility doctrine is an instrument developed in U.S. law, later also introduced in European and German Law. If the plaintiff can prove that the good or service to which access is denied is essential for her business, the courts can enforce access to the good or service in question. *See* also section 2.3.1 and footnote 38. For a detailed discuss of the essential facility doctrine, *compare to* Doherty 2001 and Lipsky/Sidak 1999.

"it concerned a product or service which was either essential for the exercise of the activity in question, in that there was no real or potential substitute, or was a new product whose introduction might be prevented, despite specific, constant and regular potential demand on the part of consumers." (Ladbroke, para. 131)

Nevertheless, in this case the CFI concluded that the television coverage of horse races in France was not essential for the business of bookmaking, especially because it was carried out after the bets were taken (Ladbroke: para. 132). That is, in this case neither the indispensability criterion nor the new product criterion has been met.23 Moreover, the court pointed out that Ladbroke was acting in a geographically different market than PMU and PMI and that there was no competition between these markets that could be eliminated or constrained (Ladbroke: para. 128-130).

In the *Bronner* case,[24] no intellectual property rights were involved. Nevertheless, the case is worth being mentioned for at least two reasons. First, the court refers a great deal to the cases discussed above in its decision, further illuminating the indispensability criterion. Second, the ruling in the *Bronner* case is highly relevant for subsequent cases (Derclaye 2003: 687). The facts are as follows: Mediaprint, a dominant newspaper publisher in Austria, refused to open its home delivery service to Oscar Bronner, who published a newspaper with only local distribution and a low circulation. Thus, Bronner accused Mediaprint of infringing Article 102 TFEU. Bronner argued that the distribution system was essential to compete in the market and that it would be too costly for him to reproduce this system (*Bronner*: para. 8).

The Higher Regional Court, Vienna, Austria, asked the ECJ for a preliminary ruling in this case. The ECJ decided that access to the home delivery distribution system was not essential to be active in the market. Since other distribution methods like mailing or sales in shops or at kiosks were still open to Bronner, the refusal to deliver did not eliminate Bronner from competition (*Bronner*: para. 41-43). Furthermore, no technical, legal, or economic reasons existed that made it impossible for Bronner to build his own home delivery system. According to the court, it was not sufficient to argue that due to Bronner's small circulation, the creation of his own distribution system was not a realistic alternative (*Bronner*: para. 44-45). Thus, the court rejected the claim of Bronner.

In the *Bronner* judgment, the ECJ based its decision primarily on the indispensability of the access to a facility, without, however, discussing the new

---

23 In detail, the CFI argued that the retransmission of the sounds and pictures of the horse races indeed constituted an additional and even suitable service for the bettors, but this service was not essential for the exercise of the main activity, that is, the taking of bets (*Ladbroke*: para. 132).

24 See Oscar Bronner GmbH v. Mediaprint c.s. (Case C-7/97), 1998, ECR I-7791 [hereinafter Bronner].

product criterion. Basically, this indispensability implies that: (i) access to the facility is essential for the intended activity or product of the competitor; and (ii) it is not possible to duplicate the facility. Hence, with these criteria the court provides clarity that the abusive conduct in refusal to license cases has its foundation in the indispensability of the access/use of the tangible or intangible property to maintain or develop competition in a downstream market (Eilmansberger 2003: 14). Moreover, with this judgment the court underlines that it is not necessary to put the competitors on an equal footing with the dominant firm regarding access to the facility (Kaestner 2005: 187-188). Aside from this clarification regarding the indispensability criterion, after the *Bronner* case it still remained unclear whether the new product criterion introduced in the *Magill* Test must also be fulfilled in refusal to license cases. Since in the *Ladbroke* case the accusation of abuse was already rejected because of no proof of indispensability, it was still open to debate whether the indispensability criterion and the new product criterion should apply cumulatively or alternatively. Some might argue that since in the *Bronner* case the decisive criterion was the indispensability requirement, either indispensability or new product has to be fulfilled. However, another strand of argument is that the court did not require a new product in the *Bronner* case because this case did not involve intellectual property rights (Byrne 2007: 327; Thyri 2005: 391).

The last modification of the *Magill* Test by the ECJ (before the *Microsoft* case) was in the *IMS Health* case.[25] *IMS Health* was a company that conducted market research for the pharmaceutical market. In Germany, it provided regional sales data on pharmaceuticals bought by pharmacies or wholesalers. Therefore, *IMS Health* bought raw sales data from wholesalers and broke them down into 1,860 different geographical regions. Finally, these data in the so-called "1860 brick structure" were sold to pharmaceutical manufacturers who used them to compare their own market share with competitors and to analyse developments (Gitter 2003: 163 et seq.). The brick structure was developed in close coopera-

---

25   See *IMS Health GmbH & Co OHG v NDC Health GmbH & Co KG (Case C-418/01)*, 2004., E.C.R. I-5039 [hereinafter *IMS Health* 2004]. This order of the caselaw is at the very least imprecise, as the Commission's decision in the *Microsoft* case is dated March 23, 2004 whereas the decision of the court in the *IMS Health* case stems from April 29, 2004. Thus, the Commission was not able to rely on the *IMS Health* decision in its analysis of the *Microsoft* case. Nevertheless, I choose this order because in the *IMS Health* case the court clarified last the criteria that should be considered in assessing abuse of intellectual property rights before it itself turned to the *Microsoft* case. Moreover, the judgment in the *IMS Health* case does not evoke significant changes in how to judge abusive behaviour but further clarifies the criteria applied. Therefore, this order shall help the reader to understand the different criteria. Due to the complexity of the facts, I will be more detailed in describing this case than the previous cases.

tion with the pharmaceutical sector. Thus, firms set their analysis methods to the 1860 brick structure (Gitter 2003: 266).

In 1999, NDC Health[26] entered the market for pharmaceutical sales data. The company tried to be successful with another regional structure, containing of 2,201 segments. As the customers rejected the product because they could not compare the new results with older data, NDC changed to a structure based on the 1860 brick structure of IMS Health (Kaestner 2005: 166 et seq.).[27] In consequence, IMS Health sued NDC for infringing its copyrights on the 1860 brick structure. According to the Regional Court and the Higher Regional Court, Frankfurt, the 1860 brick structure constituted a database and as such it was copyright-protected. Thus, the courts enjoined NDC from using the brick structure.

As IMS Health rejected to license the structure to NDC, NDC filed a complaint at the European Commission that IMS Health was abusing its dominant position. According to NDC, the brick structure had become an industry standard that was essential for any activity in that market (Kaestner 2005: 166 et seq.). After analysing the facts, the Commission confirmed the complaint of NDC and obliged IMS Health to license.[28] Specifically, the Commission found that the 1860 brick structure had indeed become a de facto standard and was therefore essential to compete in the market for regional data service. By refusing to license the structure, IMS Health was eliminating all competition in that specific market. Moreover, no argument put forward by IMS Health was capable of constituting an objective justification (*IMS Health* 2001: para. 180 et seq.). Regarding the requirement established in the caselaw in the foregoing cases that a downstream market must be involved, the Commission compared the circumstances of the *IMS Health* case with those of the *Magill* case,

"in that use of 1860 brick structure is an indispensable input to allow undertakings to compete in the market for regional sales data services in Germany. [...] there is an important distinction between the product, which is regional sales data services, and the brick structure in which data used to create these services is formatted." (*IMS Health* 2001)

---

26   To be more precise, the companies AzyX and PI were entering the market. But as NDC Health took them over shortly after that, I will – to simplify the case description – only speak of NDC Health.

27   Nevertheless, the service offered by NDC differs from the one offered by IMS Health; according to the later findings of the Commission, it contains different information. *See* Commission Decision of 3 July 2001 (Case COMP D3/38.044 – NDC Health/ IMS Health: Interim measure), OJ L59/18, 28.02.2002, para. 16.

28   See Commission Decision of 3 July 2001 (Case COMP D3/38.044 – NDC Health/ IMS Health: Interim measure), OJ L59, 28.02.2002, pp. 18 et seqq [hereinafter *IMS Health* 2001].

Therewith, the Commission distinguished between an input market – even though this was more or less theoretical – for the brick structure and the market for regional sales data services that was affected by the refusal to license. Due to this distinction, the Commission concluded that an abuse of dominance was present and thus obliged a compulsory license.

IMS Health appealed the decision at the CFI and applied for a suspension of the compulsory license. In a first hearing the court suspended the license as the decision of the Commission seemed at least to be problematic.[29] According to the CFI, the circumstances of the *Magill* and the *IMS Health* cases were not comparable.[30] For example, in contrast to the *Magill* case, both complainant and defendant were competitors in the same market in the *IMS Health* case. Thus, the Commission dispensed with the criterion of a new product, since NDC basically wanted to offer the same service as IMS Health. Moreover, the indispensability criterion seemed to be applied in a less strict way than it was in the *Bronner* case. Hence, in *IMS Health*, the Commission interpreted the three criteria developed in *Magill* as alternatives rather than as cumulative conditions. For these reasons, the CFI suspended the decision of the Commission.[31]

At the same time as these proceedings were taking place on the European level, IMS Health continued to enforce its rights in the German courts. The Regional Court, Frankfurt found that IMS Health should not be allowed to enforce its copyrights if the refusal to license constituted an abuse in the sense of Article 102 TFEU (*IMS Health* 2004: para. 17). Thus, it suspended the proceeding and referred the following three questions for a preliminary ruling of the ECJ (ibid.):

> 1. Does a refusal to license a copyright fulfil the requirements of Article 102 TFEU when the potential buyers of the competitors refuse products that do not rely on this copyright?
> 2. Does the extent to which third parties (that is, the buyers) participate at the development of the brick structure influence the abuse question?
> 3. Are switching costs of potential buyers of the competing product of relevance to assess the abuse of dominance?

With these questions, the Regional Court wanted to clarify: 1) whether it is a sufficient reasoning that the rejection by consumers of the product of a competitor makes the independent development of an alternative product impossible and

---

29 See Order of the President of the Court of First Instance of 10 August 2001 in case T-184/01R, E.C.R. II-02349.
30 For the following see Order of the President of the Court of 11 April 2002 in case C-481/01 P(R), E.C.R. I-03401.
31 In August 2003, the Commission withdrew its decision as there was no longer any urgency for an interim decision. One of the competitors, AzyX, as mentioned in footnote 26, had left the market, whereas NDC Health gained market share by using a 4000 brick structure. Commission Decision 2003/741/EC of 13 August 2003, OJ L 268, 18.10.2003, pp. 69-72.

therefore the refused good is indispensable for being active in the market; 2) whether the participation of consumers should be considered in the analysis since it may be responsible for the strong dependency on the dominant firm; 3) the role that switching costs plays in assessing the indispensability of the refused intellectual property right (*IMS Health* 2004: para. 22-23).

In regards to the second and the third questions, the ECJ stated that both the degree of participation and the level of switching costs of the potential buyers need to be considered in the analysis of abuse since these factors influence the degree of indispensability of the intellectual property right (*IMS Health* 2004: 30). In terms of the first question, the ECJ reverted to the criteria first applied in *Magill*. This time, the statement of the ECJ made clear that in addition to the criteria mentioned in *Bronner*, the prevention of the development of a new product was essential to constitute an abuse in the sense of Article 102 TFEU. That is, the firm that requested the license needed to intend to offer a product that was not offered by the owner of the intellectual property and for which there existed a potential consumer demand (*IMS Health* 2004: para. 48-49). Regarding the indispensability criterion, the court restated the conditions outlined in the *Bronner* judgment (ibid.: para 28). To prove indispensability, the existence of alternative solutions had to be examined, even though these solutions might be more expensive than or not as technologically advanced as the concerned product or service. At the very least, it had to be proven that the use of these alternative solutions would lead to an unprofitable production of goods or services whereas the use of the existing good or service would allow a viable supply (ibid.). The judgment also confirmed the necessity that two markets be involved. As the CFI explained, it was sufficient that a potential secondary market could be defined. In other words, the existence of two production stages was necessary in the sense that the product or service on the primary stages was indispensable for the production on the second stage (*IMS Health* 2004: para. 44-45). Therewith, the CFI defined the relevant market in the same manner as the Commission already did. But more importantly, the court emphasized that the refusal to license must be likely to exclude any competition on that secondary market (*IMS Health* 2004: para. 38). In general, the judgment of the court clarified the previous *Magill* test in the following manner (ibid.):

> 1. The intellectual property rights protected item must be indispensable for being active in a secondary market.
> 2. The refusal prevents the emergence of a new product for which there is a potential consumer demand.
> 3. The refusal is such as to exclude any competition on a secondary market; and
> 4. The refusal is not objectively justified.

Finally, on June 6, 2008, the Regional Court, Frankfurt rejected the complaint of IMS Health against NDC, thereby following the suggestions of the court.

2.3 Comparison with American Caselaw

Before discussing the most recent case concerning refusal to license intellectual property rights, that is, the European *Microsoft* case, we will turn to American caselaw[32] in order to analyse whether we can learn something from the decisions made on the other side of the Atlantic. In contrast to European caselaw, there are only a few refusal to license cases in American caselaw in which the courts forced an intellectual property right holder to license. Instead, in most cases, the courts found that the right holder indeed had the right to refuse to license. Still, it is unclear whether the U.S. proceeding significantly differs from the European. Before we turn to a comparison of both U.S. and EU decisions, I will give a brief introduction to American caselaw under Section 2 of the *Sherman Act*, involving refusal to license intellectual property rights.

2.3.1   An Overview of Abuse of Intellectual Property Rights Cases

In *Data General*,[33] independent service organizations (ISOs) were repairing computer hardware produced by Data General. Data General was not only manufacturing computer hardware, but it also offered service for the computers. In an attempt to increase its market share in servicing computer, Data General terminated the license for the necessary diagnostic software. As the ISOs continued using the software without its permission, Data General sued for copyright infringement, and Grumman, one of the ISOs, reacted with a complaint for violating Section 2 of the *Sherman Act* (Hovenkamp/Janis/Lemley 2005: 30).[34]

---

32   Please note that the following provides only a very small and incomplete part of the relevant caselaw. The purpose of this section is not to give a comprehensive overview but to show to give a better understanding of the U.S. cases. A detailed analysis of the American caselaw on intellectual property rights would go beyond the framework of the present thesis and would contribute only to a limited degree to a better understanding of the research question.

33   *Data General Corporation v. Grumman System Corporation*, 36 F.3d 1147 (1st Circuit 1994) [hereinafter Data General].

34   Section 2 of the *Sherman Act* is essentially the American equivalent to Article 102 TFEU. However, even though both rules are quite similar, there are some differences. In Article 102 TFEU, the focus is on abuse of dominance as described in section 2.1 above, whereas Section 2 of the *Sherman Act* prohibits the illegal acquisition or maintenance of a monopoly in a market. Thus, the focus of Section 2 of the *Sherman Act* is on *monopolization* or *attempts at monopolization*. Following the interpretation of the DoJ, "monopolization requires (1) monopoly power and (2) the willful acquisition or maintenance of that power as distinguished from growth or development as a consequence of a superior product, business acumen, or historic accident," (DoJ 2008: 5), whereas attempted monopolization "requires (1) anticompetitive conduct, (2) a specific intent to monopolize, and (3) a dangerous probability of achieving monopoly power." (DoJ

In trying to avoid counterbalancing the two statutes, the First Circuit tried to read the laws of intellectual property rights and antitrust in light of each other (ibid.). However, the court made the following presumption:

> "[W]hile exclusionary conduct can include a monopolist's unilateral refusal to license a copyright, an author's desire to exclude others from use of its copyrighted work is a presumptively valid business justification for immediate harm to consumers." (*Data General*: para. 1187)

In a footnote, the court added that there might be cases in which antitrust liability does not conflict with the objectives of copyright law. Nevertheless, the First Circuit acknowledges that even though Data General may extend its substantial market power, it has already created a software program that significantly benefits the users and further sets out to improve the quality of its products. Although Data General's refusal to license may harm competitors, consumers are likely to be better off not only in the short-term but also in the long-term. Therefore, and due to the absence of any significant market entry barrier, the court rejected the accusation of exclusionary conduct (*Data General*: 1189).

Three years later, the Ninth Circuit heard the case of *Image Technical Service v. Eastman Kodak*.[35] In this case, Kodak, a manufacturer of photocopiers, also refused to sell parts to the ISOs to extend its market power in the servicing market. In contrast to General Data, Kodak first did not refer to its intellectual property rights to justify its behaviour. It took almost 10 years of litigation before Kodak used its intellectual property rights in its defence (Hovenkamp/Janis/Lemley 2005: 31). Overruling the objection that the goods were intellectual property right-protected, the court found Kodak guilty of engaging in monopolization (*Kodak*: 1212). However, the Ninth Circuit did acknowledge the presumption in the *General Data* case, stating that it is not in general anticompetitive if a monopolist or a firm with market power refuses to license its intellectual property right-protected goods (*Kodak*: 1216). Nonetheless, the court found that in *Kodak* case, the reference to the intellectual property rights were of only pretextual nature (Pate 2002: 432, 433), especially as Kodak did not refer to its intellectual property rights from the outset of the case.[36] The court also referred to the fact that Kodak had not differentiated between patented and not-

---

2008: 6). For a detailed overview on the principles of Section 2 of the *Sherman Act*, compare exemplarily to DoJ 2008.

35 125 F.3d 1195 (9th Circuit 1997) [hereinafter *Kodak*].

36 As McCullen (2001) explains, this judgment can be regarded as a rebuttable presumption. Accordingly, a patent holder's refusal to license or sell an intellectual property right-protected good is presumptively a legal-business method to exclude others. However, the (potential) licensee or buyer may rebut this presumption if she is able to show that the intellectual property right holder's rejection was not based on the objective to protect its intellectual property and its fruits, but rather uses the intellectual property rights as pretext for anticompetitive behavior (ibid.: 470).

patented parts, instead refusing to sell any of them to the ISOs, while continuing to sell them to its major customers. Thus, the court concluded that the refusal of Kodak to sell was solely motivated by the objective of conferring its market power to the downstream market, that is, the servicing of Kodak photocopiers (Pate 2002: 433).

In *Aldridge v. Microsoft Corp.*,[37] Aldridge, the seller of a disk caching program, sued Microsoft for infringing Section 2 of the *Sherman Act*. With the introduction of Windows 95, Microsoft had included its own disk caching function in the computer operating system. At the same time, Microsoft denied access to Windows 95 so that Aldridge's program was no longer able to run on the operating system. Aldridge argued that the access to Windows 95 was an essential facility for its disk caching program since otherwise it could not reach the majority of the users (Hovenkamp/Janis/Lemley 2005: 22). Referring to the Essential Facilities Doctrine, the court denied that access to Windows 95 was essential. The doctrine is fulfilled when the following criteria are met: 1. the essential facility is controlled by a monopolist; 2. the competitors are practically or reasonably not able to duplicate the facility; 3. the use of the facility is denied to the competitor; and 4. access or provision to the facility is feasible.[38] Stating that it might be indeed necessary for the plaintiff, the court nevertheless explained that access to Windows 95 was not an essential facility under antitrust law. A product or service can only be qualified as an essential facility when it is not only vital to the business of the plaintiff but also to the whole market.[39] Furthermore, the court expressed its concerns regarding punishing a monopolist for improving its products.

> "Such a result would inhibit, not promote, competition in the market. The antitrust laws do not require a competitor to maintain archaic or outdated technology; even monopolists may improve their products." (995 F. Supp. 728, 753 (S.D. Tex. 1998) 753)

With the introduction of Windows 95, Microsoft had corrected problems in its previous system that Aldridge used to rectify. Thus, even though the court did

---

37   The David Aldridge Company et al v. Microsoft Corporation, 995 F. Supp. 728 (S.D. Tex. 1998).

38   *MCI Comm. Corp. v. AT&T*, 708 F.2d 1081 (7th Circuit 1983). The Essential Facilities Doctrines basically goes back to the 1912 Supreme Court decision in *United States v. Terminal Railroad Association of St. Louis*, 224 U.S. 382 (1912). In this case, the defendant, a consortium of different companies, had a monopoly over all railroad connections servicing St. Louis. Railroad companies not involved in the association therefore could not offer any connections to St. Louis. Thus, the Supreme Court ordered that the association either open up its membership or charge fees that put other railroad companies on an equal level (Doherty 2001: 399).

39   Basically, the essential facility requirement can be compared to the indispensability criterion in European caselaw.

not refer to intellectual property rights, it clearly states its concerns about Microsoft's incentives to innovate (Hovenkamp/Janis/Lemley 2005: 23).

The courts also employed the essential facility doctrine in *Intergraph Corp. v. Intel Corp.*[40] Intergraph, a computer hardware manufacturing company using Intel microprocessors and Intel architecture, sued Intel for discontinuing the supply of microprocessors and proprietary information. The disruption of supply had been the response of Intel to a threat by Intergraph to sue Intel's customers for infringing Intergraph's patents. Thus, Intel suspended its supply to Intergraph unless Intergraph abandoned the patent suit (*Intel*: 1350). In Intergraph's claim against Intel, Intergraph argued that the access to Intel's chips and technical know-how was indispensable to its business and therefore an essential facility (Hovenkamp/Janis/Lemley 2005: 21). In finding that the intellectual property rights connected to the chips and technology indeed constituted essential facilities, the district court granted a preliminary injunction (ibid). The Federal District rejected this decision. According to the court, an essential facility claim is only valid when the owner of the essential facility and the plaintiff are competing in the market for which the access to the essential facility is vital. The court found that Intel and Intergraph did not compete at all and thus Intergraph could not rely on the essential facility argument (Intel: 1357 et seq.).

Similar to the *Kodak* case, in *In re Independent Service Organization Antitrust Litigation*,[41] better known as the *Xerox* case, Xerox, a producer of high-volume photocopiers and laser printers, suspended selling parts to independent service organizations. These parts were used to service Xerox photocopiers and printers. Only end-users were now able to buy the parts. When both end-users and ISOs brought a class action against Xerox, Xerox agreed in 1994 to sell parts again to ISOs whereas the end-users could now license the diagnostic software. The ISOs were allowed to act as the agents of the customers and to order as well as use the software for the end-users (Melamed/Stoeppelwerth 2002: 408). One of the ISOs, CSU, decided to file a lone complaint against Xerox, claiming that Xerox's previous conduct, that is the refusal to sell the parts and license the software, violated Section 2 of the *Sherman Act*. Xerox, in response, defended its refusal with the intellectual property rights protecting both the parts and the software. Accordingly, the refusals were in line with the law and could not be punished under antitrust law. The district court agreed with Xerox, explaining that unless the intellectual property rights were unlawfully acquired, the refusal of the intellectual property right holder to deal could not constitute anti-competitive conduct, independently of the motivation of the

---

40   *Intergraph Corp. v. Intel Corp.*, 195 F.3d 1346 (Federal Circuit 1999) [hereinafter: *Intel*].
41   In re Independent Service Organizations Antitrust Litigation, 203 F.3d 1322 (Federal Circuit 2000) [hereinafter Xerox].

property right holder (Melamed/ Stoeppelwerth 2002: 408). The Federal Circuit confirmed this judgment, asserting that there was "no reported case in which a court has imposed antitrust liability for a unilateral refusal to sell or license a patent" (*Xerox*: para. 1326). Furthermore, the court held that besides "illegal tying, fraud [...], or sham litigation, the patent holder may enforce the statutory right to exclude [...] free from liability under the antitrust laws" (*Xerox*: para. 1327).

In sum, to date there is no consistent approach as to how to deal with intellectual property rights in U.S. law. Until now, no intellectual property right has been identified as an essential facility; however, in neither the *Intel* nor the *Aldridge* case did the court ultimately deny that an intellectual property right *can* constitute an essential facility (Schweitzer 2007: 9). The only case in which abusive behaviour has been contested is the *Kodak* case, which was unique in that the company did not really rely on its intellectual property rights.

Nonetheless, the debate as to how to deal with the unilateral refusal to license is still ongoing in the U.S. In *Trinko*[42] – a non-intellectual property-related case – the court took a very clear position in favour of the dominant company, that is, no duty to deal. According to the U.S. Supreme Court, the duty to share erodes incentives to investments and innovation. Furthermore, the court stated that it has never held that there is an essential facility demanding access to a facility as well in the absence of anticompetitive conduct. The court highlighted that antitrust does not impose obligations to dominant firms only because one might assume that consumers are better off (Fox 2008: 31).

Together with the other, intellectual property-related decisions, this judgment leads to the assumption that U.S. courts are in general unwilling to restrict the behaviour of dominant firms, especially if significant investments are involved. Instead, the courts highlight the importance of not undermining incentives for innovation and investment.

2.3.2   Are There Systematic Differences Between U.S. and EU Decisions?

Having briefly reviewed the most important cases in American caselaw, the question is now whether those decisions differ from the European decisions and, if so, in what regard and what can we learn from this. Even though, at first glance, one might tend to argue that U.S. courts are more reluctant to interfere

---

42   *Verizon Communications Inc. v Law Offices of Curtis V. Trinko, LLP*, 540 US 398 (2004) [hereinafter *Trinko*]. Trinko, an incumbent telecommunication company, refused to give full access to the local loop to its local competitors. Thus, the question was whether antitrust law can impose a duty on Trinko (Fox 2005: 154). For a detailed discussion of the *Trinko* case, *compare* exemplarily Economides 2005, Fox 2005, and Rubin 2005.

with intellectual property rights and more highly value them than do European courts, we have to be careful about drawing such a conclusion. First, it notable that, in most cases, U.S. courts refer to similar criteria as the ECJ and the European Commission. The similarity becomes obvious when comparing the Essential Facilities Doctrine with the *Magill* Test. Generally, we can say that the "essential requirement" equals the indispensability requirement. It relates to a downstream market, that is, access is necessary to compete on the downstream market, and competitors are not able to duplicate it. That is to say, the refusal to license must be connected with the possibility of leveraging.[43] Even though the European Commission has never explicitly based a decision on the Essential Facilities Doctrine, the doctrine has been associated with the criteria in *Magill*, *Bronner*, and *IMS Health*.[44]

Generally, the U.S. courts and also the U.S. intellectual property guidelines highlight the equality of tangible and intangible property in regards to the responsibility against antitrust law (e.g. *Microsoft* 2001; DoJ/ FTC 1995). As Melamed and Stoeppelwerth (2002) explain, neither the *Copyright Act* nor the *Patents Act* or even their legislative history gives any hint as to an intent on the part of Congress to apply competition law differently to intellectual property than to tangible property (ibid.: 410).[45] Thus, although the importance of creation and the protection of original works are highly regarded by Congress and the courts, this does not mean that the *Sherman Act* explicitly exempts those activities from antitrust liability. According to the Supreme Court and the 10th Circuit, a monopolistic refusal to license a copyright should not be deemed as a *per se* violation of antitrust laws but still might be anti-competitive under a *rule of reason* analysis.[46] In highlighting that a refusal to license intellectual property rights can only be anti-competitive under *exceptional circumstances* (e.g. *Magill*: para. 50), the European Commission basically follows a similar approach.

As pointed out in *Mallinckrodt v. Mediapart*, the decisive criterion in the U.S. is whether a restriction having an anticompetitive effect lies within the scope of the patent grant:

---

43 A more comprehensive discussion of the indispensability criterion is provided in section 5.1.2.

44 Compare exemplarily Derclaye 2003; Gitter 2003; Lang 2008; Lévêque 2005; Müller/ Rodenhausen 2008. Nevertheless, the *Magill* Test differs from the doctrine since it requires in addition the impediment of a new product.

45 From this point of view, it is either not clear why an application of competition law to abuse of intellectual property cases should evoke inconsistent legal standards for the intellectual property holder (Melamed/Stoeppelwerth 2002: 410).

46 See *Broadcast Music, Inc. v. CBS, Inc.*, 441 U.S. 1, 19, 99, S.Ct. 1551, 1562, 60 l.Ed.2d 1 (1979); *Rural Tel. Serv. Co. v. Feist Publications, Inc.*, 957 F.2d 765, 767-769 (10th Cir.).

"Should the restriction be found to be reasonably within the patent grant, i.e., that it
relates to subject matter within the scope of patent claims, that ends the inquiry."
(*Mallinckrodt, Inc. v. Mediapart Inc.*, 976 F.2d. 700, 708 (Fed. Circ. 1992)

The intellectual property right holder is only liable under competition laws when
her conduct goes beyond the scope of the right; for instance, when the right holder tries to control competition in another market (ibid.). In contrast, competition law will tolerate a monopolist or a company with substantial market power
competing on the merits, even though competitors might be hampered.[47] In so
doing, the court recognizes that innovation is connected with risk and uncertainty. Restricting the exploitation of the successful innovations would have a
negative effect on competition. However, if a firm behaves anti-competitively
beyond the innovation and beyond the scope of its intellectual property rights,
that is if it is not competing on the merits but trying to impede competition, then
the firm is liable under competition law. It is notable that this approach again
does not significantly differ from the European one. Consider, for instance, the
Volvo/Veng case. Here, the Court highlighted that abusive conduct can only be
present if the dominant firm's refusal to license affects competition in another
market (*Volvo/Veng*: para. 9). In *Magill*, the CFI noted that the refusal to license
and the accompanying prevention of competition in the downstream market

"clearly went beyond what was necessary to fulfil the essential function of the copyright as permitted in Community law. [...]The applicants' [the television companies;
my remark] conduct could not, in those circumstances, be covered in Community
law by the protection conferred by their copyright in the programme listings."
(Magill: para. 30).

---

47   Most of the judgments that reject an antitrust infringement of intellectual property rights
      and highlight the importance of innovation refer to the *Berkey* case (*Berkey Photo, Inc.
      v. Eastman Kodak Company*, 603 F.2d 263 (2nd Cir. 1979) [hereinafter *Berkey 1979*]).
      In that case, Eastman Kodak, a vertical integrated company, introduced a new amateur
      camera together with a new film, both in a different and smaller format. Due to this
      changed format, competitors were at a disadvantage because not only would customers
      who were interested in a smaller camera buy the new Kodak one but also customers
      who wanted to use the new and improved film. Disadvantages also arose in regards to
      developing and finishing the film, because competitors needed to buy new tools and
      technologies. Thus, Berkey filed an action against Kodak, complaining inter alia that
      Kodak engaged in monopolization by not pre-disclosing its innovations. The court over-
      ruled this allegation, stating that keeping innovation secret from rivals is normal busi-
      ness behaviour. In fact, the feasibility of success in the market motivates innovation and
      the aim for superior performance. Forcing a successful firm to share its knowledge with
      its competitors would conflict with this incentive (*Berkey 1979*: 281). Further, the court
      pointed out that according to Section 2 of the *Sherman Act*, a monopolist is not only al-
      lowed but also encouraged to compete aggressively on the merits. Consequently, any
      success achieved through efforts in research and development is tolerated by competiti-
      on laws (*Berkey 1979*: 281).

By mentioning the essential function of copyrights, the CFI acknowledges the role of intellectual property rights for the promotion of innovation. The requirement that a downstream market must be involved can be understood as a proxy that the specific subject matter of the affected intellectual property right remains untouched.

It is notable that all of the aforementioned U.S. cases did not impede innovation by the competitors. The plaintiffs did not complain in any of the cases that the refusal impeded the development of a new product. Instead, competitors were mostly: a) active on the same market as the intellectual property holder, and b) intending to offer the same services or products. Thus, from my point of view, the refusals to license might have an effect on price but not on innovation. Hence, we cannot reason that the U.S. approach towards refusal to license intellectual property rights differs from the European approach. We simply do not know how U.S. courts would find if a refusal would impede innovation. Even though the U.S. courts always emphasize the effects on the monopolist's innovation incentives, this does not imply that they value innovation more greatly than do European courts. The new product requirement in the *Magill* Test ultimately also comprises innovation effects. Thus, we can conclude that we cannot clearly differentiate between an American and a European approach, and we cannot revert to criteria from U.S. caselaw as to how to deal with refusal to license cases if innovation is impeded.

Having said this, I will now go back to the European caselaw, and clarify the *Microsoft* case.

2.4 The European *Microsoft* Case: Introduction of the Incentives Balance Test?

The Commission's inquiries in the European *Microsoft* case were initiated by a complaint of Sun Microsystems in 1998. As Microsoft refused to license interface information for its working group server operating systems to Sun Microsystems, Sun Microsystems accused Microsoft of violating Article 102 TFEU. Without this interface information, Sun Microsystems feared that consumers would no longer buy its product as the company could not guarantee interoperability with Microsoft's products. In the course of its investigation, the Commission launched a second accusation against Microsoft; it charged Microsoft with incorporating a software product called "Media Player" into its PC operating systems. That is, it the Commission accused Microsoft of tying Media Player to its Window Operating system, conduct which would also infringe Article 102 TFEU.

However, in the following section, I will solely focus on the interoperability case and will not further discuss the Media Player case.[48] After starting with a detailed description of the decision of the European Commission, I will continue with a discussion of the CFI judgment on this decision.

2.4.1   The Decision of the Commission

In 2004, the EU Commission confirmed the suspicions of Sun Microsystems and found that Microsoft had abused its dominant position in the marketplace for client PC operating systems, because it refused to license certain interface information of its working group server (WGS) operating systems to its competitor Sun Microsystems.[49] Without this interface information, the competitor's WGS operating systems could not communicate with Microsoft's (ruling) client PC operating systems. Furthermore, the Commission discovered in the course of its investigations that the refusal to license Sun Microsystems was not a singular case, but rather part of a general pattern. Many other competitors confirmed that they did not receive sufficient interface information and therefore suffered a disadvantage compared to Microsoft (*COMP Microsoft*: para. 573-577). An additional aggravating factor was that Microsoft only disclosed its interface information with the introduction of Windows 2000. Not until that point, it refused the disclosure (ibid.: para. 579, 584). The Commission took it for granted that Microsoft pursued the strategy to displace its competitors in this market (ibid.: 588, 589). Thus, the refusal to disclose the interface information caused a risk of eliminating competition on WGS operating systems (ibid: para. 692), which would have a negative effect on technical development and consumer welfare (ibid.: para. 693-708).

Specifically, the Commission showed that the client PC and WGS operating systems markets are closely connected due to several commercial and technical links. Accordingly, the WGS operating systems market is strongly affected by Microsoft's dominance in the client PC operating system market (*COMP Microsoft*: para. 526). Interoperability between the two systems is of high importance for the WGS operating systems. When Microsoft first entered the market for WGS operating systems, its competitors already had a strong lead. Therefore, there were incentives for Microsoft to invest in the interoperability of both its client PC operating systems and non-Microsoft WGS operating systems. As the Commission pointed out,

---

48   For a discussion of this issue, *compare* exemplarily Dolmans/Graf 2004 and Evans/Padilla 2004.

49   European Commission decision in case COMP/C-3/37.792 Microsoft, C(2004) 900 final [hereinafter *COMP Microsoft*]. The background of the decision can be found in Banasevic et al. 2004.

"[w]hile entering the work group server operating system market, pledging support for already established technologies was important in gaining a foothold and the confidence of the customers." (ibid.: para. 587)

But as soon as Microsoft achieved sustainable success in the WGS operating system market, its incentives changed and it refused to license the interoperability information not only to Sun Microsystems but also to other competitors. Herewith, Microsoft tried to eliminate the competition and establish a dominant position in this market as well. Consequently, the Commission found that this behaviour was part of a general leveraging strategy, especially due to the interruption of previous business relations (ibid.: para. 586-589).

Highlighting the importance of interoperability, the Commission showed that without access to this information Microsoft's competitors would not be able to offer WGS operating server products that were compatible with the Windows systems to a convenient degree (ibid.: para. 572). Therewith, Microsoft's conduct risks the elimination of competition in the market for WGS operating systems (ibid.: para. 692). In consequence, "an increasing number of consumers are locked into homogenous solution at the level of work group server operating systems" (ibid.: para. 694). This implied that those consumers could not profit from innovations supporting the systems brought to the market by Microsoft's competitors. At the same time, this lock-in effect hampered the success of competitors in the market and therefore also constituted a disincentive to innovate.[50] Facing only limited or even no interoperability information, competitors could not make their innovative features available within the framework of the Windows systems as they had previously done when Microsoft had disclosed the interface information. In other words, the refusal to disclose precluded follow-on innovation for vendors other than Microsoft (ibid.: para. 696-697). Accordingly, the Commission concluded, "Microsoft's refusal to supply limits technical development to the prejudice of consumers" (ibid.: para. 701).

Even though the criteria applied in the Microsoft case seem to vary from the *Magill* test, the Commission attached importance to the fact that its analysis was in line with the previous caselaw (ibid.: para. 554).[51] Thus far, the Commission had proven that: the interoperability information was necessary to ensure that WGS operating systems were compatible with the de facto standard in client PC operating systems; the refusal to license on the part of Microsoft was likely to eliminate competition in this market; and the refusal prohibited technological

---

50 *See COMP Microsoft*, para. 694. "In a longer-term perspective, if *Microsoft*'s strategy is successful, new products other than *Microsoft*'s work group server operating systems will be confined to niche existences or not be viable at all. There will be little scope for innovation – except possibly for innovation coming from *Microsoft*," ibid, para. 700.

51 However, at the same time the Commission noted that the criteria from previous caselaw do not constitute an exhaustive checklist (*COMP Microsoft*: para. 555).

development to the prejudice of consumers, which the Commission equalled to the criterion of the prevention of a new product.

In regards to the objective justification, Microsoft defended its refusal to license with its intellectual property rights on the interface information. Restricting its intellectual property rights would diminish any future incentives to innovate (ibid.: para 709).[52] Microsoft further argued that disclosure would make it easy for Sun and other competitors to clone its product (ibid.: para. 713). The Commission rejected Microsoft's objection that its intellectual property rights already constituted a justification for the refusal to license. Instead, the Commission pointed out that it is one objective of intellectual property rights to promote innovation for the public good. A refusal to license can therefore be counterproductive when it impedes innovation (ibid.: para. 711).

Scrutinizing the argument that a compulsory license would allow competitors to clone Microsoft's products, the Commission argued that this fear is causeless. In the Commission's opinion, Microsoft's competitors were at a disadvantage with regards to the quality of the implementation of the relevant specifications in comparison to Microsoft's own product. Furthermore, Microsoft would have an advantage in time compared to its competitors as it would disclose the specifications only after it already had a working implementation. Thus, in order to compete with Microsoft, the other software firms would have to offer additional services to their customers to convince them to buy their products instead of Microsoft's. The interoperability of the competitors' products with Windows alone would not be enough to guarantee success in the market. Consequently, there was no rational explanation for Microsoft's fear of being cloned (ibid.: 721-722).

Since Microsoft had no reason to fear cloning of its product, its argument that an obligation to disclose would diminish its innovation incentives could only relate to the specifications underlying the interface information (ibid.: para. 723). According to the Commission, this approach was wrong. Instead, it stressed that it was important to consider "Microsoft's incentives to innovate its products as a whole, not only in the design of its products' interfaces" (ibid.: para. 724). That is to say, even though Microsoft might have fewer incentives to improve its interfaces, it still had incentives to invest and to innovate with the WGS operating systems. Moreover, the effects on innovation had to be consid-

---

52   "The objective justification for *Microsoft*'s refusal to disclose its intellectual property rights is self-evident: those rights are meant to protect the outcome of billions of dollars of R&D investments in software features, functions and technologies. This is the essence of intellectual property right protection. Disclosure would negate and eliminate future incentives to invest in the creation of more intellectual property," NERA Report, para. 53, appendix to Microsoft's submission from 17.10.2003, quoted at *COMP Microsoft*, para. 709.

ered in comparison with the effects arising out of a continuance of the refusal to license. The Commission argued that if Microsoft continued to refuse disclosure, it would diminish competition in the market. At the same time, Microsoft's innovative efforts were driven by the competitive pressure and the innovative steps of its competitors. If the refusal results in a reduction of competition, Microsoft would have less or no incentives to innovate at all (ibid.: para. 725). If, in contrast, Microsoft were obliged to disclose its interface information, then its WGS operating systems would have to compete with the performance of other firms. Consumers would no longer be locked-in to Microsoft's products and consequently Microsoft would have more of an incentive to innovate in order to keep and expand its customer base (ibid.: para. 725). Thus, the Commission came to the conclusion that

"on balance, the possible negative impact of an order to supply on Microsoft's incentives to innovate is outweighed by its positive impact on the level of innovation of the whole industry (including Microsoft)." (ibid.: para. 783)

Simply put, the Commission conducted a balancing of the different innovation incentives. Generally, this proceeding has been called the "Incentives Balance Test."[53] Accordingly, this test comprises a consideration of the effects on innovation incentives on the whole market evoked by a refusal to license and of the effects on the likely innovation incentives evoked by a disclosure. These effects are weighed against each other. If the expected innovation incentives due to a disclosure are higher, then a compulsory license would be imposed. With that proceeding the Commission allow for its consideration that intellectual property rights are inter alia granted to promote innovation for the public good. Thus, according to the Incentives Balance Test, a compulsory license is adequate if a refusal to license is likely to diminish innovation whereas a disclosure would spur innovation.

In the *Microsoft* case, the Commission explained that, even though in the short run a compulsory license may have negative effects on Microsoft's incentive to innovate, these negative effects were outweighed by the positive impact a compulsory license would have on the innovative behaviour of Microsoft's competitors (ibid.: para. 693-700). Moreover, in the long run, the compulsory license would also strengthen Microsoft's incentive to innovate as it would need to defend its leading position in the market against its competitors. Thus, after conducting this balancing, the Commission concluded that the positive effects of the disclosure on innovation incentives outweighed the negative effects on Microsoft's incentive to innovate.

In reaching this conclusion, the Commission established that Microsoft had abused its dominant position in the client PC operating systems market by refus-

---

53   *Compare* exemplarily *to* Lévêque 2005; Vezzoso 2006.

ing to license its interoperability information (ibid.: para. 779-784). Hence, the Commission obliged Microsoft to disclose the interface information.[54]

In sum, while the objective justification has played only a minor role in the determination of abusive behaviour to date, it was front and centre in the *Microsoft* case. In response to Microsoft's argument that a duty to license would diminish its innovation incentives, the Commission introduced the Incentives Balance Test, which, first, put this argument under inspection and, second, aimed at analysing the innovation incentives of the whole industry due to both a duty to license and a refusal to license. Specifically, such a balancing would be comprised of an evaluation of the innovation incentives of Microsoft and its rivals evoked by a refusal to license and an evaluation of the (expected) innovation incentives of Microsoft and its rivals arising out of a compulsory license.

2.4.2   The Judgment of the CFI

The approach of the Commission to the *Microsoft* case raised questions regarding its legitimacy, i.e. whether the Commission's proceeding was in line with previous caselaw. In its plea in front of the CFI, Microsoft complained that the Commission applied a "new and legally defected balancing test"[55] and did not stick to the criteria developed in the previous caselaw. Since its judgment had a false basis, the denial by the Commission of Microsoft's right to rely on its intellectual property rights was illegitimate.[56]

Consequently, the CFI dealt in its judgment[57] with the issue of clarifying the criteria for the assessment of abusive conduct. The Commission had found that, in its understanding, the *IMS Health* judgment did not establish a final list of exceptional circumstances (*CFI Judgment*: para. 303). The CFI, however, noted that it followed the criteria established in *Magill* and *IMS Health*, and only if these criteria were not fulfilled would it consider other arguments (CFI Judgment: para. 336). Thus, the CFI analyzed the case and the decision according to the following criteria:

> 1. Does the refusal to license concern a product or service which is indispensable to compete in a secondary market?

---

54   Of course, Microsoft was allowed to demand a "fair and non-discriminatory" royalty for access to the interoperability information (*COMP Microsoft*, Article 5a).

55   Action brought on 7 June 2004 by Microsoft Corporation against Commission of the European Communities (Case T-201/04), Official Journal of the European Union, C-197 10.7.2004, pp. 118ff.

56   In my comments, I will solely focus on European law. International aspects, like Microsoft's accusation that the Commission decision infringes against the TRIPS agreement, will not be considered here. For the courts remarks on this issue, *compare* CFI judgment: para. 777-813.

57   *See* Judgment of the Court of First Instance in Case T-201/04, 17.09.2007 [*hereinafter* CFI Judgment], para. 690.

2. Is it likely that the refusal eliminates competition in this secondary market?
3. Does it impede the appearance of a new product which is not offered by the dominant firm and for which exists a potential consumer demand?
4. Is there an objective justification for the refusal to license?

First taking the indispensability criterion, Microsoft rejected the opinion of the Commission that the interface information was indispensable to competing in the market (ibid.: para. 337). According to Microsoft, at least five other ways existed to ensure the interoperability with working group server operating systems that were already used by suppliers of competing systems. Even though these methods did not ensure perfect substitutability to the required interface information, they were sufficient to ensure effective competition (ibid.: para. 345). However, the CFI decided that it was necessary that the competitor's operating systems provide a comparable interoperability with Windows domain architecture as Microsoft's own products (ibid.: para. 374). Furthermore, the court found that due to the very narrow linkages between the Windows client PC and the work group server operating systems, Microsoft had established a "de facto" standard for working group computing (ibid.: para. 392). Therefore, the Commission was correct in its appraisal that the full provision of the interface information was required. The CFI also pointed out that the Commission based its decision on complex economic assessments, and thus, the court was limited in its review. According to the court, the arguments put forward by Microsoft did not convince that the Commission's assessment was wrong (ibid.: para. 378-381, 388-391).

Concerning the *elimination of competition, Microsoft* argued that the refusal to license would not eliminate all competition in the secondary market. It complained that the Commission only mentioned the *mere risk* of elimination of competition in the market. It could be observed that there were still other competitors on the market for work group server operating systems (CFI Judgment: para. 437-442). Pointing out that it was not in line with Article 102 TFEU to wait until the elimination of competition had been realized, the CFI rejected this plea. The existence of competitors in some niches was not sufficient to maintain effective competition. As the market was characterized by significant network effects, the Commission was correct in intervening before competition was eliminated (ibid.: para. 561-563).

Furthermore, Microsoft challenged the development of a *new product* in dependence of the interoperability information. The Commission failed to identify a new product that would be developed on the basis of this information. Moreover, the Commission did not prove that there was a consumer demand for this product. Microsoft suspected that its products would be copied (ibid.: para. 621-625). In its judgment, the CFI emphasised that Article 102 TFEU prohibited abusive conduct, which limited production, markets, or technological developments to the prejudice of consumers (ibid.: para. 643). Following this line, the

previous decisions in Magill and IMS Health did indeed emphasise the requirement of a new product. But this criterion had to be seen in light of consumer interests. That is, the new product condition in the aforementioned cases was an
indicator as to whether the prevention of competition in a secondary market
prejudiced consumers. But as Article 102 TFEU stated, not only may the prevention of markets and products constitute a prejudice to consumers, but also the
limitation of technological development. Thus, the decisive criterion in this context was whether consumer welfare was being reduced (ibid.: para. 645-655). In
the Microsoft case, due to the lack of interoperability, consumers were locked in
to Windows products and thus, competitors could not offer successfully their
own innovative products. Hence, the CFI explained that, due to these circumstances, the resulting effect is similar to the prevention of a new product (ibid.:
para. 655-665).

Regarding the *objective justification*, the CFI first pointed out that the mere
ownership of an intellectual property right could not in itself constitute an objective justification. Otherwise, a refusal to license could never be considered to
constitute an abuse in the sense of Article 102 TFEU (CFI judgment: para. 690).
The CFI rejected Microsoft's allegation that the Commission used a new, and
legally not founded, test to analyze the objective justification and found that Microsoft misread the Commission decision and the Commission did not base its
decision on a balancing test (ibid.: para. 704-710). In fact, the Commission
showed that there was no evidence for an objective justification to refuse licensing. According to the court, the Commission, firstly, established that the exceptional circumstances defined by the court in the *Magill* and *IMS Health* cases
were present and then, secondly, proceeded to analyze the arguments put forward by Microsoft. The Commission assessed whether the justifications put
forward by Microsoft outweighed the exceptional circumstances that establish
the infringement of competition (ibid.: para. 710). In its judgment, the CFI demonstrated that the Commission convincingly proved that Microsoft had no reason to fear that its products would be cloned. Moreover, the CFI agreed with the
Commission that none of the other justifications[58] put forward by Microsoft were
solid (ibid). Therewith, the court circumvented the discussion of whether the
Incentives Balance Test might be an appropriate legal instrument for refusal to
license intellectual property rights cases.

To sum up, the CFI found that all of the exceptional circumstances identified in *Magill* and *IMS Health* were fulfilled. Therefore, there was no necessity
to consider other arguments (ibid: para. 712). Based on this argument, the CFI
confirmed in large part the decision of the Commission. The only aspect where
the Commission had to accept defeat was in regards to the "independent moni-

---

58   For a detailed discussion of all arguments put forward by Microsoft to justify its refusal
      to license, *compare to* CFI Judgment: para. 337-436.

toring trustee," which the Commission wanted to appoint in order to observe whether Microsoft complied with its decision (CFI judgment: para. 1230-1237). In this regard, the CFI found that the Commission had exceeded its authority (ibid.: para. 1251-1279). However, the CFI agreed with the Commission on all other points.

2.4.3 Discussion of the Microsoft Decision

Although the judgment of the CFI confirms the decision of the Commission and seems to refer to the previous caselaw, the judgement and the decision evoked discussion in literature. For instance, it has been criticized that it is unclear what criteria will be used in future cases to assess potentially abusive conduct. Obviously, the CFI applied a less strict standard for abusive behaviour in the *Microsoft* case than in previous cases. This is evident for the following reasons:

1. The indispensability standard is lower;
2. The likeliness of elimination of competition is only derived;
3. The new product requirement is not fulfilled; and
4. The content of objective justification is still unclear; no discussion of the Incentives Balance Test as a new instrument.

In the next section, I will explain these departures and briefly review the discussion surrounding them.[59] However, my focus will lie on the fourth criterion, that is, the objective justification and the Incentives Balance Test.

2.4.3.1 The Requirement of Indispensability

Both in the *Bronner* and in the *IMS Health* cases, the court made clear that a good or service was only indispensable if no other alternative existed that would allow a viable solution for the competitor requesting the license. Furthermore, the *Bronner* judgment explicitly stated that it was not decisive whether the good or service to which access was demanded was the cheapest possibility or the most technically advanced. Rather, it was decisive if there were alternative possibilities, irrespective of whether they provided the same quality or price as long as the competitor remained viable. Even though in the *Microsoft* decision the Commission referred to the criterion clarified in *Bronner*, it did not explain how it interprets this criterion. According to Killick (2004), the Commission simply repeated the wording of the *Bronner* case without further explaining the criterion in the context of the *Microsoft* decision (ibid.: 35-36).

To refute the determination of indispensability, Microsoft referred alternative possibilities as a means of achieving interoperability. Microsoft pointed out that its competitors could legally use five different methods to communicate

---

59 Please note that the following discussion makes no claim to be complete. For a broader discussion of the *Microsoft* decision, compare to Ahlborn/Evans 2008; Larouche 2008, Lévêque 2005; Scopelliti 2010; Vezzoso 2006.

with a Windows client PC or server operating system. Microsoft illustrated the practicability of these methods with the example of Linux. According to Microsoft, Linux had an increasing market share of the work group server operating system market, and its products were continuously gaining ground on Windows server operating systems, despite the fact that Linux had no access to the interface information (CFI Judgment: para. 345-347).

However, the CFI overruled this objection. According to the CFI, the degree of interoperability was decisive. As Microsoft inhabited a de facto standard, the CFI agreed with the Commission that it was necessary that the competitors' operating systems achieve the same operability with the Windows domain architecture as Microsoft products. This "equal footing" could only be achieved if the competitors disposed of the complete interface information. Thus, the CFI confirmed the opinion of the Commission that even though a certain degree of interoperability was already possible, this degree was not sufficient to permit the competitors to remain viable in the market (CFI Judgment: para. 220; 221; 229; 374; 377).

Like the Commission in the decision before it, the CFI applied a very low standard for indispensability in this case (Ahlborn/Evans 2008: 10; Larouche 2008: 8). As long as the alternative solutions did not generate an outcome that would put Microsoft's competitors on equal footing as Microsoft's products, they could not constitute appropriate alternatives to the demanded interface information. Only the disclosure of the interface information would allow the development of equivalent products; therefore, the information was indispensable. Therewith, the CFI diverged from its former ruling that competitors could not require an equation with the dominant firm as long as long as there were other possibilities. This inconsistency had already been criticized in the Commission decision (Killick 2004: 41; Körber 2007: 1213).

2.4.3.2   Elimination of Competition

The identification of elimination of competition goes hand in hand with the detection of indispensability. If the good or service to which access is demanded is indispensable to compete in the secondary market, then the refusal to supply is on the verge of eliminating competition in that market (Dolmans/ O'Donoghue/ Loewenthal 2007: 129). Thus, at first glance, it seems coherent that the court approved the elimination of competition after it has already confirmed the indispensability criterion.

Still, there is a distinction between the *Microsoft* judgment and previous judgments (Ahlborn/Evans 2008: 10). For instance, in the *Magill* case, the refusal to license the information for the television programs made the sustainability of Magill magazine virtually impossible. By refusing to license this program information, Magill could not provide its weekly magazine for television programs. Hence, due to the refusal, competition was actually eliminated (Killick 2004: 39).

The situation in the *Microsoft* case is quite different. According to the Commission and the CFI, there was only a *risk* of eliminating competition. As opposed to in the *Magill* case, Microsoft's competitors could remain in the market since, for instance, they had other possible ways in which they could ensure at least a minimum degree of interoperability. That is, Microsoft's refusal to disclose the demanded interface information obviously impeded competition, because the competitors could not offer perfect substitutes to Microsoft's own products and because the interoperability with Windows products was restricted, at the very least. Nevertheless, in contrast to *Magill*, this refusal did not evoke immediately the elimination of competition. For instance, the firm Linux entered the market after the refusal took place (Killick 2004: 40). Of course, the CFI recognized this and therefore stated that there was a *risk* of eliminating effective competition. In other words, there was a fear that, in the long run, the disadvantages of the competitors due to incomplete interoperability would lead to a further extension of Microsoft's already dominant position, thereby eliminating competition.

Thus, it is obvious that the criterion in *Magill* was stricter. In the *Bronner* judgment, the court also referred to the decisions in *Commercial Solvents* and *Telemarketing*, in which the refusals to supply *risked* eliminating all competition. Despite this weak language, in these both cases the refusal to supply, like in *Magill*, would have resulted in an immediate crowding out of the competitor (Killick 2004: 39). Moreover, in the *IMS Health* judgment, the court emphasized that the test is "elimination of all competition" and not "risk of elimination of competition" (ibid.). Hence, the benchmark was significantly higher than in the *Microsoft* case (Ahlborn/Evans 2008: 10-11). In confirming the decision of the Commission, the Court released its own standard.

2.4.3.3   The New Product Requirement

In the previous judgments (at least in intellectual property cases), it was clear that the emergence of a new product was essential. In particular, the ECJ pointed out in the IMS Health judgment that the refusal to allow access to the indispensable good was abusive,

> "only where the undertaking which requested the license does not intend to limit itself essentially to duplicating the goods or services already offered on the secondary market by the owner of the intellectual property right, but intends to produce new goods or services not offered by the owner of the right and for which there is a potential consumer demand." (IMS Health: para. 49)

In the *Microsoft* case, the Commission failed to prove the prevention of a new product (Killick 2004: 38). According to the CFI, the prevention of the appearance of a new good could not be the only parameter by which to determine whether the refusal to license may cause disadvantages for the customers. Rather, such a prejudice could also be caused by the impediment of technical development (CFI Judgment: para. 647). Due to the lack of interoperability with the products of Microsoft's competitors, the buying decisions of consumers were channelled towards Microsoft products. This conduct, in turn, deterred the competitors from developing WGS operating systems with innovative features. Thus, in comparison to Microsoft, the competitors were placed at a disadvantage, which prejudices the consumers (CFI Judgment: para. 653). The CFI affirmed the position of the Commission that as soon as the competitors have access to the interoperability information,

"those competitors will be able to offer work group server operating systems which, far from merely reproducing the Windows systems already on the market, will be distinguished from those systems with respect to parameters which consumers consider important." (ibid.: para. 656)

As such, although the court CFI declared that it was following the new product requirement, it extended this criterion in a manner that also comprehended technical development, which does not necessarily result in the development of a new product but may comprise some technical improvements or add-ons (Ahlborn/Evans 2008: 11, 12;).[60] Such a broad interpretation of the new product criterion gives room for interpretation. The extension of the new product cases makes it impossible to predict how the Commission (and the CFI) will apply the criterion in prospective cases (Killick 2004: 38). Giving access to intellectual property rights would evoke in almost every case the possibility for improvement (ibid: 43). With this judgment, the Court also departed from its standard expressed in the *IMS Health* case (Larouche 2008: 11). In that case, the Court insisted that competitors must intend to produce new goods or services that are not yet offered by the dominant firm (*IMS Health* 2004: para 49). According to Stratakis, such a loose interpretation of the new product criterion may motivate free-riders to demand access to a production simply by arguing that it would change some features (Stratakis 2006: 440).

2.4.3.4   Objective Justification and the Incentive Balance Test

With regards to objective justification and the application of the Incentive Balance Test, the CFI argued that Microsoft misinterpreted the Commission decision. The Commission did not base its decision on a balancing test, but showed that the arguments put forward by Microsoft were not solid (CFI Judgment: para. 704-710). In other words, Microsoft had failed to prove the existence of any objective justification (ibid.: para. 697 and 711). Consequently, as no objective justification existed and no negative innovation incentives occurred, a bal-

---

60   According to Lévêque (2005), the Commission did not consider the new product criterion at all but focused solely on the balancing of the incentives to innovate (ibid.: 85).

ancing of the different effects was not necessary and was not conducted by the Commission. The CFI clearly identified the necessity of an objective justification and supported the Commission in its assessment that an insistence on intellectual property rights was simply not enough. At the same time, the CFI was also clear regarding the burden of proof, which was on Microsoft to prove that its refusal to license was objectively justified (ibid.: para. 711). In more detail, the CFI changed the burden of proof – the Commission need not analyse whether there might be a normal business justification for Microsoft's conduct, but rather Microsoft must show why its conduct does not infringe Article 102 TFEU (Ahlborn/Evans 2008).

Regarding the Incentives Balance Test, the CFI was very cautious in its judgement. On the one hand, the CFI did not endorse the test, but on the other hand, it did not reject it either. Instead, the CFI simply found that the Commission had not based its decision on the test and that Microsoft's arguments were not convincing. This is important because if the court had rejected the applicability of the Incentives Balance Test, then it would have closed the door on such a balancing in the future. By more or less ignoring the test, the CFI allowed for the possibility that the test may be applied in future cases.

In general, the idea of the test seems suitable to solve the trade-off between competition policy and intellectual property law. For example, Lévêque (2005), in highlighting the positive effects of the test, explains that firms tend to invent valuable improvements for consumers mostly when incentives to innovation occur. Only then are consumers willing to buy the new or improved product. Thus, incentives to innovate constitute a good equivalent of consumers' benefits (ibid: 76).[61] From this perspective, focusing on innovation incentives might be a good alternative for the previous new product criterion (ibid.: 75). In his conclusion, Lévêque goes a step even further than the Commission. While the Commission applied the balancing only at the fourth step of the analysis, that is, as a test for the objective justification, Lévêque indirectly suggests analysing the effects on innovation incentives even earlier. Such a proceeding would put even more weight on innovation. In contrast, the new product requirement has some shortcomings. For instance, the term of a new product is misleading since – from a microeconomics perspective – a product consists of a bundle of different characteristics; for instance, the speed of a car, size, number of doors, and so on. Consequently, the value of a certain product is determined by its specific characteristics; for instance, the speed a car can drive. Against this background, a new product may be produced with new characteristics or even improved characteris-

---

61   According to Lévêque (2005), firms will not invest in the improvement or the modification of a good or service if they do not believe that consumers are willing to pay for it. Thus, if the refusal to supply reduces incentives to innovate, technological development will be limited to the detriment of consumers (ibid.: 76-77).

tics (Lévêque 2005: 76). Thus, such a definition of newness does not really constitute guidance as to whether a refusal to license constitutes consumer harm, especially as from an economic perspective, the decisive criterion is not the consumer value but the consumers' willingness to pay and if this willingness to pay outweighs the costs (ibid.).[62]

With the application of the Incentives Balance Test, the Commission focuses on the question of how to foster innovation, and consequently consumer welfare (Stratakis 2006: 441). Therewith, the Incentives Balance Test goes directly to the heart of the economics of intellectual property rights (Lévêque 2005: 77; Vezzoso 2006: 386). Traditionally, intellectual property rights are justified because they promote innovation as they overcome the free-riding problem and thus solve the appropriablity problem.[63] Nevertheless, there are also situations where intellectual property rights are detrimental to innovation and therefore Lévêque argues that the incentives balance test constitutes an appropriate instrument to solve this imbalance of intellectual property rights and innovation (Lévêque 2005: 77 et seq.). Similarly, Vezzoso (2006) illustrates that, if intellectual property rights are dedicated to spur innovation, it is only logical to restrict them in specific cases when it can be proved that they hamper innovation (ibid: 386). With the application of the Incentives Balance Test, competition authorities would shift their attention to identifying those circumstances in which intellectual property rights fail the goal of promotion innovation (ibid.).

Besides these advantages, the proceedings of the Commission in the *Microsoft* case has some flaws. For instance, Lévêque criticises that the application of the Incentives Balance Test seems to be based solely on the assumption that more competition automatically evokes more innovation than in a monopoly situation (ibid: 79; similar: Ahlborn/Evans 2008: 18). Without providing any evidence, the Commission argues that a compulsory license would stimulate innovations by competitors and that these innovations would in turn force Microsoft to innovate as well. However, the Commission did not properly consider the negative effects on Microsoft's innovation incentives and took it as a presumption that lower firm concentration (and therewith more innovation) would outweigh these negative effects.[64] The Commission stopped the application of the

---

62   Besides that, Lévêque criticises the new product criterion as very vague since according to the *IMS Health* decision, the *intent* of producing a new product is not a sufficient criterion for detecting anti-competitive conduct. (ibid.: 76).

63   We will expand on the economic justification of intellectual property rights in Chapter 3.

64   Besides that, such a simplistic argument (that is, more competition equals more innovation) does not consider that, especially in the IT branch, innovation is not necessarily connected to the expected reward (for instance, in the case of open source software). Thus, competitors might not be deterred by the circumstance that customers only have a

Incentives Balance Test at the first step; that is, it argued that a refusal to license would significantly reduce competitors' innovation incentives but it did not discuss the effects on Microsoft in detail (Vezzoso 2006: 385). Even though it is not evident that the decrease of Microsoft's innovation incentives outweighs the increase of the rivals' innovation incentives, this rough balancing is not robust. However, according to the Commission, the burden of proof is on Microsoft (Lévêque 2005: 79). Had Microsoft shown that on the one hand a compulsory license would negatively affect its innovation incentives and that on the other hand the refusal to license would not significantly reduce innovation incentives of the competitors, it would have passed the Incentives Balance Test (Vezzoso 2006: 385).

In addition to these more or less "practical" objections, Killick notes that such an Incentives Balance Test makes it impossible for firms to assess ex ante whether their conduct would infringe Article 102 TFEU. The Commission did not give any guidance as to how a company can determine whether its innovation incentives due to the refusal to license outweigh the positive effects of a compulsory license on its competitors (Killick 2004: 44). Moreover, Killick argues that intellectual property rights themselves already constitute a balancing of long-term and short-term innovation incentives: they comprise the short-term prejudice of exclusivity and the long-term benefit of innovation (Killick 2004: 44; Thyri: 397). Correcting ex post this balance would further diminish legal certainty (ibid.).

Against this background, it is disappointing that the CFI did not give any opinion about this test, even though Microsoft very explicitly challenged it.[65] To date, it is not at all clear how the criterion of objective justification should be interpreted (Howarth/McMahon 2008). Recent caselaw has been very vague about this. In fact, as the review of caselaw has shown, we do not know of any Article 102 TFEU refusal to license case in which an objective justification has been accepted or even in which what would have been accepted has been made clear. As a consequence, so far it is only clear that the exercise intellectual property rights might be challenged through Article 102 TFEU, but how the specific conflict between intellectual property rights (and the argument of their function of providing innovation incentives) and competition law should be solved is no clearer than before. The *Microsoft* decision of the CFI has not contributed to the clarification of this issue.

In sum, the above discussion has shown that the criteria applied in the *Microsoft* case differ from the criteria developed in *Magill*, *Bronner*, and *IMS Health*. As such, the Commission and the CFI offer some flexibility in interpre-

---

limited willingness to pay for products that are not 100 percent compatible to Microsoft's client pc operating system (Vezzoso 2006: 387).

65   For a similar point of view, *compare* Körber (2007).

tation. In general, the test applied in *Microsoft* is much looser than the *Magill* Test (as elucidated by the court in *IMS Health*). In regards to indispensability, the Commission decision and the judgment of the court diverge from the principle that less economic advantageous alternatives are sufficient to rebut indispensability. Furthermore, the Commission and the court failed to prove the prevention of a new product, and it only requires a risk of eliminating competition (Killick 2004: 38). Although the Commission maintains that its analysis follows the criteria of the *Magill* Test, it added that it rejects the idea of putting forward an exhaustive checklist for detecting the abuse (*COMP Microsoft*: para. 555). Nevertheless, the court agreed with the Commission that the *Magill* Test had been applied. Thus, both the Commission and the court did not give any clear guidance for dominant companies as to how to assess their actions in regards to abusive behaviour (Killick 2004: 36). However, as mentioned at the beginning of this chapter, in December 2008 the Commission introduced its guidance paper to Article 102 TFEU. While I presented some of the general principles behind these new guidelines, I have not focused on the different case groups yet. Hence, in the following section, I will present the principles in regards to refusal to license cases in order to analyze whether the Commission clarified which criteria it intends to apply in prospective cases.

2.5 Criteria for Refusal to License in the Article 102 TFEU Guidance Paper

In the recent guidance paper, the Commission first acknowledges that it is the right of every company to dispose of its property and to choose with whom to deal (European Commission 2009: para. 75). However, under certain circumstances, a refusal to deal may harm consumers. Accordingly, competition problems most likely arise in those cases in which the dominant company competes in the downstream market with its buyers to whom it refuses to supply (ibid.: para. 76). To assess the anticompetitive effect, the Commission will analyse whether the following three criteria are cumulatively fulfilled:[66]

    1. the refusal relates to a product or service which is objectively necessary to compete effectively on a downstream market;

    2. it is likely to lead to the elimination of effective competition on the downstream market; and

    3. the refusal is likely to lead to consumer harm.

At first glance, these criteria are very similar to those applied in the previous caselaw, that is to say, those from the *Magill* Test. Still, there are differences. Regarding the first criterion, the Commission explains that a product or service is objectively necessary when competitors in the downstream market cannot re-

---

66   For the following, *compare to* European Commission 2009: para. 81.

place the refused item with a substitute and cannot "effectively duplicate" the needed input (European Commission 2009: para 83). Even though the Commission uses almost the same wording we know from the *Bronner* judgment, the difference is that it requires that the competitors are able "to exert a competitive constraint" on the dominant company and that they are able to "compete effectively." At this point, it is unclear what this precisely means. In the *Bronner* case, the court explicitly states that it is not enough to argue that it is not "economically viable" for the competitor to duplicate the input in question only because the competitor is significantly smaller than the dominant company or because the alternative is not as advantageous (*Bronner*: para. 43-47). Conversely, in the *Microsoft* case, both the Commission and the CFI have been criticized because they demanded equal footing for the competitors and the dominant company (Lévêque 2005; Vezosso 2006). From this perspective, the requirement of competing effectively gives leeway to the Commission to apply this criterion more flexibly. Regarding the "downstream market," the Commission borrowed from the *IMS Health* case in that it is not necessary that an actual market for the input exists. Instead, it is sufficient if a potential market can be identified (European Commission 2009: para. 79). Therewith, the Commission avoids the problem in cases of intellectual property rights that the dominant company might argue that no downstream market is affected as the intellectual property right is directly connected with a good or service and not sold separately.

The second criterion does not seem to part from the previous case law. In the corresponding explanation, the Commission alludes to the fact that the criterion can mean both immediate elimination of effective competition as well as elimination over time. According to the guidance paper the Commission will assume that the criterion of elimination of competition is fulfilled with the proof of indispensability (ibid.: para. 85).

The most interesting change is in regards to the last criterion of consumer harm. With this requirement, the Commission replaced the new product requirement. In the words of the Commission, it will

> "examine whether for the customers, the likely negative consequences of the refusal to supply in the relevant market outweigh over time the negative consequences of imposing an obligation to supply. If they do, the Commission will normally pursue the case." (European Commission 2009: para. 86)

Consumer harm may arise when competitors are prevented from introducing innovative products or when follow-on innovation is impeded due to the refusal to supply (ibid.: para. 87).

> "This may be particular the case if the undertaking which requests supply [...] intends to produce new or improved goods or services for which there is a potential consumer demand or is likely to contribute to technical development." (European Commission 2009: para. 87)

Accordingly, the criterion of consumer harm has already been fulfilled when innovation is impeded. Thus, the prevention of a new product and the prevention of a follow-on innovation are mentioned by the Commission as mere indicative examples of consumer harm (Killick/Komninos 2009: 8). This is obviously another reaction to the *Microsoft* case. In the *Microsoft* case, the Commission was criticized for not strictly applying the new product criterion (compare to section 2.4.3.3), while the court pointed out that Article 102 TFEU was not restricted to the impediment of new products but focused on consumer harm (Microsoft Judgment). With this approach, competition policy now spurs innovation in general and not only new products. However, even though this approach might be welcome, it is also very vague. The "intend" and the "likely" contribution to technical development do not guarantee that the competitors will in fact innovate and or undertake any efforts to innovate. Moreover, the Commission does not make any statement as to what it will consider as likely negative effects of an obligation to supply. At first glance, one might argue that the Commission refers to the Incentives Balance Test. The Commission argued that the positive innovation incentives due to a compulsory license outweigh the negative effects on Microsoft's innovation incentives. Thus, it might be possible to argue that a refusal to license intellectual property rights is anti-competitive if the negative effects on innovation in the relevant market (that is, the innovation incentives of competitors) due to a refusal to supply are greater than the negative effects on the dominant firm's innovation incentives with a duty to supply. However, since the Commission does not spell this out, this interpretation remains speculative. Besides this focus on innovation, the Commission also contemplates the price effects of a refusal to license. In other words, if the refusal leads to an increase in prices in the downstream market, the requirement of consumer harm as well is fulfilled (European Commission 2009: para. 88).

The former fourth step of the examination, the objective justification, is replaced by the efficiency defense. Within this efficiency defence, the Commission acknowledges that a dominant firm may refuse to supply a certain input to realize appropriate returns on its investments and to maintain future incentives to invest. Further, the Commission explains that it will consider the objections of the dominant company that an obligation may negatively affect its innovation efforts (European Commission 2009: para. 89). Obviously, with this statement the Commission refers again to the *Microsoft* case. Nevertheless, while in that case the Commission answered Microsoft's objection that a duty to license would diminish its innovation incentive with the application of the Incentives Balance Test, the Commission once again fails to clarify this point in the guidance paper. It remains unclear how the Commission will assess these efficiency or innovation arguments in comparison to the anti-competitive effects, especially in regards to consumer harm. The burden of proof for negative effects on innovations due to a duty to supply lies in the responsibility of the dominant company. However, the Commission also highlights that these efficiency claims must be within the scope of the general criteria for objective necessity and efficiencies introduced earlier in the guidance paper. This is interesting, because reading the general requirements of an efficiency claim within Article 102 TFEU shows that effective competition has to be maintained for a successful efficiency claim (European Commission 2009: para. 29). Nevertheless, one of the assessment criteria in refusal to deal cases is just the likely elimination of competition. Even though one might argue that likely elimination is a weaker criterion than actual elimination of competition, this inconsistency evokes at least confusion whether an efficiency defence in refusal to deal cases can ever be successful.[67] Other criteria are that the claimed efficiencies arise out of the refusal to deal and that no other, less harmful, way exists to realize these efficiencies. Further, the likely efficiencies outweigh the potential negative effects on competition and consumers. Thus, the Commission puts a high burden on the efficiency defence.

In conclusion, with regards to the criteria for refusal to supply case, the guidance paper borrows heavily from the previous caselaw. However, while the Commission was criticized in the *Microsoft* case for not sticking closely to the criteria from the *Magill* Test, the Commission has now responded by broadening the criteria. Thus, instead of providing a final clarification of the decisive criteria or giving (dominant) firms clear guidance as to when a refusal to license intellectual property rights would be deemed to be anti-competitive, the guidance paper remains vague.

2.6 The Incentives Balance Test as a New Instrument in Competition Policy?

The case law described above and the attitude of the Article 102 TFEU guidelines to cases like *IMS Health* and *Microsoft* show that the abuse of intellectual property rights continues to be an ongoing topic in European competition policy and enforcement. At the same time, this chapter has shown that neither in the U.S. nor in Europe a consistent approach exists regarding how to deal with those cases. There remains no consensus as to what criteria should be used to asses such a refusal to license. In the *Microsoft* decision, the Commission applied a new criterion, the Incentives Balance Test. However, in its judgment, the court failed to expand on this test, and the new guidelines are also more confusing than clarifying.

Still, due to its explicit focus on innovation, the Incentives Balance Test as applied in the *Microsoft* case might constitute a good possibility of how to deal with abuse of refusal to supply intellectual property rights. Nevertheless, neither

---

67   For a similar point of view *compare to* Motta 2009: 598.

the judgment of the court in the *Microsoft* case nor the guidance paper gives a clear answer as to when such balancing should be applied in detail and what role it should play in reaching a decision. In the *Microsoft* case, it was clear that the balancing took place at the last step of the examination, within the objective justification. In the guidelines, this is not so clear; the Incentives Balance Test seems to be divided into two different assessment steps: in the determination of consumer harm and in the efficiency defense.[68] The Commission is also quiet about how the effects on innovation should be measured.

In sum, there are many facets of the Incentives Balance Test that have yet to be clarified. It remains unclear how and when an Incentives Balance Test should be applied, what criteria it will contain, and how it will measure different innovation incentives. In short, the economic rational is missing. While in this chapter, we only mentioned that the Incentives Balance Test might be an appropriate instrument to solve refusal to license intellectual property rights cases, we will discuss why this is so in the next chapter. Consequently, I will give an economic interpretation of the Incentives Balance Test. Basing on this, in Chapter 4 we will than review economic theories in order to analyse whether they provide criteria which can be applied within the Incentives Balance Test. However, at this point it is not clear whether the Incentives Balance Test is the best solution or whether the following analysis will demonstrate that it is not economically feasible and we must, therefore, develop an alternative instrument

.

---

68   Killick and Komninos are of another opinion. According to them, the third criterion already echoes the Incentives Balance Test as applied in the *Microsoft* case (Killick/Komninos 2009: 8). I agree with them only to a limited degree because interpreting the criterion already opens the question of how the dominant firm can demonstrate negative effects on its innovation.

3 Do Competition Policy and Intellectual Property Rights Stand in Conflict With Each Other?

Before we start discussing whether the Incentives Balance Test is an appropriate instrument from an economic point of view, it is important to mention that a debate exists concerning the question as to whether competition policy can interfere with intellectual property rights at all. The underlying assumption is that competition law and intellectual property law pursue diverging goals and therefore promote legally conflicting outcomes. Due to such different goals, intellectual property rights will almost always infringe competition law. From the other perspective, interference from competition policy will unduly restrict the intellectual property holder's right. However, this approach is disputed. Today most scholars argue that competition policy and intellectual property rights are complementary to each other.

Against this background, however, it is still necessary to shed some light on this issue before we continue with the Incentives Balance Test. On that account, I will briefly review the two strands of argument regarding whether intellectual property rights and competition law are conflicting or rather complementary laws. For final clarification I will then explain why we need intellectual property rights and oppose the results with the economic goals of competition policy. On this basis, we shall be able to determine the relationship between the two laws. This comparison will be concluded with a short reconciliation with European legislation.

Assuming that competition law is complementary to intellectual property law, we will turn back to the Incentives Balance Test. We will first elaborate in detail as to why and under what conditions competition policy can restrict intellectual property rights. Based on this, I will give an economic interpretation of the Incentives Balance Test.

3.1 Interface between Competition Law and Intellectual Property Law

In the cases described in Chapter 2, the defendant usually argued that it is the inherent right of both patents and copyrights to protect the right holder from imitation and that these rights permit the exclusion of other parties from the usage. Hence, if competition policy interferes with intellectual property rights and, moreover, imposes duties to license, this would undercut intellectual property rights. At the same time, the Commission pointed out that intellectual property rights are assigned to promote innovation for the public interest. Thus, if a refusal to license leads to a decrease of innovation, competition policy may interfere to correct this development.

Coming from this perspective, it is necessary to analyse whether competition policy indeed unduly restricts intellectual property rights or whether both laws complement each other in the sense that they pursue the same goal and may exist side by side. For this purpose, I will give an overview on the literature discussion on this topic in the next section. Generally, we can differentiate between two opposing approaches towards the relationship between competition law and intellectual property law: the conflict theory and the theory of complementarity.

3.1.1   Conflict Theory

Historically, there was a general consensus that competition law and intellectual property law conflicted. The underlying rationale of intellectual property rights is a stimulation of innovation. An investor or inventor is only willing to fund R&D if she is able to appropriate the benefits of it, that is, she receives a return on the investment for at least a limited period of time. Competition, on the other hand, sets out incentives to innovate by offering the innovator market success in terms of increasing market share. At the same time, a non-innovative competitor must expect to face market share losses due to the innovations of her rival. The competition incentive to innovate is reinforced by adaptive competitors who are imitating innovative outbreaks. Competitive pressure maintains the innovation incentive on creative market participants and, thus, plays an important role in favour of innovation (Linge 2008).

As a result, a conflict occurs when property rights protection leads to a restriction or abolishment of competition – the appropriation incentive to innovate limits the competition incentive to innovate. The intellectual property right conveys a legal monopoly to its owner that impedes competition. Therefore, the welfare-enhancing property rights protection turns into welfare-reducing restriction of competition. Whereas competition policy is aimed at preventing market power and restriction of competition, intellectual property rights policy is directed at the creation of market power or, in other words, at the restriction of (immediate) competition.[69] This conflict is also apparent at the level of prices; while intellectual property law promotes higher prices by excluding at least some competition, competition policy promotes lower prices by prohibiting conduct that would restrict competition (Gilbert/Weinschel 2007: 2).

From an antitrust point of view, one might easily argue that certain conduct can only be approved if it does not infringe competition law. An action typically violates competition law if it is anti-competitive. Then again, intellectual property laws are aimed at rewarding inventors by restricting competition. Thus, it

---

69   Compare exemplarily Gallini/ Trebilcock 1998; Katz 2007; Melamed/ Stoeppelwerth 2002; Ohly 2007; Schmidtchen 2007.

can be concluded that any potential infringement of competition law by intellectual property right holders is protected by intellectual property laws (Kaplow 1984: 1817). Out of this situation, the question arises as to which law should be preferred. As Kaplow illustrates, there is no unambiguous solution to this problem. In his model, Kaplow differentiates between two extreme regimes. Regime 1 deems an intellectual property right holder's practice to be illegal if it violates any aspect of competition law. Regime 2 assumes that competition law cannot restrict intellectual property right holders because they have an absolute privilege (ibid.: 1818). Under the first regime, the intellectual property right holder can indeed exercise her rights but cannot get involved in potential anticompetitive practices like cross-licensing. Under the second regime, the right holder can exercise her right without any restriction. Obviously, the reward for the inventor would be bigger under regime 2 than under regime 1, since the inventor has more opportunities to exploit her intellectual property rights.

Having recognized this, one might argue that the court or competition authorities should adopt the regime that offers the reward that is considered to be an appropriate return of investment. That is, at this point we are not looking for a solution of the conflict but rather for a precedence rule to decide which law should be preferred (Heinemann 2002: 11). However, as Kaplow points out, legislators have already determined the reward they deem to be appropriate when settling on the scope of intellectual property rights (Kaplow 1984: 1819). From this perspective, the discussion of the appropriate reward does not seem to lead to a solution of the conflict between antitrust and intellectual property law. As an alternative approach, Kaplow suggests what he calls the "Ratio Test."[70] The Ratio Test is an instrument that courts or competition authorities should use to assess the desirability of permitting a currently forbidden practice by comparing the cost it imposes on society with the costs of an extension of the patent life to achieve an equivalent reward (Kaplow 1984: 1829). The underlying assumptions are that the patent life: 1) is given; and 2) has been set at an optimal level.[71] Figure 3-1 (compare next to next page) provides an overview of the examination steps.

In Step 1 of the examination, whether a permission of the practice would entail more costs than would result from a lengthening of the patent life in order to provide the same reward to the patentee must be assessed. The consideration of the costs of lengthening is only hypothetical as we are assuming that the patent has already been set on an optimal degree. If the forbidden practice imposes more costs than the lengthening does, the practice should remain prohibited be-

---

70   As Kaplow restricts his remarks to patents, I will refer also only to patents in the following.

71   Therefore and for the following, compare to Kaplow 1984: 1829-1831. The assumptions refer to the fact that the legislator already determined the optimal patent life.

cause first, it is more costly than extending the patent life and second, the extension of the patent is not desirable anyway. If the reward imposes fewer costs on society per unit of incremental reward than a lengthening of patent life, we should proceed with Step 2. At this point, it is not possible to permit the practice straight away because, again, the existing patent life is considered to be optimal. An increase in reward due to the current practice is not defensible at this point. Thus, in Step 2 we have to assess whether permitting the practice would impose less costs per unit of incremental reward than would be saved by lowering the patent life in order to maintain the optimal level of protection. If the practice causes more costs, then it should remain prohibited. If it imposes fewer costs, then the practice should be permitted because permitting is less costly than adding the final increment in the patent life to provide the same reward. However, at the same time this implies that the patent life needs to be shortened in order to maintain the optimal reward, which was originally set.

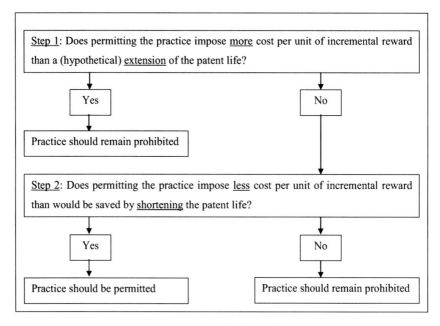

Figure 3-1: Examination steps of Kaplow's Ratio Test

To simplify, the preceding analysis may be summarized in the following ratio (R_K):

$$R_K = \frac{Patentee\ Reward}{Monopoly\ Loss}$$

The terms "patentee reward" and "monopoly loss" describe respectively the incremental reward and loss due to the forbidden practice. The higher the ratio, the more desirable the practice (Kaplow 1984: 1831).

While this procedure seems plausible, some difficulties remain. Remember that the underlying assumption is that the patent life is given; however; the result of Step 2 might be that we need to adjust the patent life. This leads to the conclusion that competition law and patent law (or more generally intellectual property law) need to be set up in interdependency (Kaplow 1984: 1840). In other words, to solve the patent-antitrust conflict we would need an institutional solution, that is, one superior entity setting up the optimal level of intellectual property law and the enforcement of competition law (ibid: 1841). As Kaplow concludes, in most countries this is not possible to constitute because legislators and courts (or competition authorities) act separately and independently from each other.

Thus, Kaplow suggests a second-best and a third-best solution. The second-best solution would be to foster a close interaction and co-ordination of both institutions (which also does not seem very practicable). The third-best alternative would allow the courts and competition authorities to decide independently from the legislators whether they will allow greater or fewer anti-competitive practices. This decision should depend on the estimation, guided by the application of the ratio test, of whether the current intellectual property law ensures just enough, too little, or too much reward (Kaplow 1984: 1841-1842).

From this point of view, it can be concluded that the patent-antitrust conflict could only be solved when both laws are set up in dependence of each other. As this is generally not the case, we can only try to adjust the conflict between restricting competition with intellectual property rights and fighting market power with competition policy. However, this conflict only occurs when we assume that an intellectual property right conveys market power to its owner.

3.1.2 Theory of Complementarity

At present, most scholars consider competition law and intellectual property law to be complementary (Anderman 1998: 5). Competition scholars accept that the exclusivity rights granted by intellectual property laws are necessary incentives for investments in R&D and, therefore, pursue the same objective as competition policy; that is, the promotion of innovation (Anderman 1998:5; Gilbert/Weinschel 2007: 2). At the same time, intellectual property scholars acknowledge that intellectual property rights are not immune to competition laws (Anderman 1998: 5-6; Ohly 2007: 48). According to Sullivan and Grimes (2006), laws can only conflict when the underlying values differ markedly. In case of intellectual property law and competition law, Sullivan and Grimes point out that both laws try to enhance consumer welfare by achieving allocative efficiency. Moreover, both laws try to achieve dynamic efficiency by fostering changes, innovations, and technological progress (Sullivan/ Grimes 2006: 841). Thus, the basis of the theory of complementarity is that both competition law and intellectual property law pursue the same goals (Drexl 2004: 792). Intellectual property rights aim at the promotion of innovation by offering exclusive grants while competition policy seeks to foster innovation by maintaining pluralism in the market. From this perspective, intellectual property is an ex ante tool and competition law an ex post tool (Montagnani 2007: 631).

While in some cases intellectual property rights turn out to be so successful that the intellectual property right holder achieves a dominant position, this is not inherent in the intellectual property rights scheme. As Kitch (1986) pointed out, even patented goods have to compete in the market, either against direct substitutes or against older or obsolete products that remain in the market (Kitch 1986: 31-32). A dominant position or monopoly rather is the result of a market development in that consumers prefer an intellectual property-protected good so much that they do not consider other products as substitutes and reject buying them (Drexl 2004: 792). Thus, the intellectual property right gives the right holder the possibility of exclusive usage, but this right does not prevent others from developing a competing product (Drexl 2004: 793). In other words, patents and copyrights always assign legal monopolies. Whether the possession of a protected asset also establishes an economic monopoly depends on the particular good, its characteristics and the market.[72] Since the conflict theory argues that intellectual property rights – depending on the scope of protection – confer market power, this strand of argument at least enfeebles the conflict theory.

Some would even go further, arguing that the pure intellectual property rights do not provide an incentive for innovation, but rather incentives arise from the competition in which the intellectual property-protected good is launched (Ullrich 1996: 566). That is, competition is decisive for innovation incentives, not the intellectual property right itself (ibid.). From this perspective, the intellectual property right is only a means to an end; that is, the exclusivity right of the intellectual property allows the necessary freedom of choice, which is crucial for the optimal allocation of resources in the market (Ullrich 1996: 566). In this regard, intellectual property is not different from any other property. Property in itself constitutes the legal acknowledgement of entrepreneurial ambition for profit and, therefore, protects the autonomy of the enforcement and exploitation of these rights in the market (ibid.). At the same time, property rights do not protect the right holder from liability against competition laws

---

72   For instance, the copyright over an Italian cookbook prevents the copying of this particular book, but it does not mean that no other author or publisher can sell another Italian cookbook. Thus, even though the author of the cookbook has a legal monopoly over this book, she cannot demand the monopoly prize because then consumers would simply buy an Italian cookbook from a different author.

when she undertakes actions restricting competition (Drexl 2004: 793). Thus, even though the assumption of an inherent conflict between competition law and intellectual property law can be neglected, there may be cases in which certain forms of exercising intellectual property rights may jeopardize competition (Anderman 1998: 6). Consequently, presuming a thesis of harmony from this would go too far. As with all other rights, intellectual property rights might be used as a starting base for anti-competitive strategies (Heinemann 2001: 1).

3.2 Innovation as a Common Objective

As we have seen above, while the conflict theory assumes diverging goals, the basic principle of the theory of complementarity is that both competition policy and intellectual property rights pursue the same goal. Thus, in this section we will analyse whether we can support this assumption from an economic perspective and also whether we can find support for it in EU legislation. In doing so, we will start with a derivation of the economic justification of intellectual property rights. We will analyse why we need intellectual property rights and what they shall achieve. Afterwards, we will compare these goals with the goals of competition policy in order to analyse whether the two laws indeed follow the same goal.

3.2.1 Justification of Intellectual Property Rights

The utilitarian perspective[73] has its origins inter alia in the wording of Thomas Jefferson, who once stated

---

73 An alternative strand of argumentation for the justification of intellectual property rights is the so-called Natural Law Approach. The foundation of the natural law approach to intellectual property rights can be found in Locke's famous Second Treatise of Government. The basic argument is that labour provides a foundation of property: "[t]he 'labour' of his body and the 'work' of his hands, we may say, are properly his. Whatsoever, then, he removes out of the state that Nature hath provided and left it in, he hath mixed his labour with it and joined to it something that is his own and thereby makes it his property. It being by him removed from the common state Nature placed it in, it hath by this labour something annexed to it that excludes the common right of other men. For this 'labour' being the unquestionable property of the labourer, no man but he can have a right to what that is once joined to, at least where there is enough and as good left in common for others." (Locke 1698, cited after Menell 2000: 157). Obviously, Locke did not have intellectual property rights in mind when developing his theories. Nevertheless, applying his theories to intellectual property rights has a certain charm. Invention and creation are the fruits of intellectual labour and therefore the property of the intellectual worker. For the interested reader, a broad introduction to the moral and philosophical approaches to intellectual property rights can be found in Drahos 1996. Further discussion on natural law and intellectual property is provided in Becker 1993; Craig 2002; Damstedt 2003; Gordon 1992, 1993; Hughes 1988; McGowan 2004; Moore 1997; Oddi 1996; Sterk 1996; Weinreb 1998; Yen 1990.

"Inventions then cannot, in nature, be a subject of property. Society may give an exclusive right to the profits arising from them, as an encouragement to men to pursue ideas which may produce utility [...]." (Jefferson 1854: 181)

Today, not only American lawyers refer to the utilitarian perspective to justify intellectual property, but rather most scholars and lawyers would agree on the incentives effect of intellectual property rights. Therefore, modern international legal and economic scholars mostly refer to this economic rationale. Accordingly, intellectual property rights[74] are justified by the necessity to appropriate the returns of R&D efforts, that is, the benefits of the production of information goods. This can be explained as follows: Information and knowledge are usually considered to be quasi-public goods. According to this approach, once an idea is created, it is difficult to prevent others from using it ("non-excludability") and the marginal costs of producing an additional unit are zero, that is to say, the usage of the idea is non-rival. As a result, the private production of knowledge is afflicted with problems. First, firms and innovators have reduced incentives to invent because they cannot prevent knowledge spillovers. Spillovers are R&D externalities influencing the research endeavors of other companies and researchers (Griliches 1992: S30). That is to say, the innovator cannot appropriate the returns of her R&D investments because others can profit from their innovative effort and imitate the innovative output. Thus, even though these knowledge spillovers can also be evaluated as positive externalities, they negatively influence the incentives of the innovator. In developing the theory of externalities, Pigou (1924) described externalities as:

"instances in which marginal private net product falls short of marginal social net product because incidental services are performed to third parties from whom it is difficult to exact payment." (Pigou 1924: 162)

Consequently, there is an underproduction of ideas and knowledge, because firms and innovators do not value them correctly. Due to this insufficient appropriability, fewer innovations would be made than desirable from a total welfare perspective (Pigou 1924: 161 et seqq.). Assigning property rights would solve this externality problem (Coase 1960; Demsetz 1967: 348 et seqq.).[75]

---

74   In economic terms, intellectual property rights define usage rights on information goods (Schmidtchen 2007). The production of information goods can increase society's welfare in at least four different ways: 1) when a new product is developed (product innovation) for which a significant demand exists; 2) when the quality of an already existing good is improved; 3) when there is a reduction in production costs (process innovation); 4) when a new information good reduces transaction costs (institutional innovation), like in case of trademarks (Schmidtchen 2007: 13). Throughout my thesis, I will mainly refer to the first three welfare benefits.

75   More precisely, Coase explains that a market for externalities would evolve through the creation of property rights. However, this model, also known as the Coase Theorem, is based on the assumption that no transaction costs exist. Obviously, this is not the reality.

Demsetz' famous article "Toward a Theory of Property Rights" (1967) plays a central role in this line of argument. Demsetz points out that property rights are necessary to give incentives to internalize these externalities or, in other words, to improve the internalization (Demsetz 1967: 348). Demsetz argues that whereas common ownership gives insufficient incentives, private ownership of transferable property rights allows internalization (Demsetz 1967: 349). Regarding copyrights and patents, Demsetz explains that if ideas and knowledge are freely appropriable by all, there are no incentives to develop them because the originators cannot benefit from them. Thus, extending private rights to the originators would result in a spurt of in the development of new ideas (ibid: 359).[76]

According to Arrow (1959), intellectual property is characterized through three kinds of market failure: indivisibility, uncertainty, and inappropriability (Arrow 1959: 2 and 9). Regarding indivisibility, knowledge-generating activities like R&D often result in high fix costs, starting with costs for setting up a laboratory and employing specialized labor. As such, economies of scale arise with every further use (Geroski 1998: 92). Uncertainty exists in two regards. First, the firm undertaking the R&D activities faces technological uncertainty in regards to how to create and develop a new product. Second, after overcoming the first uncertainty, the innovator is confronted by market uncertainty, that is, how to sell the product and how to intertwine consumer wishes with technological conditions (Geroski 1998: 92). Inappropriabilty is related to public goods in that other companies and innovators can profit from the generated knowledge without paying for it (positive externalities). If the owner would sell her information on the open market, then the purchaser could reproduce and sell this information at little or no cost and thereby destroy the monopoly of the inventor (Arrow 1959: 9). Therefore, without legal protection, these market failures would lead to an underproduction of ideas and knowledge.

While this approach sounds quite similar to Demsetz's approach, Arrow's argument is different in a number of respects. In his approach, Demsetz aims mainly at the internalization of externalities, because otherwise the inventor has the wrong incentives and does not produce a socially optimal amount. Thus, Demsetz starts with the problem of non-excludability. In contrast, Arrow bases his argument on the public good characteristics, that is, on non-excludability *and* non-rivalry. According to Arrow, the producer cannot cover her developing costs because the marginal cost of an additional unit equals zero. In a world of

---

Thus, with this assumption, Coase shows a failure in our markets as optimal allocation will never be realized due to transaction costs (Frischmann 2007: 655).

76   However, it is important to note that intellectual property rights are not exclusively assigned to internalize (positive) externalities (Cohen 1998: 514). Instead, they are assigned both to create incentives to innovate and to enable access to the intellectual good (Frischmann 2007: 653).

perfect competition, the market price matches the marginal cost. Together with the characteristic of non-excludability, the creator or inventor has no possibility of covering her costs and, as a result, will not produce. Keeping the information secret is the only solution for the inventor to use it exclusively and to appropriate the return of her efforts. However, this monopoly is not only socially inefficient but might not be desirable for the original producer herself because she is not necessarily able to exploit the ideas as effectively as others (Arrow 1959: 9).

Therefore, intellectual property law has two different aims: 1) it tries to provide incentives for innovation (reward function) and therewith to correct market failure; and 2) it aims at supporting the disclosure of innovation (knowledge diffusion function) (Schmidtchen 2007). Without intellectual property protection, firms would tend to keep their innovations secret. This secrecy would lead to two inefficiencies.[77] First, the resources spent on keeping the information confidential are diverted from other productive uses. Second, as other economic agents cannot profit from the developed knowledge, the pace of technological progress is slowed (Régibeau/ Rockett 2004). Thus, if the knowledge or the information is protected by intellectual property rights, the right holder can disclose the information to other companies (for example, for licensing agreements) without fear of imitation.[78] Conversely, the other party can assess the value of the information before making the decision to buy (Arora/ Ceccagnoli 2004: 3).

Obviously, these two functions of intellectual property rights lead to a tradeoff between incentives on the one hand and access on the other hand, since the greater the incentive to innovate due to higher protection, the less the access to the information of these innovations (Towse/ Holzhauer 2002: ix). However, to this day, intellectual property rights are deemed to be essential to promote innovation.

3.2.2   Economic Goals of Competition Policy

Generally, in economics the overall goal of competition policy is the enhancement of welfare.[79] In detail, two concepts of welfare can be differentiated, the consumer welfare standard and the total welfare standard. Under the approach of total welfare, economists and competition authorities do not consider distribu-

---

77   Still, in Chapter 4 we will see that secrecy can also be related to a number of benefits.

78   Please note that in case of patents the right holder must disclose the underlying information, compare Article 29 of The Agreement on Trade-Related Aspects of Intellectual Property Rights (TRIPS Agreement), adopted in Marrakesh, Annex 1C, Agreement Establishing the World Trade Organization, 1869 U.N.T.S. 299, 33 I.L.M. 1197 (1994).

79   For the various objectives of competition compare also to Budzinksi 2008; Kerber/Schwalbe 2007 and Motta 2004.

tional effects.[80] In contrast, the conception of consumer welfare measures only the effects on consumer surplus and does not account for changes in producer surplus.[81] That is to say, competition authorities analyze the firms' conduct only in relation to consumer surplus. If a conduct, for instance a merger between two firms, tends to lead to redistribution from consumer surplus to producer surplus (that is, the growth of producer surplus is at the expense of consumer welfare), then it is very likely that the authorities will find this conduct to be anti-competitive. Even though the consumer welfare is not indisputable, nowadays it is the generally accepted standard in competition policy (Christiansen 2008: 409).[82]

Means for the measurement of welfare and effects on welfare are the subor-dinated goals allocative, productive and dynamic efficiency. Generally, a market is assumed to be allocative efficient when market processes lead resources to an allocation according to their highest value use among all competing uses and no reallocation could further increase utility (Kolasky/ Dick 2003: 242). To put it in

---

80 Thus, the total welfare standard considers both the effects on consumer and producer welfare. Accordingly, a particular action of a firm would not reduce welfare and there-fore be not anti-competitive if it leads to a redistribution of consumer welfare to produ-cer welfare as long as the total welfare maintains or increases. For further discussion of the benefits of total welfare compare exemplarily to Carlton 2007; Crampton 1994; Far-rell/Shapiro 1990; Heyer 2006; Posner 2001; Motta 2004; Williamson 1968.

81 Heyer (2006) differentiates between three different welfare standards. The first one is a standard he calls the "Actual Pareto" consumer welfare standard. Under this concept, antitrust authorities would not intervene in a merger or other potential anti-competitive conduct when the welfare of the consumers in each impacted market is improved or at least not worsened as compared to before (Heyer 2006: 2). With the "Potential Pareto" consumer welfare standard, the decisive criterion is whether the net welfare of the con-sumers across the impacted markets increases. That is, even though in certain markets consumers may be worse off, this does not count if the benefit of consumers in other markets outweighs those losses (Heyer 2006.: 2). Finally, the third standard is the total welfare standard consisting, as described above, of the sum of producer and consumer surplus. Furthermore, Crampton (1994) also distinguishes the total welfare standard. He defines the sum of consumer surplus and producer surplus as total surplus, whereas total welfare also incorporates welfare effects on third markets (ibid.: 59, 60).

82 The reasons for this preference are manifold. For instance, it is argued that that competi-tion policy should also consider distributional effects, since consumers are the weaker party. Since consumers cannot enforce their rights in the same manner as companies can, it is appropriate that competition policy advocates for them. Besides that, the con-sumer welfare standard has the advantage that it is more practicable than the total welfa-re standard (Salop 2005: 22-23; Lande 1989). According to this point of view, it is ea-sier to assess solely the effects of anti-competitive conduct on consumers or even only on prices (Carlton 2007: 159; Motta 2004: 21; Werden 1996). For a detailed discussion about the advantages of both consumer and total welfare standard, *compare to* Christi-ansen 2010.

simpler words, allocative efficiency presupposes that the price mechanism is working (Anderman 1998: 17).[83] This implies that producers produce at optimum costs or at least close to optimum costs because competition drives the price down to the marginal cost per unit. Productive efficiency is closely related to allocative efficiency. Productive efficiency is fulfilled when, for example, a firm produces a given output with the fewest input or the reverse, a firm produces the biggest possible output with given resources. No rearrangement of resources could increase the output or further alleviate the costs (Kolasky/Dick 2003: 244). That is, the firm produces at minimal costs. Both allocative and productive efficiency are static concepts, that is, they consider price effects ceteris paribus. Under the assumption of perfect competition, efficient allocation is achieved at the intersection of the demand and the supply curve when prices equal marginal costs and both consumer and producer surplus[84] are maximized. Thus, in the context of efficient allocation competition policy aims at the maintenance of a working price mechanism. Under the consumer welfare standard, actions aiming at the reduction of consumer surplus to the advantage of producer surplus are considered to be anti-competitive – alleging that the growth in producer surplus is not a result of an improvement of production processes or of other efficiency improvements but a result of change of prices.

In contrast, dynamic efficiency does not focus on price effects but on the promotion of technological progress (Brodley 1987).[85] In detail, dynamic efficiency comprises the request for improvements in technologies, which can include the enhancement of a product's quality, the development of new products, or the development or improvement of production technologies. Competition may foster dynamic efficiency by putting pressure on single firms to innovate

---

83   In economics, the concept of efficient allocation is associated on a theoretical level with the general equilibrium theory and from a normative perspective with the Pareto criterion. The latter is fulfilled in a situation where it is impossible to improve the utility of any person without worsening the utility of any other person. The criterion is based on the assumption that interpersonal utility comparisons are not possible and on the assumption of perfect competition. Efficient allocation is achieved when the resources of the economy are allocated to production that they fulfil the Pareto criterion. For further explanations compare to Varian 1992 or any other intermediate textbook on microeconomics.

84   The individual surplus of a consumer is the (positive) difference between her willingness to pay and the actual price she is paying. The aggregation of the benefits of all consumers constitutes the consumer surplus or consumer welfare. Likewise, the individual producer surplus is the difference between the production costs and the market price or, simply put, the profit the producer makes when selling the good. Consequently, producer surplus pictures the aggregate profit of all producers. Compare to Varian 1992 or any other intermediate microeconomics textbook.

85   Please note that Brodley (1987) refers to innovation efficiency instead of dynamic efficiency.

continuously, to try to develop new or better products, or at least to try to lower the production costs. If firms do not act accordingly, they will fear being replaced by more innovative and consequently more successful firms in the market (Anderman 1998: 17). Thus, dynamic efficiency alludes to the growth of knowledge in an economy, embracing technical progress, and the introduction of new products and processes (Schwalbe/Zimmer 2006: 10). It enhances welfare in numerous ways, since consumers are better off because of increased quality and diversity of products and services and there are lower product prices due to improvement of production processes and reduction of production costs. The producers or suppliers profit from dynamic efficiency through Schumpeterian rents, which are based on their innovative success (Kantzenbach 1967; Röpke 1977).[86] Hence, whereas allocative and productive efficiency are primary static goals, dynamic efficiency aims at the enhancement of innovation. From an economic perspective, static and dynamic efficiency are at least equally important. Since dynamic efficiency aims at the creation of new products and therewith new values one might even argue that dynamic efficiency is more important for a sustainable maintenance and increase of welfare than marginal competition in price in already established markets (Schumpeter 1942: 83-84).

3.2.3 Interface of Competition Policy and Intellectual Property Law from an Economic Perspective

This leads us again to the initial question whether – from an economic point of view – competition law and intellectual property law are conflicting or whether they pursue the same goal. If we take a short-term perspective, it is possible to argue that the two laws stand in conflict with each other. Under that perspective, competition policy can only focus on price effects since the realization of technical progress cannot be observed and analysed yet. Thus, competition policy can only take into account effects that occur in a predictable time period and, therefore, it focuses on static efficiency or, in other words, on price effects. At the same time, intellectual property rights allow an inefficient allocation of resources and may lead to a deadweight loss. Due to the prohibition of imitation, the innovator is the only one offering that particular product, that is to say, she has a legal monopoly. Even though a legal monopoly does not necessarily go along with market power in the sense that the innovator can raise the price above

---

86   Furthermore, dynamic efficiency also generates or increases adaptive flexibility. This is a function of competition, which was originally described by Kantzenbach (1967) as "Anpassungsflexibilität." According to this concept, dynamic efficiency has two main effects; first, it boosts knowledge generation and accumulation within an economy; and second, it fosters the ability of an economy to adapt both to exogenous and endogenous changes (Linge 2008: 19). In other words, this adaptive functionality of dynamic efficiency determines the ability of markets to evolve in the future (Budzinski 2008: 312).

market (equilibrium) price, in some cases it gives leeway to set a higher price. Clearly, with an exclusive focus on the goal of static efficiency, a conflict between competition law and intellectual property law would be on hand.

However, as the remarks in the previous section have shown, static efficiency is only one aspect of (consumer) welfare. If we broaden the scope and take a ·long-term perspective, competition policy promotes technical progress, that is, innovation. Therewith, it pursues the same goal as intellectual property law does. The difference between the two laws is rather instrumental: both laws aim at the promotion of innovation, intellectual property law does so by protecting from direct imitation and competition policy by maintaining competitive pressure and pluralism. From this perspective we can argue that even though both intellectual property rights and competition law pursue the same goal, the instruments used to achieve this goal are oppositional. Still, we can assume that the promotion of innovation through intellectual property rights does not evoke competition policy concerns. Instead, competition policy acknowledges that a certain reward is necessary to create innovation incentives. This reward is also a driver of competition since competitors have incentives to innovate themselves, either to find possibilities for inventing around or to develop an innovation that replaces the one of the intellectual property right holder. Hence, an intellectual property right does not impede competition but rather direct imitation. From an economic perspective we would therefore argue that since competition law and intellectual property law pursue the same goal, that is the promotion of innovation and welfare, no general conflict between the two goals exists.

3.2.4 Tension between European Competition Rules and Intellectual Property Rights

Having outlined the interface between competition policy and intellectual property rights, we will now briefly turn to the tension that exists between them in the context of the European Community.

As highlighted by the former Competition Commissioner Monti, in the European Union, competition policy protects consumer welfare by maintaining a high degree of competition within the common market in order to achieve: 1) low prices; 2) a broader choice of goods; and 3) technological innovation (Monti 2001). Thus, the goals of European competition policy basically mirror the objectives as stated from an economic perspective. First, European competition policy is based on the consumer welfare standard, which is evident in various regulations. For instance, both Articles 101 and 102 TFEU consider effects on consumer welfare as decisive for the establishment of anti-competitive conduct. Second, the goal of lower prices complies with the goal of static efficiency. For illustration, in the "Guidelines on the application of Article 81 of the EC Treaty to technology transfer agreements," the European Commission states that it is the aim of Article 81 (now Article 101 TFEU) to protect competition on the market with a view on efficient allocation.[87] And finally, the broader choice of goods and technical innovation previously mentioned corresponds to dynamic efficiency. This goal is expressed, for instance, in Article 101(3) TFEU. Accordingly, cartel agreements are exempted from the cartel prohibition if they contribute to "improving the production or distribution of goods or to promoting technical or economic progress [while allowing consumers a fair share of the resulting benefit]."[88]

Besides these more or less purely economic objectives, European competition rules also aim to defend small and medium-sized firms (Motta 2004) and to promote the integration of a single market. As established in previous treaties as well as in the Treaty of Lisbon (ToL), the promotion of market integration is one of the main objectives of the European Union.[89] European competition policy essentially pursues two main objectives; first, the maintenance of competition embracing all the goals mentioned above; and second, fostering single market integration (Jones/ Sufrin 2004: 36). According to the European Commission, a functioning internal market is an inevitable condition for the development of an efficient and competitive industry.

This goal of market integration is also the driving force for European intellectual property rules. Intellectual property rights that have only national validity or are designed differently within each member state may lead to restrictions of free trade (Lang 2008: 23). Thus, Article 97 of the ToL establishes that the Parliament has to initiate measures for uniform protection of intellectual property rights. Besides the goal of stronger market integration, such European regulation of intellectual property rights aims at the stimulation of innovation. This goal becomes evident in several directives concerning the harmonization of intellectual property rights.[90] For instance, the Convention on the Grant of European Patents (ECP) that establishes the grant of European patents is motivated by the desire "to promote innovation and economic growth in Europe".[91] Regarding

---

87 Commission Notice - Guidelines on the application of Article 81 of the EC Treaty to technology transfer agreements, OJ EC 2004 No. C 101, para. 5.

88 As the bracketed part of this excerpt shows, this exemption is only valid if consumers benefit from these developments. Thus, besides the goal of promoting innovation, this paragraph also contains another goal: the enhancement of consumer welfare.

89 *Compare to* Article 2 of the Treaty of Lisbon and *to* Article 3 TFEU.

90 For an overview of all guidelines and directives aiming at a harmonization of intellectual property rights compare exemplarily to Pierson/Ahrens/Fischer 2007: 23.

91 *Act revising the Convention on the Grant of European Patents* (European Patent Convention) of 5 October 1973, last revised on 17 December 1991, of 29 November 2000, Preamble (p. 488).

copyrights, the Directive on harmonisation of copyright[92] states that copyrights protect and stimulate the development of new products and services (ibid.: para. 2). More generally, in the Directive on the enforcement of intellectual property rights[93] the Commission states that

> "[the] protection of intellectual property should allow the inventor or creator to derive a legitimate profit from his/her invention or creation. It should also allow the widest possible dissemination of works, ideas and new know-how." (ibid.: para. 2)

From this statement it becomes evident that a second goal besides the promotion of innovation is the distribution of knowledge. Hence, the goals of intellectual property rights in European legislation conform to the economic objectives: the promotion of innovation and the dissemination of knowledge. So what is now the tension between intellectual property rights and EU competition rules?

Since we found that both the goals of competition law and intellectual property law coincide with the economic objectives, we might assume that the relationship between the two is the same in European law. Reviewing the publications of the EU in regards to this tension, the relationship between competition law and intellectual property law finds clearest expression (at least in the legal texts) in the Guidelines on technology transfer agreements. In the Guidelines, the Commission states:[94]

> "The fact that intellectual property laws grant exclusive rights of exploitation does not imply that intellectual property rights are immune from competition law intervention. [...] Nor does it imply that there is an inherent conflict between intellectual property rights and the Community competition rules. [...] Intellectual property rights promote dynamic competition by encouraging undertakings to invest in developing new or improved products and processes. So does competition by putting pressure on undertakings to innovate. Therefore, both intellectual property rights and competition are necessary to promote innovation and ensure a competitive exploitation thereof. "

Therewith, we can conclude that within European legislation there is no conflict between both laws. Instead, there is agreement that intellectual property law and competition policy aim at the promotion of innovation. Again, this result corresponds to our findings from an economic perspective: in lieu of being contradictory, the overall objective is the promotion of innovation and therefore, competi-

---

92   Directive 2001/29/EC of the European Parliament and of the Council of 22 May 2001 on the harmonisation of certain aspects of copyright and related rights in the information society, OJ L 167, 22.6.2001, pp10-19.
93   Corrigendum to Directive 2004/48/EC of the European Parliament and of the Council of 29 April 2004 on the enforcement of intellectual property rights (OJ L 157, 30.4.2004), OJ L 195, 2.6.2004, pp. 16–25.
94   Commission Notice - Guidelines on the application of Article 81 of the EC Treaty to technology transfer agreements, OJ EC 2004 No. C 101 p. 2 para. 7.

tion policy and intellectual property law are just different instruments to achieve this goal.

3.3 Interplay of Competition Law and Intellectual Property Rights as a Means of Fostering Innovation

The sections above have shown that neither from an economic point of view nor in the European jurisdiction do intellectual property rights and competition policy conflict with each other; instead we found that they are complementary. Nevertheless, so far we still did not clarify whether competition policy can restrict intellectual property rights and, if so, under which conditions. Thus, in the following sections we will turn to the question regarding when competition policy ought to interfere. Based on these results we will then turn back to the Incentives Balance Test in order to analyse whether this specific test is an appropriate means for an interference with intellectual property rights.

3.3.1 Under Which Circumstances Should Competition Law Interfere with Intellectual Property Rights?

As already pointed out, both competition policy and intellectual property rights aim at the promotion of innovation, or, in other words, the enhancement of dynamic efficiency. The difference between the two is only instrumental – whereas intellectual property rights foster innovation by rewarding a successful innovator with monopoly profits, competition policy tries to stimulate innovation by protecting competition and free market entry (Kerber/Schmidt 2008). But when or under what circumstances can competition law restrict intellectual property rights? Since the mutual goal is the promotion of welfare, it seems only consistent that competition policy ought to interfere when such a restriction would further spur innovation. Hence, we have to analyse whether an impediment to innovation justifies the interference of competition policy into intellectual property rights. In order to determine this we will employ the property rights theory.

From an economic perspective, property rights aim at the promotion of social welfare. According to the property rights theory, not the asset itself is owned but rather a bundle of rights to use this asset (Alchian/Demsetz 1973: 17). Owning a property right implies the right to use the property, to modify its form and to transfer it to other parties, e.g. through rental or sale (Furubotn/Pejovich 1972: 1139-1140). The strength of a right is determined by the extent to which the right holder can actually decide on the use of the right. The restrictions to a right may also contain the prohibition of a certain conduct. As Alchian and Demsetz describe, a person owning an apple tree may have the right to pick the apples but she still may not have the right to fell the tree (Alchian/Demsetz 1973: 17). Therefore, a property right holder does not have an absolute or unrestricted right over the asset; rather, the right is assigned to optimize welfare (Lueck/Micelli 2007). At the same time, a property right allows the right holder to harm or benefit others. With the assignment of a specific bundle of rights the property right specifies to which extent the right holder can harm third parties and the right also specifies who has to pay whom to modify the activities of the right holder (Demsetz 1967: 347). Applying this to intellectual property rights, a patent, for example, confers the right to exclusive usage and, hence, the exclusion of others. If a competitor wants to use the patent as well, she has to negotiate the usage and the usage conditions with the patent holder. In other words, she has to pay the patent holder, for instance, a license fee. Thus, while a property right usually creates benefits for the right holder, it might create externalities for third parties concurrently. Referring again to intellectual property rights, the negative externality could be that competitors cannot participate in the further development of a certain idea or innovation since they are excluded from the use of the patent or copyright.

According to Demsetz, an externality occurs when the costs of integrating the (positive or negative) effect into the decision making process is too high to make it worthwhile (Demsetz 1967: 348). The property right allows the owner to economize on the usage of the protected asset and therefore she has no incentives to consider the effects of her actions on the rights of others (ibid.: 356). From this we can conclude that if the (social) costs of the externality exceed the (social) benefits of the right it is necessary to consider internalizing those effects. It is an important function of property rights to create incentives to accomplish a greater internalization of externalities. In terms of the property rights theory, internalization alludes to a process that renders possible the full realization of (negative) externalities by all concerned parties. Usually, such an internalization process involves a change in property rights (Demsetz 1967: 348). As Furubotn and Pejovich (1972) point out, if no short-run technical progress or innovation can be expected that is capable of correcting the negative effect – in the case of intellectual property rights this might be an innovation replacing an existing patent – policy makers should be concerned with finding an optimal pattern of correction. In other words, if the outcome of the usage of the property rights differs from that which would be achieved by considering all social costs and benefits, it is necessary to consider an alternative property rights assignment. Hereby, this new assignment or correction should take into account how it affects the use of the assets as well as the output mix (ibid.: 1145).

Thus, this brief excursion into the principles of property rights theory shows that property rights 1) have the purpose to enhance welfare, 2) are not absolute rights but rather have inherent restrictions and 3) can be modified when they do not enhance welfare. So how can we transfer this to intellectual property rights? First, as already highlighted, intellectual property rights are assigned to create incentives for innovation, and more generally to enhance social welfare. However, the extent of these rights is determined by the scope of protection. Does the patent cover not only of the invention but also related areas or does it only protect the invention itself and allow for further innovation by other parties? The exact design of the rights specifies how the owner can use her rights and it also specifies to which extent competitors or other inventors are excluded from the usage. Hence, as with other property rights, they create externalities – positive ones attributed to innovation and the creation of knowledge and negative ones due to the restriction of usage and exploitation by other innovators and firms. In the cases described in Chapter 2 we already saw that in some cases the exploitation of the intellectual property rights can evoke high negative effects since the exclusion of competitors prohibits new products or technological developments. Without judging whether these negative effects overweigh the positive, welfare enhancing effects of intellectual property rights in those particular cases, the question here is how policy makers and legislators should deal with those intellectual property rights that greatly restrict new innovations.

Following the approaches of Demsetz and Furubotn/Pejovich, in such cases it is necessary to consider a redefinition of the (particular) intellectual property rights in order to internalize the negative effects and to reinstall the welfare enhancing effects. However, the question is whether it is necessary to do that through competition policy or whether it is possible to solve this problem with intellectual property law. Consider a solution within intellectual property law. At first glance, there are two different possibilities regarding how to deal with these problems of socially undesirable effects. First, it might be a solution to design intellectual property rights on a case-by-case basis. Taking into account the administrative effort for such an undertaking and also the – probably – small number of cases in which the negative effects of intellectual property rights are higher than the benefits, this approach is not convincing. Second, one might introduce the possibility of redefining intellectual property rights ex post within intellectual property law. Obviously, the approach is advantageous compared to the first suggestion. An intellectual property right would only be subject to redefinition if there is some evidence that the negative effects evoked by the exercise of this right supersede the benefits. To put it differently, such an ex post interference would only occur when the intellectual property right demonstrably restricts innovation, for instance on secondary markets. However, without further elaborating on this, the difficulty with this proceeding is the existing variation among national intellectual property laws. In contrast to competition law and despite efforts at harmonization, at this point there is no uniform European intellectual property law. From this perspective, it would be difficult to incorporate such a correcting mechanism equally in all national laws.

Therefore, using competition policy for a redefinition of intellectual property rights has a certain charm. Since we have a European competition law and also a European authority, the Commission, which investigates those cases in which an impediment to competition seems to occur, the same rules would apply to all cases. Moreover, using competition policy for such a redefinition is also advantageous because it already offers an instrument to detect those cases in which it seems likely that intellectual property rights impede innovation (and competition). If competition policy ought to interfere with intellectual property rights, this implies that an ex post correction only occurs when competition has already been impeded. This proceeding would greatly limit the number of cases in which such a redefinition would be conducted especially if we – as described in Chapter 2 – use Article 102 TFEU to detect such cases. Under these criteria only dominant firms would be subject to ex post correction of their intellectual property rights. If a competition policy investigation finds that the negative effects through exclusion from the right, that is to say, the negative effects due to a refusal to license, supersede the benefits of the intellectual property rights, it would redefine the particular intellectual property right by imposing, for instance, a compulsory license. Simply put, if the exercise of the right to exclude by refusing to license significantly impedes technical progress, competition authorities ought to step in and correct the scope of the intellectual property right. Such a proceeding corresponds to the property rights theory that demands that property rights be assigned to enhance social welfare. The interference by competition policy would reaffirm this objective. Consequently, this correction should be in such a manner that the redefined intellectual property right gives consideration to all the effects on innovation, that is, the effects on innovation of the right holder and on innovation of competitors. In the words of Demsetz, the redefinition of the intellectual property right should lead to an internalization of the externality. As a consequence, more innovation can occur. From this perspective, imposing a compulsory license would be a possibility to tailor ex post the concerned intellectual property right with competition policy. Since competition policy, like intellectual property rights, aim at the promotion of innovation, such interference would only occur when innovation is at stake.

3.3.3   The Incentives Balance Test as a Means to Redefine Intellectual Property Rights

Having said that competition policy should be applied to intellectual property rights in those cases in which the right seems to be detrimental to innovation, we will now analyse which role the Commission's Incentives Balance Test can play in this setting.

As already outlined, the decisive criterion for a restriction of intellectual property rights is the impediment to innovation. Thus, before competition policy can interfere with intellectual property rights it is necessary to analyse whether innovation is actually impeded. As Furubotn and Pejovich highlighted, a new assignment of property rights or – in our case – the ex post tailoring of intellectual property rights - requires a careful analysis of the effects of such an action (Furubotn/Pejovich 1972: 1145). Thus, the investigating authority has to analyse the effects of a restriction of intellectual property rights on both the innovator and the competitors. To achieve an improvement over the current situation, it is inevitable that the redefinition of intellectual property rights, that is, the imposition of a compulsory license leads to an enhancement of overall innovation activity. This is actually what the Commission tried to achieve with the application of the Incentives Balance Test.

Recalling the Incentives Balance Test as described in Chapter 2, the test aims to compare the innovation incentives present when the innovator refuses to license, that is, no interference by competition policy, with those incentives present when a license is given. Thus, the Commission intends to compare the situations with and without refusal to license. Only if the overall effects on innovation incentives through an interference of competition policy outweigh the innovation incentives when the intellectual property right is not restricted should competition policy step in to impose a compulsory license. This proceeding is also in line with the property rights theory: Intellectual property rights are assigned to promote innovation. In those cases in which this goal is endangered policy makers, that is, competition authorities, intervene in order to analyse what actions are capable of internalizing or correcting this externality. By doing so, they analyse the effects of a specific action, such as the imposition of a compulsory license, on all involved parties. When competition authorities find that welfare (in our case innovation) would be enhanced through the action, they redefine the property right.

From this perspective, the Incentives Balance Test is an optimal instrument to analyse whether a refusal to license intellectual property rights impedes innovation and competition. If the test proves that a narrower scope of the intellectual property right would significantly enhance innovation, it restricts the intellectual property right by imposing a duty to license. To put it simply, the Incentives Balance Test analyses whether in a specific case the intellectual property right is defined correctly, that is, welfare enhancing. Only if in this specific case the intellectual property right leads to a reduction of welfare, competition policy would correct it ex post. In a nutshell, we can understand the Incentives Balance Test as an instrument of competition policy tailoring too extensive intellectual property rights that would otherwise impede the innovative efforts of competitors and, as a result, restrict competition and decrease social welfare. Thus, the application of the Incentives Balance Test competition policy could indeed focus on the mutual goal of promoting innovation.

Conducted in the legal framework of Article 102 TFEU, intellectual property rights would only be restricted in those cases which notably affect competition and impede innovation. That is to say we do not deal with cases in which smaller firms without significant market power decide to refuse to license. With such an approach we lower transactions costs and maintain legal certainty for firms. In the *Microsoft* case, the Commission applied the Incentives Balance

Test as the fourth step in its examination. Thus, we can interpret the three fore-going investigation steps as filters (Kerber/ Schmidt 2008). Only when the other requirements for an abuse under Article 102 TFEU are fulfilled, that is, when we can prove an impediment to competition and innovation, would the Incentives Balance Test, which is now used as "objective justification," be employed. Ap-plying the test only as the fourth step in the analysis has the positive effect that competition cannot wrongfully correct intellectual property rights. Such restric-tions also minimize the negative effects such a proceeding might otherwise have on innovators (Kerber/ Schmidt 2008). Since the Incentives Balance Test also considers the effects of a duty to license on the dominant firm, we ensure that the innovator's incentives to innovate are also not cut back unduly. Hence, the Incentives Balance Test would directly go to the heart of the interplay between intellectual property rights and competition policy by focussing on the effects on innovation. This proceeding would rebut any objection that a restriction of intel-lectual property rights would evoke negative effects on innovation. Instead, the application of the Incentives Balance Test provides an ex post correction of ill-defined intellectual property rights that foster too many negative effects. Impos-ing a compulsory license can be understood as an instrument to correct this par-ticular right in order to enhance welfare.

However, even though the concept of the Incentives Balance Test seems to be an optimal solution to solve refusal to license cases, the application of the Commission has some shortcomings. The problem lies in the realisation of the Incentives Balance Test. The Commission did not elaborate on what economic criteria it applied to assess whether a compulsory license would spur or decrease innovation. Basically, the Commission stops its investigation after explaining the idea of the Incentives Balance Test. It argues that more competition always leads to more innovation and therefore a compulsory license would result in a higher overall innovation level. Thinking this argumentation line out, we might wonder whether we need intellectual property rights at all, since imitation would lead to higher competitive pressure and therefore more innovation. However, such a point of view ignores the likely market failure due to the public character-istics of information and it fails considering properly the effects on the dominant firm but also on its competitors. In other words, the Commission failed to ade-quately flesh out concrete criteria and guidelines for the test.

3.4   Conclusion: What We Have Learned So Far

The analysis of the relationship between competition law and intellectual prop-erty law on a theoretical level shows that the intervention of competition au-thorities in intellectual property rights is justified. Since both competition policy and intellectual property law aim at the promotion of innovation, competition law may restrict the exercise of intellectual property rights in order to foster innovation and therewith social welfare. It is the interplay of both laws that upholds the mutual goal of promoting innovation.

Having developed an economic framework for competition political interference with intellectual property rights, the Incentives Balance Test constitutes a convincing approach how to deal with those cases in which the exercise of intellectual property rights or, in more detail, a refusal to license may impede innovation. From an economic point of view, the idea of the Incentives Balance Test is to analyse whether in a specific situation the intellectual property rights of a dominant firm are designed correctly, that is, in a welfare enhancing manner, or whether they lead to a reduction of welfare. If the application of the Incentives Balance Test shows that the intellectual property rights may in fact result in less innovation instead of more innovation, a compulsory license or any other remedy would be imposed. This remedy can than be understood as an ex post redefinition of the intellectual property rights in order to enhance welfare and therewith, to restore the common goal of both competition policy and intellectual property law.

Nevertheless, we still do not know what actually fosters innovation and on which criteria an optimal test should focus. While acknowledging that the concept of the Incentives Balance Test is convincing, so far we miss solid economic criteria with which we can assess whether the intellectual property rights are in certain cases too broad and create negative effects in the sense that they lead to a reduction of innovation and therewith, welfare. Thus, in the following chapters, we will analyse whether it is possible to fill the basic principle of the Incentives Balance Test with sound economic criteria or whether we might search for an alternative solution that has a similar effect as such an "optimal" Incentives Balancing Test as interpreted above.

4 The Appropriation of Innovation: How Can We Assess the Necessity of Intellectual Property Rights?

Having outlined a framework for the Incentives Balance Test, in this chapter we will review economic theories in the hopes of finding theories and criteria that can be applied to assess how much intellectual property protection is necessary for providing sufficient incentives for innovation. In detail, we will now analyse what criteria economic theories can offer to conduct the Incentives Balance Test.

The chapter starts with a review of the law and economics theories of intellectual property rights that discuss the optimal degree of protection. The purpose of proceeding as such is twofold: first, to analyse whether a standardized assignment like we have in most countries might lead to an inefficient result; and second, to analyse whether we can use these theories to derive criteria for our test. Thus, the first purpose aims at a confirmation that it is possible that intellectual property rights are not always optimally designed and that competition policy can therefore intervene. The second purpose aims at the development of criteria for an assessment from competition policy in refusal to license intellectual property rights cases.

In the second part of this chapter, I employ insights from innovation economics, starting with an analysis of preconditions for innovation and imitation and exploring appropriability instruments beside intellectual property rights. This is in order to examine whether these results can be used to complement the theories and criteria of optimal intellectual property design or whether they are even better suited for an application within the Incentives Balance Test.

In the last section, I will shed some light on the discussion of the influence of market structure on innovation. The review of the corresponding literature underscores that a general statement is not feasible and that the effects depend on several facts like the strength of the innovation. The discussion of network industry will further show how important it is to consider industry specifics before making judgments regarding the influence of competition on innovation. Again, the motivation behind this step is to assess whether it is possible to deduce insights from these theories that we can consider for the analysis of competition policy of the abuse of intellectual property rights.

The chapter will close with a short summary of the presented results and a discussion of the implications for the Incentives Balance Test.

4.1 The Optimal Design of Intellectual Property Rights in Law and Economics

In Chapter 3, we saw that intellectual property rights do not only aim at providing incentives to innovate, but they also aim at an optimization of social welfare. Thus, we can argue that a case-by-case assignment of intellectual property rights should actually equal a balancing within an idealized Incentives Balance Test as described in section 3.3.3. Similar to the assignment of intellectual property rights, an optimal Incentives Balance Test asks whether in a specific case the intellectual property rights (and their exercise) really spur innovation or whether they might have detrimental effects. Thereby, the Incentives Balance Test does not only focus on the innovation incentives of the first innovator, that is, the incentives of the dominant firm, but also on the effects of later innovators, that is, the incentives of competitors. From this perspective, it seems as if the application of criteria stemming from the law and economics of intellectual property rights within an Incentives Balance Test is the most apparent solution to fill the test with life. Thus, in the following section we will analyse what criteria we can deduce from the mainstream law and economics theories of intellectual property rights.

4.1.1   Patents

Patents are the strongest form of intellectual property protection. Traditionally, they have been justified under four different theses: 1) the "natural law" thesis; 2) the "reward by monopoly" thesis; 3) the "monopoly profit incentive" thesis; and 4) the "exchange for secrets" thesis (Machlup 1958:21).

The "natural law" thesis assumes that man has a natural right to his own ideas and that the usage of these ideas by others should be considered to be stealing.[95] The "reward by monopoly" thesis assumes that man should be rewarded for his services to the extent that they are useful to society. As inventions are considered socially useful, patents are the appropriate way to ensure this reward.

In contrast to the first two theses, which stem more or less from a moral argument, the last two theses are derived from an economic point of view. The "monopoly profit incentive" thesis presumes that inventors and firms will only invent and exploit if they can expect to yield profits from their efforts. The easiest way for society to offer these incentives is to grant patent rights on the invention. The "exchange for secrets" thesis holds that it is in the best interests of society for an inventor to disclose her secret. This would allow the use of the inventor's knowledge for other prospective inventions. Giving the inventor patent

---

95   For this and for the following, *compare* Machlup 1958 and Machlup/ Penrose 1950.

rights on her invention allows her to disclose her ideas without fearing imitators. Hence, a patent does not only offer the inventor the appropriation of returns, but it also prohibits her from keeping the knowledge secret.

Of course, these theses have not been without their critics, but I will not go into the details here.[96] In general, we can summarize that both the "natural law" and "reward by monopoly" theses have lost importance over time and they are now subordinate to other justifications for patents. Today's economic justification focuses on the "monopoly profit incentive" for patents as well as the "exchange for secrets" function of patents (Gallini 1992: 52). Against this background, patents are a policy instrument to spur private innovation. They are granted to firms and individuals to protect their inventions from direct copying. If the innovation is successful, the patent grants the patent owner the opportunity to recoup at least part of the innovation cost and to make some profit. In other words, patents assign (legal) monopolies to patent holders for a limited time period.

However, the creation of innovation incentives with patents produces deadweight losses and thus imposes not only benefits but also costs on society.

> "Stimulating the invention and development of new products and processes is without doubt the most important benefit expected of the patent system. For it society pays a price: the monopoly power it conferred by patent grants." (Scherer 1980: 442)

Achieving the optimal design of patents, that is, mastering the trade-off between sufficient incentives and imposing as few costs as possible on society, is a difficult and important challenge for legislators. Basically, the optimal structure of a patent is determined both by the patent lifetime (patent length) and the patent breadth. Before I explain the socially optimal mixture of length and breadth, I will briefly introduce them separately.

4.1.1.1 Optimal Length

The term patent length determines the period in which the invention is legally protected from imitation and in which other firms are prevented from entering the market (Takalo 2001). The basic model for determining patent length goes back to Nordhaus (1969). Generally, he differentiates between two effects. On the one hand, a lengthening of the patent protection increases the expected reward of the innovation and therewith the incentives to invest in research and development (R&D).[97] The resulting increase of (expected) innovations leads to an

---

96   For a detailed discussion of the four theses, *compare* Machlup/ Penrose 1950.
97   Nordhaus describes this relationship with the invention possibility function (IPF), which describes the relation between the level of inputs (to realize the invention) and the percentage of resulting cost reduction. He assumes that an increase in the inventive input increases the size of the invention (Nordhaus 1969: 73). Regarding the optimal patent li-

increase in social welfare. On the other hand, the longer the patent lifetime, the longer the deadweight loss incurred by the monopoly lasts. This has an opposite welfare effect. Patent length is optimal when the marginal utility of an additional increase in patent lifetime equals its marginal costs (Nordhaus 1969: 76).

In detail, Nordhaus' model is based on the assumption that the patent completely protects the invention from imitation (Nordhaus 1972: 428). The level of research is generally an increasing function of the output and the patent life and a decreasing function of the interest rate (which equals the social discount rate) and the cost of research (Nordhaus 1969: 74). In other words, while a longer patent life and a higher expected output spurs innovative activities, a high interest rate and high research cost have the opposite effect. Assuming that the patented innovation leads to a reduction of production costs, Nordhaus examines the effects of the patent lifetime for process innovations on social welfare.[98] Accordingly, the optimal patent life is a finite and positive number of years, determined by factors like the demand elasticity or the ease of invention (ibid.: 79). The lower the demand elasticity, the longer the optimal life. This can be explained with the deadweight loss – with an increase of the demand elasticity, the deadweight loss increases too. In contrast, if the demand elasticity of the product is zero, that is, the demand does not react to prices, the deadweight loss would tend to be zero as well. In this case, an infinite patent would be optimal (ibid.).[99] Figure 4-1 (compare to following page) illustrates this relationship between deadweight loss and demand elasticity.

The graph on the left side depicts a process innovation in a market with an elastic demand. Due to the innovation, the inventor has lower production costs, which lead to a shift of the supply curve S to S'. However, the inventor cannot realize the monopoly price p^M and the monopoly quantity q^M because the monopoly price would be higher than the price before the innovation. Thus, she prices slightly under the competition price p^c and therewith gets the whole demand. As she could have offered the quantity q' to the price p', a deadweight loss $\overline{ABC}$ arises. If, as pictured in the right graph, the demand is inelastic, that is, the demand does not react to changes in price, no welfare loss arises. Again, the supply curve changes from S to S'. The inventor charges slightly under the competition price p^c, which is just enough that she gets the whole demand. As consumers do not react to the price changes, she can skim the total surplus

---

fe, Nordhaus deviates from that: "If there is no relationship between pecuniary rewards and inventive inputs on the one side and inventive output on the other, the optimal life is zero." (Nordhaus 1969: 74) Accordingly, the longer the patent lifetime, the higher the incentives to invest and the higher the amount of resulting innovation.

98   Nordhaus defines social welfare as consumers' surplus plus producers' surplus minus resource costs (Nordhaus 1969: 76).

99   For a detailed mathematical depiction of these interrelations, compare to Nordhaus 1969: 76-86.

$\overline{EBAp^C}$. In this case, an infinite patent would create optimal incentives for innovation and no social loss would occur. Obviously, we can hardly imagine a case in reality in which this criterion is fulfilled. However, this relationship shows that with decreasing demand elasticity the deadweight loss decreases, whereas high demand elasticity would evoke a higher social loss. Therefore, the patent length should be adjusted according to the respective elasticity.

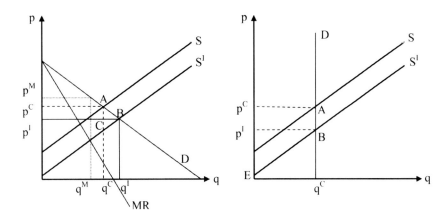

Figure 4-1: Process innovation with elastic demand (left) and inelastic demand (right)

The relationship between the ease of the invention and the patent length is more intuitive. An invention is easier when a higher cost reduction (or a bigger output) can be achieved with a given level of research (Nordhaus 1969: 79). Or, vice versa, in some industries a certain cost reduction can be achieved with a lower research effort. Thus, the "easier" an invention, the shorter the optimal patent lifetime (ibid.).

However, according to Nordhaus, the exact optimal patent length is impossible to determine as long as we do not know the exact values of the different parameters (ibid.: 79). But if we know the data of the demand elasticity, the discount rate, the reduction in per unit costs for the invention, and the curvature of the invention function, we could still specify if the actual patent lifetime is too long or too short (ibid.: 80). Still, as Nordhaus points out, this already has difficulties because we can make only very rough estimations for the invention function. Using those estimations, Nordhaus calculates the optimal length for innovation with varying value and different demand elasticity. For non-drastic innovations that face low demand elasticity, the length is the longest. With increasing demand elasticity, the optimal length shortens. An interesting result is also that with increasing value of the innovation, the term of protection should be

shorter as well. Nordhaus demonstrates that an important drastic innovation facing higher demand elasticity should not be protected longer than two years.
(ibid.: 81).[100] According to his calculation, for most innovations the optimal
length is clearly less than 20 years (ibid.). As Scherer (1972) shows in a reinterpretation of the model, a shortening of patent lifetime[101] would most likely
affect only inventions that already have a minor influence on social welfare.
Admitting that both Nordhaus and his results are based on naïve models, Scherer
points out that this even supports their results because they do not consider other
market barriers causing imitation lags (Scherer 1972: 426).[102] Thus, even though
we do not know precisely what the optimal patent length would be in numbers,
these remarks show that one uniform patent lifetime cannot be optimal but
should at least differ from industry to industry, or even better from innovation to
innovation. Further, we can assume that the actual patent lifetime of 20 years in
most states is probably too long in a lot of cases.

4.1.1.2 Optimal Breadth

The definition of patent breadth is not as clear-cut as the definition of patent
length. In an extension of his model, Nordhaus (1972) measures patent breadth
with the part of technology or cost reduction that does not freely spill out to
competitors (ibid.: 429). Gilbert and Shapiro (1990) define the breadth of a patent as the flow rate of profit to the patent holder during patent lifetime. Gallini
(1992) determines the breadth in dependence of the costs of imitation, while
Klemperer (1990) defines it as the region of differentiated product space, that is,
the possible product differentiation, covered by the patent.[103] In contrast, Matutes et al. (1996) determine patent breadth with the protection of the patent
holder for applications based on the patented product in (varying) markets, that
is, for how many applications of the invention is the patent valid. However, the
question of patent breadth is generally one of how much monopoly power an
innovator should receive (Wright 1999: 419). Legislators can restrict the mo-

---

100 However, this calculation is based on a fixed rate of discount and a fixed exchange rate
     of capital and labour. As Nordhaus has already explained, a slight change in the dis-
     count rate would double the results of his calculations (Nordhaus 1969: 81).
101 Note that Scherer alludes only to process innovations.
102 It is to note that of course extensions to and modifications of this model exist. But as I
     do not refer to them in the following sections, I abstain from discussing them here. The
     interested reader can *compare* exemplarily *to* Bergin 2008; Gallini 1992; O'Donoghue
     et al. 1998.
103 According to this definition, consumers have to face additional costs when they decide
     to buy an imitation of the protected good because they need to "travel" to the bounda-
     ries of the patent. Thus, social loss due to patents includes not only deadweight loss, but
     also travelling costs and the reduction in demand due to these transportation costs of the
     travelling customers (Klemperer 1990).

nopoly power by defining the patent so narrowly that inventing around it is possible and competitors can offer close substitutes to the patent-protected good or service without infringing the patent.

Independently of which definition we follow, the underlying assumption of each is that a narrowing of patent breadth leads to more competition in the product market. In consequence, the innovator would earn fewer profits and competitors would gain more. The innovation incentives for innovators would decrease, whereas more competition would lead to a restriction of the monopoly and therewith to a reduction of the deadweight loss (Denicolo 1996: 251). Thus, the effects on welfare are twofold. On the one hand, welfare is negatively affected by the reduction of innovation incentives and the resultant fewer innovations. On the other hand, welfare is positively affected by the lower welfare loss. Which effect outweighs the other depends on whether due to the increased competition social welfare grows quicker than the innovation incentive decreases (ibid.).

Nevertheless, these static considerations do not consider the dynamic aspects (Merges/Nelson 1990: 843). First, usually many innovators and potential innovators exist, interacting with each other, especially as invention is not a one-round game. Thus, it is not so clear how the presence of a strong patent affects the pool of potential innovators and their incentives to innovate, especially as competitors are normally driven by the desire to stay in competition also in the long run (ibid.: 869). In other words, static models do not consider how market structure and innovation are related to each other, that is, we simply do not know for sure what evokes what (compare to section 4.3.1). Another critical assumption in these static models is that innovation is given externally. As Merges and Nelson point out, many models assume that the imitation process is very easy to realize and ignore that the substitutes created by inventing around are not solely restrained to imitation of the original innovation (ibid: 870). Not only "real" substitutes are affected by the patent breadth, but also follow-on innovations, which might add an additional value to the innovation. A too broad patent might discourage this kind of innovation (ibid.: 870). In contrast, a narrower patent leads to more innovations in a certain area that would under a broad patent regime infringe the already-existing patent. Basically, Merges and Nelson represent the opinion that competition produces more innovation and therewith enhances social welfare. Thus, they plea for a rather narrow patent breadth. This approach can be traced back to Schumpeter (1934). According to Schumpeter, competition is the driving force of innovation. To survive the competitive pressure and to persist in the market, firms have strong incentives to innovate (ibid.). From this perspective, it is arguable that narrow patents promote competition in the market and therewith maintain the incentives to innovate. However, this can be contradicted by the so-called "Prospect Theory" of Edmund Kitch (1977).[104] Under this theory, Kitch analyses how patent policy can stimulate an efficient generation of innovation with a given pool of resources (Kitch 1977: 265). Kitch acknowledges that competition due to narrower patents can evoke inefficiencies such as reciprocal exclusion from (patent) usages or also by patent races. In contrast to Merges and Nelson, Kitch argues that narrow patents lead to social waste as companies invest too much in innovation due to patent races. Instead, (broad) patent protection allows the innovator to coordinate with potential imitators and to ensure an efficient usage of resources (Kitch 1977: 279). Furthermore, if only one (dominant) firm owns a broad patent, this makes planning for other companies easier. If competitors develop follow-on innovations they do not need to fear infringing another patent[105] and only have to negotiate with one company about licensing (ibid.: 285-86). Thus, according to Kitch's prospect theory, control of a technology by a single firm is better, because rivalry and therewith waste of resources is avoided and opens instead the possibility of planning and efficient use of resources.[106]

In contrast, Merges and Nelson argue that the more firms compete, the more diverse the results as mostly different firms have different views on certain things. Moreover, if due to a broad patent only one company researches in a certain market, the company may simply oversee some research questions or innovation possibilities. Thus, narrower patents do not only increase price competition but also diversity (ibid.: 872).[107] Besides that, if a company does not have to fear any competition, it might also have no incentive to further innovate at all (ibid. 871). Having said this, Merges and Nelson conclude that, at least in markets with cumulative technologies, narrow patents are preferable because they

---

104 Kitch defines prospect as "a particular opportunity to develop a known technological possibility." (Kitch 1977: 266) Accordingly, patents always contain prospect elements. Depending on the design of the patent system, the prospect function of patents can be stronger or weaker. However, in our systems, the prospect function is generally an important part of the patent system (ibid.: 267).

105 This problem is closely connected to patent thickets and submarine patents (see exemplarily Shapiro 2001). In short, patent thickets arise when patents are assigned imprecisely. In consequence, overlapping patents might exist and infringe each other. Submarine patents, in contrast, are patents that are not used to produce but to file suits if someone uses the underlying technology accidentally (ibid.).

106 Even though allocative efficiency is enhanced when only one firm controls a certain technology, this might be to the expense of dynamic efficiency. As Kerber and Saam (2001) argue, a concentration of firms might evoke a reduction of learning opportunities in the market. Thus, focusing on efficient allocation of resources and avoidance of waste of resources ignores the fact that different outcomes could be achieved due to parallel research processes (ibid.).

107 For a comprehensive discussion of the value and influence of diversity on innovation, compare to Linge (2008).

stimulate innovation and therewith faster technological progress (ibid.: 908). I will discuss the optimal patent mix for cumulative innovation in section 4.2.1.4. I will now turn to the interplay of patent length and breadth for stand-alone innovation.

4.1.1.3 Optimal Combination of Length and Breadth for Single Innovations

Optimal length and breadth can only be determined in dependence of each other. The leading question for this determination is how a patent system should be structured efficiently to create a certain reward for the innovator. Thus, models concerning the optimal patent mix normally do not consider the question of the amount of the appropriate reward for the innovator, that is, they take the reward as a given and focus on the most efficient composition of length and breadth (Gilbert/Shapiro 1990: 106). Before I present the results of these models,[108] it is noteworthy that they are mostly based on static assumptions, as they do not consider that there is usually more than one innovator, that is, they ignore the possibility of patent races, and further they do not consider technological developments that could lead to diversity. Still, for our purposes, these models provide very valuable insights about the complexity of determining optimal patent protection.

Under the assumption of a static and predictable environment, Gilbert and Shapiro show that an infinite patent length is optimal if social costs grow disproportionately high with an increase of patent breadth. Thus, according to their model, the rather narrow patent breadth should be adjusted in a way that the appropriate reward can just be realized (Gilbert/Shapiro 1990: 106 et seqq.). Gilbert and Shapiro illustrate that these assumptions are generally fulfilled in a homogenous product market. Equalling the reward of the innovator with the price for the products, Gilbert and Shapiro show that social costs are minimized when patents are so narrow that price almost equals marginal costs and length is infinite (Gilbert/Shapiro 1990: 111).

In contrast, Klemperer defines a model with product differentiation. He assumes that consumers prefer the same product versions, but differ in regards to willingness to pay and costs for substitution between the different product versions. Starting with the determination of patent breadth, Klemperer minimizes the trade-off between social costs and the reward for the innovator. Afterwards Klemperer adjusts the patent length, which increases both social costs and innovator' profit to the same amount, to the breadth so that the given reward can be realized (Klemperer 1990: 117). According to his model, long and narrow pat-

---

108   As we will not need the detailed derivations in the course of this thesis, I limit myself to presenting only the results. The interested reader may *refer* exemplarily *to* Denicolo 1996; Gallini 1990; Gilbert/Shapiro 1990; Klemperer 1990 and Takalo 1998.

ents are optimal when consumers have the same cost of substitution. Then, for instance, broad but short patents are optimal when consumers have the same maximal willingness to pay (reservation price) (Klemperer 1990: 127).

Both models have in common that they assume imitation to be costless, and thus, imitation is always a threat to innovation. Gallini, by contrast, presumes imitation to be costly, that is, the broader the patent, the costlier the imitation, because then, for instance, the patent holder can more easily prove patent infringement and demand compensation (Gallini 1992: 60). Generally, the longer the patent life, the higher the incentives to imitate or invent around. From the perspective of a social planner, the optimization problem with imitation costs is to ensure an appropriate reward for the innovation, to minimize deadweight loss, and to avoid or at least to minimize duplicative spending from imitators (Rockett 2008). Thus, legislators should set the breadth to the extent that imitation is just avoided and then set patent life according to the desired reward for the innovator (Gallini 1992: 61). In a modification of the model, Takalo assumes that the success of an imitation is uncertain and influenced by the level of knowledge spillovers. He shows that with a low level of knowledge spillovers, patent breadth and length are substitutes for each other whereas with a high spillover level, they are complementary. Thus, Takalo suggests a short patent life and, depending on the spillovers, adjusts the breadth. For a high knowledge level, this implies that patents should be rather narrow, too, as breadth is complementary to length (Takalo 1998).

Adding a dynamic perspective by including the possibility of patent races,[109] Denicolo (1996) suggests more general rules. He shows that the optimal mix of length and breadth depends, first, on the relationship between social welfare and post-innovation profits and,[110] second, on the breadth of the patent. Denicolo further shows that optimal mix depends on several factors: the type of market,[111]

---

109 According to Denicolo (2001), patent races do not necessarily lead to a "winner takes all" situation. As long as patent length is finite, the losers of the patent race will get positive profits when the patent expires. Thus, the equilibrium-level of R&D efforts is determined by two factors: first, the "profit incentive," which describes the difference between the patentee's profit and the profit before the innovation; and second, the "competitive threat" comprising the difference between the winner's profit and the loser's profit (Denicolo 2001: 253). Further, if, for instance, the innovation is not drastic and the patent breadth is narrow, losers might sill be able to lower their marginal costs, too, because they could invent around without infringing the patent (ibid.: 258).

110 That is to say, patent length and breadth must be chosen in a way that the discounted deadweight loss over the patent's lifetime is minimized while a given incentive to innovate must be created (Denicolo 1996: 257).

111 Denicolo differentiates between homogenous and heterogeneous product markets and between Bertrand and Cournot competition.

the gradient of marginal costs and demand curves, and imitation costs.[112] According to his model, broad and short patents are more likely to be socially optimal the less efficient competition in the product market is (Denicolo 1996: 264). Denicolo suggests determining the optimal patent mix in dependence of the competitive pressure in the product market. With little competition, patent breadth should be broad, because in such an environment we do not have to fear high welfare losses due to the prevention of efforts to innovate around the patent. The reward is adjusted accordingly by a short patent life (ibid).

An alternative approach is offered by Takalo (2001). According to Takalo, the optimal patent mix should minimize the trade-off between dynamic and static inefficiencies. A longer patent increases innovation (dynamic efficiency) but leads to a longer disadvantage to the consumers because the patent monopoly got prolonged (static inefficiencies) and vice versa (ibid.: 35). Takalo shows that the optimal mixture can vary according to three different rules. First, if patent length has a relatively large effect on the innovation incentive. That is, if the marginal rate of substitution of patent length to breadth is greater for social welfare than for the incentives to innovate, then maximum length and minimum breadth is optimal. Second, if patent breadth has a relatively large influence on innovation incentives. That is, if the marginal rate for substitution is greater on innovation incentives than on social welfare, then minimum length and maximum breadth is optimal. Third, if the relative effects of length and breadth on incentives to innovate are equal, then the mixture of length and breadth does not impact social welfare (Takalo 2001: 36). Therefore, Takalo offers a universal approach for the determination of the optimal patent mix. However, it should be obvious that this is a quite complex undertaking with results differing in dependence of the underlying assumptions and the varying market circumstances. The optimal mix thus varies, at the very least, for different industries, if not for different products. In the next section, I will turn to the optimal patent protection for cumulative innovation.

4.1.1.4 Optimal Combination of Length and Breadth for Cumulative Innovation

4.1.1.4.1 Limits of Patents with Cumulative Innovation

As previously noted, the above-described models refer only to single innovations. Even though this scenario is useful to get a conception of the optimal design of patents, it does not necessarily reflect reality. More common are innovations that do not stand alone but constitute an entire innovation stream. Although the determination of the optimal protection for a single innovation is already difficult, it becomes even more complex when it relates to cumulative innovation.

---

112   For a detailed explanation and a mathematical derivation, compare to Denicolo 1996.

With cumulative innovation, one invention is essential for a later innovation, that is, the later or the follow-on innovation is based on the technology of the first innovation.[113] In other words, the first innovation generates positive externalities for future inventors and opens up the field for new research. One of the main difficulties connected to cumulative innovation is how to reward the inventors of a basic innovation for its value as a stand-alone innovation and for its value for follow-on innovators. At the same time, it has to be guaranteed that the later innovators get an appropriate reward for their innovation (Scotchmer 2004: 134). The challenge is to create sufficient incentives for the first innovator, especially if the stand-alone innovation has only a low value, but also to maintain incentives for successive innovators. Under a regime of broad patent protection, the second innovator will have few incentives to innovate because she needs to license from the first innovator and cannot appropriate all the returns from her innovation. Conversely, under a regime of narrow patent protection, successive innovators will have full incentives to invest in innovation, whereas the first innovator has reduced incentives to innovate (Scotchmer 1991, 2004).

As long as all innovation is under the responsibility of only one firm, the allocation of property rights does not matter. The company internalizes the externality, and no efficiency problems occur. In other words, we can design the patent for stand-alone innovations and need not fear the cutback of incentives for later innovation. However, in most cases, several companies compete for successive innovations. Thus, property rights are needed to distribute the benefits of the externalities created by the first innovation (Rockett 2008). As a straightforward solution for the trade-off between optimal incentives for first and successive innovators cannot be found in patent law, it is necessary to consider the

---

113 Scotchmer (2004) differentiates between three types of cumulative innovation. First, the case of basic innovation which may lead to many second-generation inventions or applications, that is, the later innovator uses the invented technology. Second, the case where a second-generation product requires the input of several first innovations. Finally, cumulative innovation may take the form of a quality ladder, that is, the first innovation is successively improved by later innovators (Scotchmer 2004: 132). However, the second type of cumulative innovation can also be interpreted as complementary innovation because if the first innovations cannot stand alone but create only value in the context of the second-generation product, the innovators face a two-way relationship to each other. Each innovator relies on the cooperation of the others to build the second-generation product. In contrast, with cumulative innovation, we have a one-way relationship: the second innovator relies on the first innovator, but not the other way around. Further, with the complementary innovation, the innovations do not necessarily build on each other but are developed simultaneously (Rockett 2008). Thus, in the following section, I will only refer to cumulative innovation as innovation building on a prior innovation.

possibility of licensing and other agreements.[114] I will further discuss licensing in the following section.

4.1.1.4.2 Licensing Agreements as Solution

As previously explained, the general problem with cumulative innovation is how to ensure sufficient innovation incentives for the first and second innovator,[115] given that the first innovator evokes positive externalities and firms other than the first innovator should participate in the development of the second innovation (Scotchmer 1991: 31). Generally, the innovators have two possibilities: either they make an ex ante licensing agreement or they negotiate ex post on a licensing term. In the case of prior licensing, broad patents are optimal. Assuming broad patents, licensing agreements allow the first innovator whose patents give her the right to all follow-on innovation, but who might not be able to develop them, to trade her right and still get access to the benefits of successive innovations. As long as enough reward remains for the second innovator to cover her costs, both parties have an interest in negotiating with each other and conducting further research (Rockett 2008).

The model of Green and Scotchmer (1995) illustrates these interplays in more detail. Assume we have an innovator who creates a research tool that has a (commercial) value on its own of zero.[116] If the innovator plans to conduct the follow-on innovation herself, no problem arises. But what if the innovator is not capable of realizing the next step? In this case, the profit must be divided between both parties so that both are able to cover the invention costs and have the incentive to invest. Obviously, since the stand-alone innovation has a value of zero, the first innovator has no incentive to invest at all if she does not receive some benefits from the second innovation (Green/Scotchmer 1995). Thus, bargaining between both innovators will occur. The outcome of this bargaining process depends on several facts, including whether the licensing agreement is made ex ante or ex post and the length and breadth of the involved patents (Rockett 2008). The patent breadth determines how the profit is divided between the two parties, as it determines whether the second innovation infringes the patent of the first and to what degree. If the second innovation does infringe the first patent, the innovator must make a license agreement. The length of the patent, in contrast, determines the total profit of both innovations. If the patent

---

114 For a detailed discussion on this topic, *compare* exemplarily *to* Scotchmer (1991).

115 For a comprehensive discussion on how to divide the profits between both first and second generation, *compare* exemplarily *to* Chang 1995, Chou/Haller 1995; Green/ Scotchmer 1995, Matutes/Regibeau/Rockett 1996 and Scotchmer 1991 and 1996.

116 Green and Scotchmer (1995) illustrate this with the invention of a laser technology. Laser technology alone has no or only a minor value for consumers whereas laser surgery constitutes a direct value to consumers. However, laser surgery is only possible on the basis of laser technology (ibid.: 22).

breadth put one side at a disadvantage, the patent length has to be longer to ensure that this party can cover its costs (Green/Scotchmer 1995: 21).

Now, consider first a situation where only ex post licensing is possible and where the second innovation infringes the first one. Both parties have an incentive to bargain because if they do not, the first innovator cannot profit from the second innovation and, as the value of her innovation alone is zero, cannot cover the cost of invention. The second innovator faces the same problem – if she does not license, she suffers losses at the level of the development costs. However, even though both innovators have an incentive to bargain, the outcome might not be optimal. For instance, if they decide to share the profit evenly, but the second innovator has higher development costs, the second innovator might have diminished innovation incentives.[117] In contrast, if the patent breadth is narrow and the second innovation does not infringe the first one, then the first innovator does not get any profits and would not invest in the development at all (Green/Scotchmer 1995: 24).

With ex ante licensing, both inventors can avoid these problems, because here the innovators share both the costs and the profit (ibid.: 23). Bargaining ex ante over the licensing agreement, both parties can ensure that they will receive at least as much profit as they would get by not licensing and doing something else instead. This action alternative determines the so-called threat points of first and second innovator (ibid.: 24). The first innovator might as well agree to a lower licensing fee as an incentive for the second innovator when she is about to start investing in the development of the follow-on product (Rockett 2008). Thereby, the second innovator can ensure to cover her costs. Thus, with ex ante licensing agreements, the second innovation will always be realized if it generates an additional benefit to the first innovation. According to Green and Scotchmer, with ex ante licensing infinite, breadth is optimal when certainty exists over the costs and value of the second innovation. In this case, all follow-on innovations infringe the patent of the first innovation. Obviously, the bargaining position of the first innovator will be better and the probable bargaining outcome is that the second innovator gets a share of the profits, just enough to cover her costs and give her a sufficient incentive to invest. The biggest part of the profit will flow back to the first innovator to reward her for the positive externality she created (Green/Scotchmer 1995: 26).

If only the costs of the innovation are known ex ante and the value of the second innovation is uncertain, infinite patent breadth is no longer optimal. The follow-on innovator is now in the situation that she cannot make an entry decision for every possible value of the innovation. If the patent breadth is very broad, the second innovator knows that her innovation will very likely infringe

---

117   In other words, the second innovator can only bargain of the improvement's profit but
      not over her sunk research costs (Green/Scotchmer 1995: 23-24).

the first innovation and, therefore, ex post licensing will be necessary. As the second innovator knows that ex post licensing will probably devour her profits, she has a credible threat not to enter the market (for the follow-on innovation), and the first innovator will agree to ex ante licensing where they share the profit evenly. With a small patent breadth, the second innovation might not infringe the first innovator's patent at all and, thus, the threat not to enter is no longer credible. As such, in an ex ante licensing agreement with narrow patent breadth, the first innovator will insist on a larger part of the profit (Green/ Scotchmer 1995: 27).

However, there are several other parameters that need to be considered to determine optimal licensing conditions and agreements. For instance, Scotchmer (1996: 323-324) differentiates between cases according to the patentability of the second innovation. In her model, she assumes that two firms compete for the second innovation. Consider a case where ex ante licensing is possible. Both firms would bid in an auction for the license of the first innovation. Without the patentability of the second innovation, the patent holder of the first innovation would receive all the surplus of the second innovation less the costs of development. As the second innovation does not receive a patent, the firm that won the auction and the patent holder do not have any incentives to bargain with the second firm; thus, the latter would not invest in the development of the follow-on innovation. If the second innovation is patentable, the loser of the auction still has the incentive to invest, as she has a one in two chance of receiving the application and therewith the patent first. In other words, if she is successful in developing and patenting the follow-on innovation, she can block the marketing of the second product regardless of the outcome of the auction. If the winning bidder cannot sell her product without infringing the patent of the losing bidder, her exclusive license becomes worthless. Thus, in this case, the winning bidder has to bargain ex post with its competitor. Scotchmer assumes that they very likely share the profit evenly. As both bidding parties know ex ante that they might have to bargain ex post over the license again and that therefore they might lose a significant part of their profits, they would not agree to an ex ante licensing agreement with the first innovator that solely covers their costs. Thus, in the case of patentability, the first innovator receives fewer payoffs than without patentability. To compensate this reduced profit – which might not even cover the costs of invention – the patent lifetime needs to be longer.

Altogether, according to Scotchmer the optimal policy would be not to allow patentability of follow-on innovation. In this case, we would ensure sufficient incentives for both innovations without creating social waste because of double development costs. However, this is only valid if no impediments for ex ante licensing exist. If those impediments might occur, patentability and longer patent lives should be preferred (Scotchmer 1996: 330).

Even though this discussion of the models of licensing agreements with cumulative innovation is far from comprehensive, it should be sufficient to get an idea of the complexity of determining optimal patent scope where follow-on innovations are concerned. In the next section, I will turn to copyrights and how to determine the optimal degree of protection.

4.1.2 Copyrights

By and large, the economic justification for copyrights ties in with the above argumentation. In contrast to patent law, copyrights do not try to promote innovation but rather to spur creative expression (Régibeau/ Rockett 2007: 517).[118] Consequently, copyrights protect only the particular expression of an idea, not the idea itself. Furthermore, copyright-protected goods differ from tangible property. An imitator or a second competitor of tangible property has the same costs as the first in the market; for instance, she must buy machines or input factors to produce the good. In case of creative works, this is different. Without protection, the second competitor can benefit from the work of the innovator and simply copy the product without developing costs. For example, an imitator can offer a book or a film at a lower cost than the innovator can. As a result, the innovator would loose all her profits and be unable to capture her development costs, because consumers would prefer to buy the same book or film for less from the imitator (Akerlof et al. 2002: 4). That is, copyrights are necessary to ensure that creators reap the fruits of their endeavours. However, it is interesting to note that the first copyright law was the Statute of Anne in Great Britain, which aimed to restrict the power of the Stationers' Company and not to strengthen the author's rights or to promote creative effort.[119] Nevertheless, the traditional approach dominates, that copyrights are necessary and desirable to allow the creator the appropriation of her work.[120]

---

118   In this context, it is also necessary to highlight that copyright protection relies much more on philosophical approaches than patent protection. Especially in Europe, the natural law thesis of Locke, the "natural obligation" identified by Kant (1895), and theories of personhood (compare exemplarily Radin 1982) have a strong influence on the understanding of the role of copyrights. In Germany, the work of an author is an expression of her individuality (Ohly 2007: 52). Still, as copyright is not only valid for books and other "classical arts" but also for software and other products, the understanding of copyright is more and more shifting towards an economic-based approach.

119   As Nicita and Ramello (2007) put it, "[T]his is a puzzling perspective that casts serious doubt on the view of original copyright as a legal device based solely on the need to provide appropriate rewards/incentives to creators of information goods and to encourage the dissemination of knowledge." (ibid.: 4).

120   For a critical discussion of the necessity of copyrights *compare* exemplarily *to* Breyer 1970 and Hurt/ Schuchman 1966.

4.1.2.1 Theoretical Approach to Optimal Design

The definition of the appropriate scope of copyright protection is also a matter of balancing innovation incentives against access to information. The broader the copyright protection, the higher the incentive to innovate. At the same time, a broader scope of copyright protection limits access to the works as authors are able to increase their prices and thereby exclude a larger group (of the public) from consumption. Lunney (1996) describes the problem as follows:

"The more desirable a work is, the greater is the need to ensure the creation of the work and the greater the need to secure its widespread dissemination." (ibid: 486)

However, copyright does not only have the task of solving this trade-off between incentives to creation and society's utility through consumption (Watt 2004: 156). Another trade-off that needs to be addressed is the balance between static and dynamic effects, which occur when the cumulative effects of creation are also considered. On the one hand, it is necessary to protect the first creation to such an extent that it provides enough incentive for the creator to innovation. On the other hand, the protection should not be so strong that follow-on protection is hampered (Watt 2004: 156).[121]

In their seminal article "An Economic Analysis of Copyright Law," Landes and Posner (1989) focus especially on the balance of incentive and access. Hence, they propose that copyright law "maximize the benefits from creating additional works minus both the losses from limiting access and the costs of administering copyright protection" (ibid.: 326). The authors divide the cost of producing a copyright-protected work into two components: first, the cost of creating the work, which they call the "cost of expression"; and second, the cost connected with the duplication or reproduction of the work. Thus, the work will only be created when the difference between the expected revenue and the cost of the duplication of the work exceeds the cost of creation (ibid.: 327). Landes and Posner draw the following conclusions in their analysis: At the optimal level of copyright protection, the amount of producer and consumer surplus per work must exceed the cost of creating the marginal work, and at the same time, the level of protection should be below the level that maximizes the number of works created. Otherwise, the additional welfare due to more creation would be outbalanced by the higher costs of expression and the greater administrative and enforcement costs. Furthermore, if, over time, growth in income and technological advances enlarge the size of the market for any given work, and the cost of copying declines, copyright protection should expand (ibid.: 343 et seq.).

Besides the higher costs of expression due to broader copyright protection, there is also the problem of optimal resource allocation as mentioned by Plant

---

121 Another trade-off Watt mentions is the conflict between copyright and competition law. Since we already discussed this trade-off in Chapter 3 I will not deepen this issue here.

(1934). With broader copyright protection, the economic return on authorship investments increases. Thus, additional works are created, luring away labour and capital resources from other productive efforts. In consequence, broadening the scope of protection is connected to the loss of the value society could have expected from alternative investments for which these resources otherwise would have been used (ibid.: 183 et seq.). In other words, at this stage we can connect too broad copyright protection with two different cost factors. On the one hand, it hampers access to information or knowledge and on the other hand, higher opportunity costs evolve due to the redirection of resources to the production of copyright-protected work.

Another aspect that should be considered before defining the scope of copyright protection is that too broad protection may lead to a monopoly and thus to a decrease of welfare. Since copyright prohibits the marketing of a perfect substitute, the creator of the relevant product can price above-average costs. Thereby, she creates a deadweight loss, as not everybody who is willing to buy the product at average costs buys at the higher monopoly price. That is to say, a social loss arises due to underutilization.[122]

Of course, there are differing opinions. For instance, in referring to underproduction, Novos and Waldman (1984) show that there might be some proof that social welfare loss decreases with an increase in copyright protection. But according to their model, there is no evidence that an increase in copyrights leads to an increase in social welfare loss due to underutilization. Rather, Novos and Waldman argue that a copier has higher copying costs than the producer's marginal costs for another unit of the copyright-protected good. Therefore, consumers are spending more resources in copying the good than would be needed by purchasing the good from the producers on the primary market. An increase in copyright protection leads to a shift from the secondary market, that is, the copying market, to the primary market, that is, the creating market. Thus, an increase in protection evokes a decrease of the social welfare loss due to underutilization (Novos/Waldman 1984: 245 et seq.).

4.1.2.2 Empirical Assessment of Optimal Copyright Scope

Irrespective of these theoretical models as to how broad the scope of copyrights should be, in most states the length of the copyright is the lifetime of the author plus 70 years. Even in the United States, where originally the copyright protection added up to 50 years after the author's death, the protection period was ex-

---

122 Nevertheless, one should be careful using the term "monopolization" in the context of IP. As long as substitutes for the relevant good exist, no monopoly in an economic sense will emerge. Consider, for example, the book market. An author of a detective story does in general not have any monopolistic power as consumers would rather buy another book than pay an inappropriate price.

tended to 70 years in 1998.[123] Obviously, this determination of duration is not based an economic consideration. This is not astonishing as most economic theories concerning the scope of protection indeed model a theoretical balance between access and incentives but do not give clear advice for the practical realisation (Derclaye 2003: 4). One reason for this phenomenon is that copyright protection, similarly to patent protection, has to be partitioned in at least three dimensions (Watt 2004: 157):

> 1. Duration: the length of time for which the legal copyright is enforced,
> 2. Depth: the particular aspects of the creation that are protected (and those that are not); and
> 3. Breadth: what particular acts are deemed to be copyright infringing (and what are not).[124]

Nevertheless, the need for more precise specifications has been recognized by economists and thus, the interest in empirical studies regarding the optimal scope of protection has grown (Watt 2004: 167). Even though empirical evidence is very rare,[125] the few existing models advocate very clearly shorter periods than in place today. For instance, Boldrin and Levine (2005) illustrate that the elasticity with which creators react to changes in copyright terms seems to be very low (ibid.: 34). That is, if the scope of protection decreases, there would be a slight reaction in the production of copyright-protected works and the output would not significantly change. Consequently, if a decrease in copyright protection would not result in a decrease in works, a longer duration of protection is not justified, because this would needlessly maintain a higher deadweight loss than with a less broad protection (Boldrin/Levine 2005: 34).

More precise recommendations regarding the optimal duration of copyright come from Pollock (2007, 2009). Basing his theory on the existing literature, Pollock develops a model to empirically analyse copyrights[126] and comes to two, complementary results. First, Pollock demonstrates in a theoretical model that the optimal protection decreases with a decline in the costs of production and distribution of the copyright-protected work (Pollock 2007). Demonstrating that the costs of creating "original works" have fallen exponentially, Pollock argues that a reduction in the strength of protection seems to be necessary (ibid.: 62). Second, by using a dynamic model and empirical data, Pollock shows that the optimal length of a copyright term should be less than 30 years (Pollock 2009:

---

123 See Copyright Term Extension Act of 1998, Pub. L. No. 105-298, 112 Stat. 2827.
124 The sum of depth and breadth are often understood as the scope of copyright protection (Watt 2004: 157).
125 As Png (2006) points out, the low number of empirical studies is first of all connected with the limited availability of data (ibid.: 4).
126 I abstain from explaining the model in detail. The interested reader may *compare to* Pollock (2009).

53). However, we should keep in mind that this value is only an approximation, depending on parameters like discount rate, cultural decay,[127] elasticity of supply, and so on, of which we have only limited knowledge. Using both empirical evidence and theoretical estimations, Pollock determines ranges of values for each parameter. Depending on the value he chooses out of these ranges, different results can occur. As Pollock shows, the term of 30 years is probably still far too long. Using point estimates, he makes a calculation showing that optimal protection should not be longer than approximately 15 years. (Pollock 2009: 52).

In sum, we can see that: 1) the current duration of copyright protection is probably much too long; and 2) the determination of the optimal duration is highly complex and demands detailed knowledge of different parameters, which are only receivable under great difficulty, if at all. We can further assume that, due to varying values of the decisive parameter – for example, the cultural decay of books is different from that of music – one size does not fit all. Thus, like in patent law, the general and very long-lasting assignment of copyrights is likely to create welfare losses in at least some cases.[128]

4.1.3   Intermediate Result: Necessity of Case-by-Case Design of Intellectual Property Rights

This section has demonstrated that a broad range of theories exist how to determine the optimal scope of intellectual property rights. Nevertheless, instead of giving us a clear recommendation, the results differ depending on the underlying assumptions. According to Nordhaus (1969), we can make the following general statements for patent length: The easier the invention, the shorter the patent length; the lower the elasticity of demand, the longer patent length; and the higher the value of the invention, the shorter the length. However, to determine exactly the optimal patent length (for process innovations), we need knowledge of the demand elasticity, the ease of the innovation, the discount rate, the reduction of unit cost for the invention, the curvature of the invention function, and the value of the invention (Nordhaus 1969). The problem becomes more complex when we want to determine the optimal mix of protection; that is to say, the optimal composition of breadth and length. Starting with the models in a static world, according to Gilbert and Shapiro (1990) in homogenous product markets, patents should be narrow if the social costs grow disproportionately high with the increase of patent breadth (ibid.: 106). In heterogeneous product markets, patents should be long and narrow if consumers have equal costs of substitution.

---

127   Cultural decay refers to the fact that the value of copyright protected works tends to decrease in the course of time (Pollock 2009: 42).

128   Please not that this brief overview about the economics of copyright is not exhaustive. For further discussion please *compare* exemplarily *to* Breyer 1970; Gordon 1989; Png/Wang 2009; Richardson et al. 2000; Towse et al. 2008; Tyerman 1971.

If, in contrast, consumers do not have the same costs of substitution but equal reservation prices, patents should be short and broad (Klemperer 1990: 127). If we further extend the assumptions and assume that imitation evokes costs, Gallini (1992) suggests that patents should be broader the higher the costs of imitation. Takalo (2001), developing a dynamic model, suggests the following rules: If patent length positively influences innovation incentives, the optimal mix for patents is maximum length and minimum breadth. If patent breadth stimulates innovation more, the optimal mix is minimum length and maximum breadth. If breadth and length have the same effects, the mix does not matter (ibid: 36). For copyrights, the determination of the optimal scope of protection is similar complex as for patents. Regarding cumulative innovation, we learned that, first, there is no straightforward definition of optimal protection because it either puts the first or the second innovator at an advantage. Second, we saw that in the case of cumulative innovation, licensing seems to be a welfare-enhancing solution.

Although it is not a comprehensive summary, this brief recall of our results demonstrates the challenges for an application within competition policy but also for an application within intellectual property law. In section 3.4 we assumed that intellectual property rights are not always assigned optimally and can therefore cause welfare losses. This section has now shown that a uniform assignment and design of intellectual property rights cannot be optimal. Consider only the model of Nordhaus. It should be obvious, that, for example, the reduction of unit cost for the invention, the ease of the invention and the value of the invention differ not only across industries but also across the varying innovations. Does the innovation replace a particular, maybe very expensive, input good or does it fasten the production process? Did the company explicitly search for this innovation and invested large amounts in R&D activities? Or did it discover the innovation by chance, maybe as a by-product of another innovation? Regarding product innovations the optimal patent breadth and length depends inter alia from the consumer structure. Obviously, consumer demand for a certain innovation may differ largely. Take, for instance, a new and innovative computer game: some consumers would have a high willingness to pay whereas other consumers would only be willing to buy the new game at a comparatively low price. Hence, it is likely that in most cases the intellectual property rights are not designed correctly, in some cases the protection is too high and in some cases too little. In these cases, intellectual property rights do not achieve their goal to enhance welfare and promote innovation. We can rather assume that in a lot of cases intellectual property rights provide either too less or too much incentives to innovate.

In sum, this section demonstrates that economics provide a broad range of theories how to determine intellectual property rights. It further shows that a case-by-case design of intellectual property rights requires manifold information. For such case-by-case assignment of intellectual property rights it is necessary to have profound knowledge on the market conditions and to quantify this knowledge. Against the background of the multiplicity of information required, the need for quantification is at least challenging. As such, it seems as if a consideration of the law and economics theories of intellectual property rights does not contribute to a simplification of an optimal design of intellectual property rights.

At the same time, these theories present only one string of economic theory that can be applied to intellectual property rights. Moreover, they mainly base on rather narrow assumptions. Coming from an evolutionary economic perspective, especially the assumption that knowledge has necessarily public good characteristics can be questioned. Thus, we will now turn to more general theories and insights from innovation research in order to extend our perspective and to examine if we can find further criteria that may also influence the design of intellectual property rights.

4.2 Innovation Research: What Do We Know about the Appropriability Conditions for New Knowledge?

The theories described above mostly refer to the assumptions of perfect competition, that is, they take innovation more or less as given; the innovator only has to choose out of a pool of new technologies. In this sense, innovation is a question of which investor is able to realize a certain innovation first. What these theories do not consider is that R&D activities are search processes that include both failure and success. Sometimes, it may take years until the results of R&D investments are workable solutions or products. As already mentioned, another shortcoming of these classical theories is that they consider knowledge and information as a public good. This assumption is at least questionable, it is not so clear that everybody can decode and use any kind of information. As such, this section will, first, analyse which factors on the level of the firms do not only influence the creation but also the handling of information and knowledge and, second, explore whether firms have alternative appropriability instruments besides intellectual property rights.

To explain both the preconditions and impediments to successful innovation as well as successful imitation, we will refer to theories from evolutionary economics and the resourced-based view of the firm. This discussion aims at refuting the notion that knowledge always features a public-good character. Instead, we want to prove that the appropriation of knowledge is connected with several preconditions and problems and, therefore, firms can also rely on other appropriability strategies to capture the returns on their investments and do not necessarily rely on intellectual property rights.

We will then review the empirical results regarding the effectiveness of intellectual property rights and other appropriability instruments. In discussing these alternative instruments, we will clarify what influence the choice of appropriability mechanisms has as well as their effectiveness in protecting innovation. Thereby, we will also consider potential barriers to imitation.

4.2.1 Preconditions for Successful Innovation and Imitation

4.2.1.1 Influence of Different Knowledge (Sources) and Routines

As emphasized in resourced-based approaches, a firm's success depends on the interplay of several factors (Penrose 1959; Rumelt 1984; Teece 1984; Werner-felt 1984). These approaches can be traced back to Coase (1937), who points out that firms do not function like markets. Within firms, prices do not direct individual actions, but rather an individual acts because an authority, such as the manager, tells her to do so. Thus, a firm is led by a manager who coordinates the activities of the members, forecasts prices, and rearranges production factors. Coase also emphasizes the importance of dynamics, because firms must be able to adjust to a changing market environment. According to resourced-based approaches, firms are heterogeneous as they have different strategic resources that are not perfectly mobile across firms (Barney 1991: 1001). With this assumption of heterogeneity, the resource-based view of the firm differs from older strategic management theories that assume for simplicity's sake that firms in one industry are more or less homogeneous and have the same resources (Porter 1980, 1981; Scherer/Ross 1980). Competitive strength arises because of an analysis of environmental opportunities and threats (Caves/Porter 1977; Porter 1980, 1985). A firm's resources comprise all assets, organizational processes, capabilities, firm attributes, knowledge, and information (ibid.) Consequently, instead of analysing firms only from the product perspective, it is also necessary to study them from the resource side (Barney 1986). Accordingly, the basic principles of the resourced based view of the firm can be described as follows: The available resources and (core) competences determine in which markets a firm can be active and influence the market success. Consequently, a firm is successful in the market if it has better resources or uses them better than its rivals. Due to these resources the firm is more efficient as well as more effective as its competitors (Burr et al. 2005: 17). According to Teece and Pisano (1994), successful companies are characterized by

> "timely responsiveness and rapid and flexible product innovation, coupled with the management capability to effectively coordinate and redeploy internal and external competences." (ibid.: 538)

These competencies can also be understood as "dynamic capabilities" (Teece 1982, Teece/Pisano 1994, Teece/Pisano/Shuen 1997). They are dynamic because the firm has to react to permanent changes in and new requirements of the environments. The term "capabilities" comprises all firm internal skills, competences, and resources that are necessary to adapt to, integrate, and re-configure both internal and external challenges (Teece/Pisano 1994: 538). In other words, a competence might be a firm's ability and experience in marketing products. However, a firm's capabilities are always restrained by its previous patterns and organizational methods. Put differently, path dependencies and routines matter.[129] Thus, the way a firm adapts to new challenges is determined by its previous reactions (Teece/Pisano 1994: 547).

Introduced by Nelson and Winter (1982), routines are decisive for future developments within the firm. Routines include the specific characteristics of a firm, starting with well-defined technical routines for production processes as well as procedures for hiring or firing, but also including policies regarding investment, R&D, advertising or business strategies, and so on (ibid.: 14). Routines are, in their functionality, similar to biological genes, as future firms build upon persistent routines and routines are selectable in the sense that some may do better than others and, thus, survive or grow in importance (ibid.). Therefore, accepting the notion of routines as genes, the future technological possibilities of firms are heavily constrained by their past technological capabilities (Dosi 1988: 225). In these routines, essential coordination information is stored and "remembered by doing," that is, the routines also depend on individual knowledge. Moreover, parts of the underlying knowledge are tacit, in that they are not consciously known or articulable by members of the organization (Nelson/Winter 1982: 134). The concept of routines implies that firms' capabilities to innovate are restricted by their previous routines. In sum, innovations are generated on the basis of existing products, processes, and technological knowledge.

In this regard, search activities are activities that scan the environment for alternatives to a firm's present routines. They take place before and after transforming a production process (the innovation) into a routine and, hence, reducing uncertainty and the costs of innovation by lessening the number of trials needed. During research activities, production processes are only simulated and thus have a lower cost than a real implementation. Thus, "search activities are ways of 'learning by not doing'" (Saviotti 1998: 844). As a result of the search activities, the firm's knowledge base grows, the characteristics of the products and processes improves, and the firm's fitness, that is, the capacity of a technology to adapt to external changes, increases (Saviotti 1998: 846).

At this point, it is important to differentiate between information and knowledge. Information is factual, whereas knowledge can be understood as a correlation structure. Knowledge generalizes certain variables and connects them to

---

129   For a broader discussion of path dependencies and routines, *compare* exemplarily *to* David 1985; Dosi 1988, 1997, Ruttan 1997.

each other (Saviotti 1998: 845).[130] Information is only valuable and understandable in the context of certain knowledge. In other words, it is necessary to possess certain knowledge to interpret and use some pieces of information.[131] Thereby, knowledge can be divided into different types: tacit, codified, and cumulative. The latter evokes both path dependencies and barriers for new members in the firm or potential entrants in the market who do not know the correlations between certain pieces of information and knowledge. The knowledge used to produce and operate in the market is the firm's collective knowledge. Since collective knowledge comprises not only factual knowledge but also the interplay between individuals that is necessary to produce, it is broader than the sum of the individual knowledge (Saviotti 1998: 845). Therefore, parts of the collective knowledge are tacit, that is, implicit and singular. Within a firm, tacit knowledge is mostly embedded in routines and capabilities (Nelson/Winter 1982). However, knowledge can only seldom be divided into solely tacit or codified knowledge. Mostly, knowledge is partly tacit as well as partly codified. Even though tacit knowledge impedes copying or imitation and therefore has advantages, the codification of knowledge is important to communicate and further improve the firm's collective knowledge base and hence spur the progress of the firm's research activities. The newer a field of research or type of knowledge, the more difficult the process of codification as individuals have different associations, intuitions, and definitions. When there are already difficulties for members of one firm (internal), this becomes even more challenging for potential entrants (external), because they do not know the firm's routines, which were part of the generation of this specific knowledge. Thus, knowledge can never be used at zero cost to others even if it is completely codified. To understand and use the information, the imitator always needs the same "code" to retrieve the information. In other words, if the person does not know the code, she first has to learn it; hence, she bears the cost of appropriation (Saviotti 1998: 848). This implies for the innovator that a higher degree of involved tacit and collective knowledge induces higher appropriability of the returns of the innovation.

However, returning to routines and dynamic capabilities, the knowledge stored in routines determines the firm's dynamic capabilities.[132] As many rou-

---

130 From this perspective, knowledge has a local character. Its scope or span can vary from being very broad, for instance a general theory, to very narrow, like a very specific theory (Saviotti 1998: 845).

131 For example, it is only possible to understand an academic publication properly if one has at least some basic knowledge in the particular subject.

132 Altogether, firms collect and combine different kinds of knowledge and capabilities, including legal, financial, marketing, technological, and scientific knowledge, which correspond, for example, to the use of certain production processes, knowledge embodied in scientific instruments (Saviotti 1998: 855), or to what Teece (1986) called com-

tines do not stand alone but are part of a set of routines, imitation is even more difficult because the imitator also has to copy the interplay of the routines. Put differently, if something in the production process has to be changed, it might be necessary to adapt the marketing of the product as well (Teece/Pisano 1994: 550). Thus,

> "the competitive advantage of firms stems from dynamic capabilities rooted in high performance routines operating inside the firm, embedded in the firm's processes and conditioned by its history." (Teece/Pisano 1994: 553).

Still, as indicated at the beginning of this section, a firm's success depends not only on existing capabilities but also on the ongoing development and exploitation of its firm-specific assets (ibid.). In the following section, I will clarify how a firm can improve its capabilities.

4.2.1.2   Spillovers, Absorptive Capacity, and Path Dependence

One factor that can be important to strengthen a firm's capabilities to innovate is knowledge spillovers. In the logic of traditional economics intellectual property rights, if information or knowledge spills out, the (inventing) company and others, in particular rivals, can benefit from this information (Spence 1984). In consequence, the rivals will apply the externally generated knowledge, and the original creator or inventor cannot appropriate the returns of her (intellectual) work. This is discussed differently in evolutionary models. In their seminal work on learning and innovation, Cohen and Levinthal (1990) put into perspective the problem of spillovers as a disincentive to innovative activity. According to Cohen and Levinthal, firms have to invest first in their own R&D capabilities, before they are able to capture external knowledge. The ability to exploit external knowledge constitutes a critical component of a firm's innovative capabilities. A firm's ability to evaluate and use knowledge from outside sources depends in large part on prior related knowledge (ibid.: 131). This prior knowledge contains both basic skills and knowledge of recent developments in certain technological or scientific fields. This prior knowledge allows the owner to: 1) recognize the value of new information; 2) assimilate it; and 3) apply it to commercial uses. Together, these three abilities constitute a firm's absorptive capacity (Cohen/Levinthal 1990: 128).

Accordingly, it can be shown that due to activity in a firm's own R&D, the ability to absorb and use knowledge from external knowledge sources increases (Patel/Pavitt 1995: 18). The same is true for activities in manufacturing opera-

---

plementary assets. According to Arora/Ceccagnoli (2004), "complementary assets are assets valuable in commercializing an innovation and are complementary in the sense that their value is greater when owned by the innovating firm" (ibid.: 4). We will further illuminate the role of complementary assets for appropriation later in this chapter (Section 4.3.2.3).

tions in certain fields; in markets in which they are active, firms have better knowledge of how to use and exploit certain developments (Cohen/Levinthal 1990: 129).

Individual capabilities are also a critical component for absorptive capacity, which makes it necessary to invest in the personal training of the firm's individual members (ibid: 131). Nevertheless, it might be problematic to acquire skills from outside, because a firm's absorptive capacity develops cumulatively and, therefore, the acquired knowledge or capabilities need to be integrated into the already-existing set of skills and knowledge. An inherent part of the required absorptive capacity is often determined by firm specifics and thus cannot be bought and easily integrated into the company (ibid. 136). Due to this cumulativeness of a firm's absorptive capacity, especially in areas of quickly moving (technical) developments, strong path dependencies exist. If a firm once missed the opportunity to invest in certain capabilities, it may never be able to make up for this omission and will not be able to assimilate and exploit new information in this area (ibid.). Cohen and Levinthal call the emergence of this effect "lockout." If the firm does not invest in its absorptive capacity from the very beginning, it will not be aware of new developments over time. Even if the firm becomes aware of new technological possibilities, it probably will not invest in them as the lack of absorptive capacity makes it more costly to adapt these new technologies. Thus, the firm is "locked-out" of subsequent technological developments (Cohen/Levinthal 1990: 136). This is related to something that Dierickx and Cool (1989) call *time compression diseconomies*. To put it simply, this means that the accumulation of knowledge takes time. The longer and the more constant a knowledge-creating process is, the bigger the knowledge base and the output. If one tries to absorb the same knowledge in a shorter period of time, ceterus paribus we can assume that less knowledge has been absorbed or created. Dierickx and Cool illustrate this with the example of two MBA students: If one program takes two years and the other one, the MBA student in the one-year-program has a smaller knowledge base even though the number of classes and lectures was exactly the same (ibid.: 1507). Thus, a firm that invests constantly over time in R&D is at an advantage compared to a company that starts investing in R&D later, independently of whether the latter company spends more money on its R&D activities.

Besides that, the existence of spillovers can also constitute an incentive to spend more on R&D. By expanding their own R&D activity, firms improve their absorptive capacity and, thus, are able to exploit spillovers from other firms' investments in innovations (Cohen/Levinthal 1989: 593). Hence, following this argumentation, it is reasonable for firms to invest in advanced research but also in basic research, even when in the latter the main results cannot be used directly for commercial proposes. However, basic research broadens the knowledge base of the firm and can be used to understand and use specific knowledge or knowledge spillovers from other firms. Due to the broad knowledge a firm earns in conducting R&D, it will be able to react swiftly to the advances of competitors and immediately exploit new and useful technological and scientific information (Cohen/Levinthal 1990: 148). This can be illustrated with the example of a bathtub. The amount of water already in the tub can be interpreted as the current knowledge stock. Through the tap, new water, that is, new knowledge, flows into the tub, whereas water flowing out through a leak can be seen as the decay of knowledge in the sense that it gets obsolete with new developments and technologies (Dierickx/Cool 1989: 1506). However, this metaphor shows that even though it is possible to control the flows in and out the tub immediately, building up a certain stock of knowledge, or collecting water in the tub, takes time (ibid.). Consequently, for a potential imitator, it is not free of cost to copy the ideas of an innovator. Even in the absence of intellectual property protection, firstly, an imitator has to observe an invention and the knowledge behind it and, secondly, she must possess the absorptive capacity to understand and implement this knowledge. Thus, an innovator probably has to suffer from immediate imitation in only a few cases.[133]

This model of absorptive capacity has been further developed by Zahra and George (2001).[134] Zahra and George divided the model into two subsets, which consist of four dimensions in total: (1) knowledge acquisition and (2) assimilation constitute the potential absorptive capacity, whereas (3) knowledge transformation and (4) exploitation constitute the realized absorptive capacity (ibid.: 186). According to this model, potential capacity equips firms with the strategic flexibility and the possibility to adapt and to evolve in fast moving environments, whereas the outcome of innovative conduct represents the realized absorptive capacity (Zahra/George 2001: 185). Firms with well-developed knowledge acquisition capabilities are better able to capture external technological knowledge as they can better integrate new information into their own knowledge. Furthermore, firms with distinct knowledge assimilation capabilities have a higher fitness in analysing, understanding, and interpreting new technologies (Zahra/George 2001: 189). Knowledge transformation, however, describes the firm's capability to develop and refine routines that ease combining existing knowledge and newly acquired knowledge. Thus, a well-developed knowledge transformation capability enables firms to better cross-apply existing knowledge

---

133 This depends mainly on the degree of involved specific knowledge and the degree of involved previous knowledge. The less knowledge is involved, the easier it is to copy.

134 Besides the model of Zahra and George, there are also two other developments or interpretations of absorptive capacity. First, Mowery and Oxley (1995) define absorptive capacity as a set of skills that is necessary to incorporate and interpret the tacit component of transferred knowledge. Second, Kim (1997 a, b, 1998) understands absorptive capacity as the capability to learn and solve problems. These two approaches will not be considered in the following section.

to new market applications. And, finally, due to the knowledge exploitation capabilities, which reflect the firms' ability to reap and incorporate knowledge into their operations, firms are better able to refine, extend, and leverage existing competences (ibid.: 190).

This interpretation of absorptive capacity stresses as well that the exploitation of spillovers is more complex than assumed in the model of perfect competition. The competitors first have to invest in their absorptive capacity before they can copy inventions of innovators. As Zahra and George's model implies, an imitator needs to establish all four dimensions of absorptive capacity before she can exploit and successfully transfer external knowledge. According to this approach, if a firm disregards only one level, this will hamper the exploitation of spillovers because all dimensions build upon each other (ibid.: 191).

In sum, it is clear that innovation and innovative success are not only a function of incentives and appropriability. Rather, R&D efforts are influenced both by the history of the firm, that is, by routines and path dependencies, but also by the capability to absorb and use knowledge spillovers. This capability, in turn, can be influenced by R&D efforts as the absorptive capacity of a firm grows with an increase in R&D activities. At the same time, it is evident that (successful) imitation is not as natural and automatic as assumed in the economics of intellectual property rights. Instead, firms need to have certain knowledge and skills to copy a successful innovator. This relativises not only the problem of immediate imitation but also the assumed cost advantage of the imitators. Even though an innovator probably still faces higher development costs, imitation is not costless. Hence, we can challenge the argument that without intellectual property rights an innovation will always be copied immediately. Having said this, the next section will, first, show how firms rate the effectiveness of intellectual property rights and, second, explore alternative appropriability mechanisms and their effectiveness.

4.2.2.   Empirical Results

4.2.2.1   Effectiveness of Intellectual Property Rights in Protecting R&D

Some empirical studies[135] have analysed whether intellectual property rights are indeed essential for the appropriability of innovation or whether other appropriability mechanisms might exist. These surveys largely support the evolutionary approach, stating that the effect of spillovers is not as detrimental to innovation as the traditional rationale for intellectual property rights describes. In fact, these empirical studies have shown that patents and other intellectual property protec-

---

135   Due to better measurability, these studies mainly focus on patents.

tions are not necessarily crucial for firms' decision to innovate. In the following section, we will review the most significant studies.

For instance, a study examining the influence of patent and other intellectual property systems on innovative activity could not find any evidence for increased inventions in countries with intellectual property protection in comparison to countries without such protection or with less of it (Moser 2005). Nevertheless, Moser demonstrates that in countries with weak intellectual property regimes, more innovations occur in industries that rely mostly on secrecy or lead time (ibid.). Hence, even though innovation takes place irrespective of the presence of intellectual property rights, in countries without or with only very little intellectual property protection, the focus of innovative activity lies on industries where there are appropriability mechanism other than patents (Dosi/ Margengo/ Pasquali 2006: 12).

In her analysis of the influence of intellectual property protection on innovation and the economic development of developing countries, Léger (2007) finds no evidence that intellectual property protection spurs innovation. Rather, she comes to the conclusion that it is more likely that weak intellectual property protection contributed to the rise of the Asian Tiger states (Léger 2007: 26). In fact, most currently industrialized countries developed under a regime of weak intellectual property protection; only when they reached a certain technical level did they strengthen their intellectual property system (Khan 2002, Lerner 2002). One reason for this phenomenon is the cost connected with obtaining protection; information, certification, and monitoring costs may outweigh the incentives due to protection in developing markets. Thus, patents and other intellectual property rights fail to fulfil their traditional functions in developing countries (Léger 2007: 27). Furthermore, Léger explains that even if patents do not provide strong incentives to innovate, their complementary roles like definition for technological transfer, strategic uses, and signalling reputation are of importance for strengthening innovation in industrialized countries (Léger 2007: 36). In contrast, Dosi, Marengo and Pasquali (2006) highlight the strategic value of patents in the sense of creating market entry barriers and of infringement and counter-infringement suits against rivals (ibid.: 9). I will elaborate on this in the next section.

Another stream of literature focuses on surveys questioning why firms patent and how patents influence inventive activity. For instance, Mansfield, Schwartz, and Wagner (1981) asked the innovating firms whether they would have invested in innovations without patent protection. Apart from the pharmaceutical industry, more than three-quarters of the interviewed firms declared that they would have pursued the innovation in any case (ibid.: 915). Following the argumentation of Mansfield, Schwartz, and Wagner, this is because the existence of patents does not decisively influence the rate of entry; thus, the absence of patent protection does not significantly enhance the competitive pressure on innovating firms (ibid.: 916). In another survey five years later, Mansfield (1986) found out that, apart from pharmaceutical and chemical industries, 80 to 90 percent of the inventions would have been placed in the market in the absence of patent protection (Mansfield 1986: 174 et seqq.). Even if the sample is comparatively small, about 100 interviewed firms, this result gives an interesting perspective on the relevance of IP protection.

Similarly, basing on data from 1983, Levin et al. (1987) examine, amongst other things, the effectiveness of IP protection in their analysis of appropriability in industrial R&D projects. In this study, Levin et al. show that firms appraise appropriability mechanisms like first-mover advantage, learning curve effects, and secrecy much higher than patents (Levin et al. 1987: 794 et seqq.). These results are consistent with the earlier findings of Taylor and Silbertson (1973), showing that patents have a significant influence in the chemical and pharmaceutical industries but not in others. Corresponding results are presented in the most recent study from Cohen, Nelson, and Walsh (2000).[136] Their survey shows that among secrecy, lead time, complementary sale or services, and complementary manufacturing, patents are the least important instrument to profit from R&D investments (ibid.: 9). Nevertheless, Cohen, Nelson, and Walsh also point out that in certain industries like medical equipment and drugs, the importance of patents and other intellectual property rights is significantly higher.[137] Moreover, most firms rely on more than one appropriability mechanism; rather, they rely on appropriability strategies. The authors identify three different strategies: first, relying on complementary capabilities and lead time; second, using legal mechanisms, especially patents; and third, employing secrecy (Cohen et al. 2000: 8). However, it is interesting to see that firms often still do not rely only on one strategy but use a bundle of them. Thereby, it is notable that even though some industries might rely mainly on complementary capabilities or lead time, no industry relies exclusively on patents and other legal protection tools. Moreover, no industry identifies patents as the most effective instrument to protect their investments (ibid.: 9). The following graph gives an overview on the effectiveness rating of the different instruments.

---

136 Even though the data stems from the year 1994, according to my knowledge there is no newer study that analyses in that depth the effectiveness of different appropriabilty mechanisms. However, the study of Harhoff et al. (2007) gives also very valuable insights of the strategic use of patents.

137 This finding is related to the fact that in these industries the underlying technologies are rather simple. In other words, they can be easily understood by an individual who has some basic knowledge and skills in the area (Kash/Kingston 2001: 12). We will come back to this in the next section when we talk about discrete and complex industries.

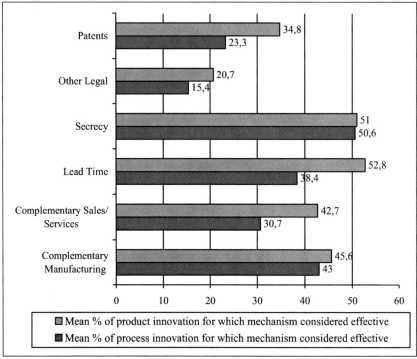

Figure 4-2: Effectiveness of appropriability mechanisms for product and process

innovations

Source: Cohen/Nelson/Walsh (2000)

Obviously, for product innovation, lead time and secrecy are the most important appropriability mechanisms, whereas patents are – after other legal mechanisms – the least effective instruments. Nevertheless, the findings that lead time and secrecy are the most important instruments to protect investments in innovation have been verified by several other studies.[138] For instance, a survey by the

---

138 *See* exemplarily Arundel 2001; Baldwin/Hanel/Sabourin 2002; Harabi 1995; McLennan 1995 cited in Arundel 2001. Arundel (2001) refers to data of the 1993 Community Innovation Survey in Europe. In this survey, manufacturing companies were asked to rank the effectiveness of different methods to enhance the competitiveness of their innovations. 54,4 % evaluated lead time advantages as most important to product innovation, 16,2% secrecy, and 11,2% patents. Arundel points out that since the response categories leave room for interpretation – they rank from crucial to insignificant – the informative value of this result is at least questionable (ibid. 615). However, comparing how many

European Commission, stemming from 2001, shows that 63,3% of the interviewed firms rate lead time (or first mover advantages) as the most effective instrument to protect their knowledge, and only 28,2% named patents and other
legal instruments as the most effective (European Commission 2001: 54, 55). To
put it in the words of Dosi et al. (2006):

> "To sum up, (i) in most circumstances, appropriability conditions sufficient to jus-
> tify private innovative efforts are in place with or without IPR protection, whereas
> (ii) IPR themselves have only limited importance as drivers of innovative efforts,"
> (Dosi/ Malerba/ Ramello/ Silva 2006: 897).

Still, besides the low ranking of the effectiveness of patents, we can observe that
the number of patent applications is growing (Arundel 2001).[139] Thus, there
must be another explanation as to why firms patent. In the next section, we will
therefore analyse why firms nevertheless use intellectual property rights.

4.2.2.2   Why Firms Do or Do Not Patent

In their survey, Cohen, Nelson, and Walsh did not only ask for an evaluation of
the appropriability instruments, but also asked the firms why they do or do not
patent (ibid.: 14). Starting with the latter, the authors asked why a firm did not
patent its last recent invention. Basically, the companies named five different
reasons: 1) difficulties in demonstrating the novelty of an invention; 2) the
amount of information disclosure required for patent applications; 3) the costs of
an application; 4) the costs incurred during litigation cases at court; and 5) the
ease of legally inventing around (ibid.). Of all reasons, the ease of legally inventing around a patent is the biggest hindrance of patenting (~65%), followed
by the demonstration of newness (~55%), and the disclosure of information
(~47%) (ibid.: 14 and also Figure 5). The significance of knowledge disclosure
becomes apparent in an empirical study by Allison and Lemley (2000). According their results, the majority of patents cites other patents, that is to say, they

---

companies ranked secrecy as more important than patents, the survey shows that – independently of firm size and research activity – the majority evaluates secrecy higher
than patents (ibid.: 617). Burr et al. (2007) differentiate between formal appropriability
mechanisms like patents and copyrights, and strategic appropriability instruments like
secrecy and first-mover advantages. Similar to the result from Cohen/Nelson/Walsh
they show that strategic instruments generally are from greater importance for the protection of innovation (ibid: 261-263).

139   For instance, Cohen, Nelson, and Walsh show that compared to the survey from Levin
      et al. (1987), patents have grown in importance (Cohen/Nelson/Walsh 2000: 13). Besi-
      des the development of the patent rating, it is interesting to note that in the 1983 survey
      no company evaluated secrecy as the most effective instrument, whereas in the 1994
      survey companies in 13 industries ranked it as the most effective and in 11 industries as
      the second most effective instrument for appropriation (Cohen/Nelson/Walsh 2000:
      Table 4 and 5).

mainly rely on knowledge developed for previous inventions (ibid.: 2102). The firms were also asked to evaluate the most important reason for not patenting, meaning they could only choose one reason out of the list. Here, the most important reason is the demonstration of novelty (32.1 %), followed by the ease of inventing around (24,6%), and disclosure of information (24,3%) (Cohen/ Nelson/Walsh 2000: Figure 6). We can assume that the ease of inventing around and the disclosure of information are closely related to each other, because the more information is disclosed, the easier a competitor can invent around the patented innovation. Even though the demonstration of knowledge is the most important hindrance to patenting, the disclosure requirement and the ease of information together total almost 50%. In these cases, we might argue that patent protection does not only fall short of its goal of promoting innovation, but might indeed evoke the contrary. In other words, patent protection might stifle innovation incentives because it makes inventing around, that is, copying, easier.

However, we should not overestimate these results. Even though in some cases companies might abstain from patenting because it is too complicated, it facilitates copying attempts, and it is costly, there are still enough reasons why firms nevertheless apply for patents. As Cohen, Nelson, and Walsh point out, when patents are rated the least effective instrument to protect an invention but the number of patents application is nevertheless rising, this demonstrates that patents can also generate other profits besides the direct revenues from the protected product or process (ibid.: 17). There are a number of reasons to patent, including: 1) to prevent copying; 2) to strengthen the firm's position in negotiation, that is, in cross-licensing agreements; 3) to earn licensing revenues; 4) to prevent competitors from launching a similar invention; 5) to prevent suits; 6) to enhance the company's reputation; and 7) to act as an indicator of the firms' performance in R&D (ibid.). For both product and process innovations, the legislator-intended reason, namely the prevention of copying, is the most important.[140] However, for product innovation, with approximately 82% of the respondents, patenting is also motivated by blocking rivals. Preventing competitors from developing similar inventions is also the second most important reason to patent for process innovation, followed by preventing suits (46,5% for process innovation; 58,8% for product innovation) and use in negotiations (37 %). This is similar for product innovations, where the use in negotiations got 47,4 % of the respondents, slightly behind the intent of enhancing their own reputation (47,9%;

---

140   For product innovations 96% and for process innovation 77% of the respondents by reason (Cohen/Nelson/Walsh 2000: Figure 7 and 8). However, some argue that this result may be exaggerated because many respondents might have considered that this reason is the most socially desirable (Allison/Lemley 2000: 2104).

for process innovation 34%) (ibid: Figure 7 and 8).[141] Hence, we can summarize that the strategic value of patents and intellectual property rights has risen in importance.[142] Patents and intellectual property rights strengthen the firm's value in merger and acquisition negotiations and can be used as a tool in licensing agreements (Hussinger 2006: 737).

However, it is important to note that across industries, differences exist regarding the motivation to patent. A not uncommon distinction is between complex and discrete industries (Levin et al. 1987, Kash/ Kingston 2001; Kusoniki/Nonaka/Nagata 1998; Merges/Nelson 1990). Kash and Kingston (2001) differentiate between simple and complex technologies. Accordingly, simple technologies are those that can be understood by experts and rebuilt on this basis (ibid: 11). An example of this is pharmaceuticals; each pharmacist or chemist can read and understand the formula and mix the drug accordingly (ibid.). In contrast, complex technologies, for instance in the computer and software industries, require large and diverse knowledge, which cannot be captured by a single individual. Furthermore, complex technology consists of both tacit and codified knowledge (ibid.).[143] Thus, it cannot easily be copied. Another feature of complex technologies is that the innovation process is often organic in character and involves several incremental innovation steps, that is, they require several patents. Therefore, the value of a complex technology is often not foreseeable and rather random (ibid.: 14) Moreover, because of the multitude of involved components, in complex industries companies often do not dispose of all required patents but need to engage in licensing agreements with other companies. This problem is also known as "the tragedy of the anticommons" (Heller/Eisenberg 1998). The term anticommons refers to the fact that in those complex technologies the different parts and involved technologies are all protected by intellectual property rights. The right holders, though, are not identical and hence, complex technologies require licensing agreements between the right holders to conduct an innovation (ibid.).[144] Thus, cross-licenses are widespread in complex indus-

---

141 For product innovation, 28,3 % of the respondents reported licensing revenues as a motivation for licensing revenues (for process innovation 23,3%) and 5,8% (5%) as a means for performance measurement (Cohen/Nelson/Walsh 2000: Figure 7 and 8).
142 For similar results compare to Harhoff et al. 2007.
143 Accordingly, discrete and complex technologies can also be differentiated by the kind of the underlying knowledge. In discrete technologies the required knowledge is mostly codified while in complex technologies it is not possible to codify all knowledge (Burr et al. 2007: 113).
144 Heller and Eisenberg call it the tragedy of anticommons since the necessity of licensing and the large number of involved intellectual property right holders can impede innovation. That is to say, if not all right holders agree in the licensing or in the licensing conditions, an innovation can be prohibited. For a detailed discussion of this problematic *compare to* Heller/Eisenberg 1998.

tries (Cohen/Nelson/Walsh 2000: 19). Based on this, Cohen, Nelson, and Walsh analysed whether the use of patents can be differentiated in regards to complex and discrete industries. Indeed, their data shows that in complex industries approximately 55% of the respondents indicated that patent applications are motivated by a better negotiation position whereas in discrete product industries only 40,6% register patents for this reason (ibid.: 19). Further differentiating and weighing the results,[145] the difference between complex and discrete industries becomes more apparent: 55% of complex industries patent for use in cross-licensing agreements, but only 10,3% do so in discrete product industries (ibid.). In contrast, in discrete product industries, patents have a stronger role in building fences in order to prevent rivals from developing competing products (ibid.: 23).[146]

In general, the authors reach the conclusion that the use of patents differs in complex and discrete product industries in three ways. First, as mentioned above, in complex product industries patents are important to strengthen the role in negotiations, whereas the possibility of earning additional revenues through licensing agreements plays only a minor role. In contrast, in discrete product industries patents are used in the traditional way, in other words, they are needed to ensure revenues for the research and development activity. This includes also possible licensing revenues. Finally, discrete product industries employ patents to impede the development of similar products (ibid. 23-24).

4.2.3 Alternative Strategies to Appropriate R&D Returns

4.2.3.1 Secrecy

Generally, secrecy has been seen as the alternative to patenting intellectual property.[147] As Machlup (1952) said, "people patent only what they cannot hope to keep secret" (ibid.: 281). Usually, when we talk about secrecy, we refer to trade secrets, that is, a piece of information or an intellectual good like a manufacturing process that has a commercial value. In keeping it secret, the possess-

---

145 For a detailed explanation of the methodology, *compare to* Cohen/Nelson/Walsh 2001: 19 et seqq.).

146 Similar results can be found in the Harhoff study. The authors differentiate two patent strategies: 1) the use of patents as bargain chips and 2) the use of patents as blocking devices. The first strategy is typical for complex industries whereas the second strategy is used in discret industries (Harhoff et al. 2007: 262 et seq.).

147 Please note that in our discussion we will not consider the effects of secrecy on social welfare, including, for instance, that secrecy can lead to a waste of resources because of double invention. Rather, our focus is on the arguments as to why firms choose to keep information secret. For a depiction of the welfare effects, *compare to* Friedman et al. 1991.

ing firm wants to prevent competitors from duplicating the protected knowledge or information (Friedman et al. 1991: 61). Especially since the disclosure of information in the patenting process is connected with certain disadvantages, for example, competitors are able to observe a new technological trend early and react accordingly, some firms prefer keeping their innovations secret (Hussinger 2006: 736). The problem of information disclosure is even greater when we relate it to a limited intellectual property protection, in that competitors have incentives to copy an innovation even though it is patented (Anton/Yao 2004: 2). For instance, Mansfield et al. (1981) show in their study that 60 percent of patented and commercially successful innovations have been imitated within four years (ibid.: 913). Reasons for the limited protection are the ease with which invention around is possible in some cases, the possibility that a patent is invalid if challenged, and the low penalty payments in infringement suits (Anton/Yao 2004: 2). The advantage of secrecy, though, is that it is free of charge and competitors cannot learn about the underlying technology so quickly (ibid.). A famous example for successful secrecy is the recipe of Coca-Cola. Had the company decided to patent the recipe, competitors would have known the ingredients right from the beginning, and they would have been able to develop substitutes far earlier. And, more importantly, after 18 years, in the year 1903, competitors would have been able to legally use the original recipe of Coca-Cola. However, the firm decided to keep the recipe secret, and until today it rejects the claim that anyone else has its original formula (Moser 2009: 1).

Secrecy may be a disadvantage, though, if someone finds a formula or any other trade secret, since the innovator has no legal instrument to protect its invention for copying or imitating (Hussinger 2006: 736). Thus, a trade secret cannot be assessed like property because the owner does not have an exclusive right over it (Friedman et al. 1991: 62). In contrast to intellectual property law, possessing a trade secret does not give the right to litigate against an imitator if the secret unintentionally leaks out (ibid.). As such, we might wonder if this insecurity does not outweigh the disadvantage of information disclosure. It is legitimate to question why a firm decides to choose a rather unsafe way of protecting itself instead of simply patenting the invention. Friedman et al. illustrate this with three examples.[148] In the first case, a firm has a patentable invention, and it thinks that imitation of the invention will take at least almost as long as the term of patent protection. Further, the invention has only a moderate value. Deciding whether to patent the invention or not, the company or the innovator weighs the costs of a patent application, including the cost of preparing the required documents, against the costs of keeping the invention secret by preventing the slipping through of information. If secrecy is connected with lower costs, the company decides against patenting.

---

148   For the following, please compare to Friedman et al. 1991: 63-64.

In the second case, the invention is again patentable, but the innovator assumes that reinventing it will take competitors much longer than the duration of patent protection. Patenting the invention would ensure a stronger protection, whereas keeping it secret has the advantage that the inventor profits longer from the benefits, provided that the information does not leak out. However, if the firm believes that it can protect the trade secret from leaking and if it expects a greater return, it will keep the information secret. At the same time, choosing secrecy means that the innovator believes that the value of her invention is bigger than supposed by the legislators of patent law.

In the third case, the invention is not patentable, but the innovator expects that imitation will take long enough to profit sufficiently from the innovation. As Friedman et al. explain in this case – similar to the previous one – the underlying assumption is that the legislator has a different estimation of the invention's value than the inventor, that is, assigning a patent would over-reward the invention. If the innovator thinks that keeping the necessary information secret will ensure a sufficient reward, she will decide in favour of secrecy.

Thus, according to Friedman et al., an inventor chooses trade secret over patent protection when she either assumes that the costs of patenting are too high compared to the value of the invention or when she thinks that the value of the invention exceeds the value of the patent and she will earn a greater profit by keeping it secret.

In modelling strategic patent behaviour, Horstman et al. (1985) further show that with an increase of the expected value, firms tend to prefer secrecy over patenting. Although this may sound counterintuitive, the reasoning behind it is plausible: Because of information disclosure, patents have a signalling function. That is, a competitor comes to know about a new technology or a new idea. While not allowed to imitate, the competitor still has valuable information about the innovation and can use that information to invent around. At the same time, the strategy not to patent valuable innovations creates a new signal – that the patented invention has only a low to moderate value and that, therefore, imitation is not worthwhile (ibid.: 839).

Anton and Yao (2004) indicate that innovators do not have to decide either for patents or for secrecy. Rather, especially with bigger innovations, innovators can decide to disclose and patent some parts of the invention and keep another part secret (ibid.: 2). Based on this, Anton and Yao differentiate three cases. First, if an innovation is rather small, competitors are less likely to imitate it. Thus, small innovations are normally patented and disclosed. Second, for bigger innovations, firms tend to rely on a mix of patenting and secrecy. As imitation occurs, this most likely leads to an implicit licensing agreement in the sense that competitors have to pay penalties for infringing. Third, for large innovations, firms would rather rely on secrecy than on patent protection (ibid.:3).

To summarize, firms keep innovations secret because, first, sometimes the costs of patenting exceed the value of the invention and, second, patenting is always connected to disclosure of information and knowledge. Even though direct duplication is not allowed, the protection is often incomplete and competitors may imitate nevertheless or the disclosure may give sufficient information to successfully invent around.

4.2.3.2   Lead Time

The appropriation strategy of lead time, also known as "first-mover advantage," is at least in part connected to secrecy. In other words, to benefit from the first-mover advantage, firms innovate inwardly and then introduce the resulting profit as the first company on the market (Argawal/Gort 1999: 2). Bain (1956) identifies three main entry barriers for later market entries: 1) economies of scale and sunk costs; 2) absolute cost advantages; and 3) product differentiation advantages of the first innovator.[149] Similarly, Lieberman and Montgomery (1988) acknowledge leadership in product and process technology, or simply technological leadership, pre-emption of access, and development of buyer switching costs as the main reasons why being first on the market can turn out to be a decisive advantage.

Regarding entry barriers, sunk costs only play a role in capital intense industries. Followers or imitators must first invest in costly technologies or manufacturing capabilities before they can start competing with the incumbent firm. This effect may be strengthened by economies of scale; some technologies may not run efficiently under a certain minimum production number (Demsetz 1982, Stigler 1968). Thus, depending on the scope of the lead time, the incumbent already might have reached a large part of the potential consumers. Before entering the market, firms therefore need to assess whether they can reach a sufficient large consumer basis and whether the market is growing quickly enough to produce at an efficient level (Stigler 1968). The incumbent, however, has the advantage that she already invested in the market; ideally, she already captured her sunk costs and can now sell the product at a lower cost than the potential entrants (Bain 1956: 54-55).

Absolute cost advantage may arise due to the disposal of scarce resources, management skills, or higher developed production technologies (Argawal/Gort 1999: 6). Lieberman and Montgomery (1988), highlighting technological leadership as one of the main sources of first-mover advantages, explain this advantage with: 1) learning curve effects; and 2) success in patent or R&D races

---

149 Please note that Bain's theory about market entry barriers is valid in general and does not refer exclusively to lead time or first-mover advantage. His theory can also be applied to explain why established sellers can demand prices above the competitive level without fearing market entry (Bain 1956: 5).

(ibid.: 42). Being first in the market gives the opportunity to learn from one's mistakes and improve; thus, if imitators later enter the market, the incumbent already has the first teething problems behind her, whereas her rivals are still at the beginning of the learning-by-doing process (Grant 1991: 123). Nonetheless, the underlying assumption is that the learning effects can be kept proprietary. Another assumption is that advances in manufacturing and production can also go back to patents and copyrights, showing an intertwining of different appropriability instruments. Intellectual property protection is not mandatory, and in the early development phase, it can be even detrimental, although it can still strengthen the first-mover advantage as intellectual property rights can extend the lead time after commercializing the product. Another possible way of maintaining technological superiority is protection by trade secrets (Lieberman/Montgomery 1988: 43).

The advantage of scarce resources can be interpreted broadly. The first-mover firm has better information regarding the purchase of input factors, for instance, it get better deals than later firms or it controls natural resources. Besides that, the first mover can also choose – both in a geographic but also product characteristics space – the most attractive or lucrative location. This is especially advantageous when the market shows only limited demand, that is, when there is only "space" for a limited number of firms. In this case, the first-moving firm can choose in which niches it wants to be, whereas later firms have to take the leftover possibilities (Lieberman/Montgomery 1988: 44).

The third barrier of entry identified by Bain is advertising, which serves as a proxy for product differentiation.[150] As a result of advertisements, consumers' demand should be influenced in favour of the advertising firm's products (Comanor/ Wilson 1979: 454). According to this argument, advertising and the development of reputation and a brand name increase the absolute cost advantages of the incumbent firm and simultaneously raise the costs for new entries. However, the argument that advertising constitutes an entry barrier has been disputed (Demsetz 1979; Schmalensee 1974, 1982). Comanor and Wilson (1979) have shown that the effect of advertising depends on the type of advertising and the demand elasticity of consumers. In other words, advertising with only an informational character may lead to a higher sensibility among consumers of quality and/or price, in other words, a higher elasticity of demand, which would reduce entry barriers. If, in contrast, the advertising is (also) persuasive, the demand elasticity is lower; consumers tend to buy the product of the incumbent, in other words, entry barriers are increased (ibid: 455).

---

150   According to Bain, product differentiation is inter alia propagated "by efforts of sellers to distinguish their products through packaging, branding and the offering of auxiliary services to the buyers, and by advertising and sales-promotional efforts designed to win the allegiance and custom of the potential buyer" (Bain 1956: 115).

This argument of product differentiation is closely related to switching costs and buyer choice under uncertainty, which also strengthen the first mover. Switching costs means that later market entries have to convince the consumer to change from the first mover's products to their products (Cohen 1996: 537). Depending on inter alia how successful the first mover has been in promoting its product(s), this constitutes a further barrier for competitors. The barrier becomes even stronger when the use of the product is related to learning processes, that is, when consumers switch to a competing product they have to get used to handling or operating the new product (Lieberman/Montgomery 1988: 46). Besides that, consumers already know the quality of the incumbent's product, while they are uncertain about the quality of the new products. As long as consumers have been satisfied with the first product, they tend to stick to that product instead of risking lower quality (ibid.).

Nevertheless, being first on the market does not necessarily guarantee long-lasting market success. Due to free-rider effects, changes in consumer demand or technological possibilities, or simply better overall performance, later entries can still outpace the first mover.[151] Thus, market success depends not only on the timing of the market entry, but also on other factors like complementary assets. We will discuss this in the next section.

4.2.3.3   Complementary Assets and Technologies

As mentioned in the previous section, it is not (always) sufficient to have a good idea, develop the product, and bring it to the market first. For the successful commercialization of an innovation, the interplay of several factors is required. This relates also to the requirement of dynamic capabilities discussed in Section 4.2.1 above. According to Teece (1986), complementary assets are decisive for the appropriation of innovation. In his article "Profiting from technological innovation," Teece illustrates that, especially in regimes with low levels of intellectual property protection, the ability to appropriate the returns of an innovation depends on the whole set of competences. Generally, complementary assets do not only include physical and material assets, but they also comprise organizational capabilities or competences. In terms of the resourced based view, a firm's competence is not based on one or more distinct resources but is rather determined by a firm's ability to make better use of its resources than its competitors. Hence, a firm's competence can be described as the co-ordinated and precise use of its assets (Burr et al. 2005: 21). To successfully commercialise an innovation, not only is knowledge in R&D or manufacturing necessary, but also knowledge in finance, marketing, legal, and other aspects (Teece 1986: 288). Thus, a firm that makes an innovation and disposes of complementary assets

---

151   For a more detailed depiction of first mover 'disadvantages' and for a critical review of first mover advantages in general compare to Lieberman/ Montgomery 1988 and 1998.

will probably be better able to appropriate the returns of the innovation than a firm without any or with fewer complementary assets (ibid.: 292). This is illustrated by the study from Cohen, Nelson, and Walsh (2000) discussed above where, according to their survey, complementary sales and services as well as complementary manufacturing were decisive in more than 40 percent of product innovations in their sample (ibid.).

Thus, a company has an advantage when it can use its own complementary assets. For instance, when a drug company wants to introduce a new product, it needs to disseminate information on the product over a particular, specialized channel to reach the right patients, doctors, and hospitals. If the company already has experience in disseminating this kind of information, its marketing capabilities will support the successful introduction of the drug (Teece 1986: 288). Similarly, the use of hardware requires specialized software. Having already skilled software engineers and a technical service department also supports the commercialization of the hardware (ibid.). Teece, Pisano, and Shuen (1997) highlight the importance of dynamic capabilities in this context, that is, "the firm's ability to integrate, build and reconfigure internal and external competences to address rapidly changing environments" (ibid.: 516). In other words, the innovating company must be able to adjust its competences quickly to the requirements of its new product. At the same time, these dynamic capabilities allow the company to react quickly to other market developments.

However, the strategic advantage of a firm decreases as the complementary assets become more generic. In other words, if competitors already have the same assets, or if the assets are easily accessible on the market, the complementary assets lose their importance to appropriating the returns of the innovation (Rothaermel/Hill 2005: 52). In contrast, the more specialized or unique the assets, the more the likelihood of a successful commercialization of the innovation increases (ibid.). Therefore, Teece differentiates between three types of assets: generic, specialized, and co-specialized (ibid. 1986: 289). Generic complementary assets can be acquired on the market and do not need to be adjusted to a particular product or innovation. In contrast, specialized assets involve a unilateral dependence between the asset and the innovation. Co-specialized complementary assets exhibit a bilateral dependence (ibid.). To illustrate the bilateral character of a complementary asset, imagine the introduction of a new engine for a car. In this example, specialized repair facilities are needed to support the engine. However, the relation is mutual because the innovation and commercialization also depend on the repair facility (ibid.). The generic capabilities are, for instance, the manufacturing facilities. Thus, the crucial determinants for the success of the firm are the specialized and co-specialized assets, because they are difficult to imitate (Rothaermel/Hill 2005: 53).

From this perspective, it is possible to argue that complementary assets can also constitute a barrier to imitation. Stephan (2003) differentiates between four barriers: time pressure, accumulated previous knowledge, cumulativeness of resources, and ex ante uncertainty. To start with the first, in a dynamic market, a potential imitator faces time pressure to accumulate the necessary resources and complementary assets. In order to react quickly and hasten the accumulation process, the imitator has to spend more to acquire the needed assets. Moreover, costs arise as the imitator does not have sufficient time to test its assets and thus, faces a higher failure or mistake rate (Stephan 2003: 102). Besides that, second, in order to build up complementary assets, certain knowledge is required. That is to say, if the imitator already has experience in a related field, she can diminish her accumulation costs. But if the imitator has rather limited experience or knowledge, she has more costs because she has to make up for this failure (Reed/DeFillipi 1990: 94). The third problem constitutes the lack of separation of complementary assets and resources. The more complex and intertwined the complementary assets of an innovator, the more difficulties an imitator faces in rebuilding these assets. This is inter alia because the imitator cannot observe which assets are related to each other and which separate assets are involved at all (Grant 1991: 127). Finally, even if a competitor already invested a lot in her complementary process, ex ante uncertainty exists as to which assets will be successful or necessary for innovation. This uncertainty increases the costs and the time period for building an asset stock (Stephan 2003: 103). However, as Reed and DeFillippi (1990) note, competitors can eventually overcome these barriers to imitation. Thus, the innovator has incentives to permanently reinvest and renew the barriers to imitation (ibid: 97).

An innovation can either be continuous or discontinuous in the sense that it makes previous (co-)specialized complementary assets obsolete or further builds on them (Rothaermel/Hill 2005: 54). Thus, if a firm introduces an innovation that discontinues the specialized assets of the competitors, the reaction rate decreases. Firms that follow need to adjust their assets or replace their specialized assets before they can compete with the new innovation (ibid.). Again, that is to say, in those cases innovation may involve large complementary investments that create barriers to entry for imitators (Gilbert 2006a: 163). The simpler the innovation, that is, the easier an imitation is to realize, the more important complementary assets become. Therefore, a company must have advantages in specialized and co-specialized assets, because it is effortless to obtain generic assets in the market. In this case, the innovating firm can rely less on price advantages, but it has to show strength in sales and after-sale services (Teece 1986: 292).

All in all, Teece shows that the degree of imitability depends, firstly, on legal protections like copyrights, patents, and trademarks and, secondly, on the inherent reproducibility of the technology for which the degree of tacit and explicit know-how is decisive (Teece 2006: 1134). That is, on the one hand, as long as the innovator does not have complementary assets, it is not sufficient to rely on IP protection to profit from innovation. On the other hand, the more specialized the complementary assets that go along with the innovation are, the more advantageous the innovating firm is, that is, the less it needs intellectual property protection.

4.2.3.4   Other Appropriation Strategies

Besides the appropriability strategies mentioned above, firms have several other methods to protect their innovations. This section will briefly introduce some of these alternate protection methods.

One mechanism for protecting innovations is *labour contracts*. Labour contracts may establish that the inventions of employees belong to the company, and they may forbid employees from leaving for direct competitors. The goal of these agreements is to keep skills and knowledge within the company and therewith to prevent easy imitation by rivals (Hurmelinna-Laukkanen/Puumalainen 2007: 97). Keeping a specialized employee in the company is not only important to keep expertise within the firm, but also because each employee takes along knowledge about internal routines and capabilities. Thus, by hiring staff from competitors, a firm would not only gain know-how but may also gain valuable insights into the procedures and work-flow of its competitors. From this perspective, binding staff to the company is also an essential component for keeping things secret (ibid.).[152] Furthermore, agreements that intellectual property rights generated by the inventive efforts of single employees subrogate to the company enhance appropriability (ibid.).

Another possible mechanism of protecting innovations is *technological fences*. Technological fences can be used, for instance, to protect unauthorized copying (Palmer 1989: 288). We know this from compact discs and videocassettes, which are protected with a certain code that makes it impossible to copy them. A further example of technological fences is evident in the *Xerox* case. Xerox, a manufacturer of copiers and repairer of parts, incorporated a special code in its copiers. As a result, independent service organizations could not exchange spare parts as the copiers would only accept parts with the corresponding code (compare section 2.2.1). While this was deemed anti-competitive because the code prevented competition on the service market, the *Xerox* case shows that there are several ways to protect innovations.

---

152 However, there is also a discussion on innovation clusters highlighting the importance of frequent changes of employers. According to this argument, innovation activities profit from the exchange of ideas that occurs following transfers between firms and also from discussion between specialists from competing firms. The underlying idea is that the exchange of know-how and experiences creates new ideas and therewith spurs development. From this perspective, firms profit from knowledge transfers and have incentives to promote the exchange. A famous example of this innovation clusters where firms choose locations within spitting distance of competitors (and suppliers) in order to benefit from knowledge spillovers is Silicon Valley in California (Swann 2009).

However, sometimes employing new technology requires highly specialized information, making extensive teaching necessary. In these cases, if the innovator does not want to profit directly from the use of the technology, she can appropriate the benefits of her innovation by not only licensing the technology, but also by providing training or licensing know-how (Gilbert 2006a: 163). Nevertheless, licensing agreements may constitute a possibility of profiting from an innovation in any case. Even though intellectual property rights may facilitate licensing agreements, it is also possible to realize them in specifying remedies contractually for cases of unauthorized uses or releases of the good to third parties (Palmer 1989: 292).

4.2.4 Intermediate Result: Limited Relevance of Intellectual Property Rights for Appropriation of R&D Returns

In general, this section shows that knowledge disposes over a public good character only to a limited degree. In most cases, at least some previous knowledge is necessary to decode certain information. Thus, imitation is almost never costless, and it also requires time to acquire the necessary skills and resources to copy a certain innovation. From this perspective, we can argue that intellectual property rights are not necessarily an essential instrument for the protection and appropriation of innovation. Instead, this section shows that firms also resort to other alternative appropriability instruments than only intellectual property rights, for instance, secrecy, lead time, and complementary assets.

Further, the survey of Cohen, Nelson, and Walsh demonstrates that industry differences regarding the evaluation of the effectiveness of patents exists. We can assume that the effectiveness of the different appropriability instruments differs in dependence of the respective industry, type of innovation, involved knowledge, and so on. Normally, firms choose the appropriability instrument or the group of appropriability instruments that seems to be the most effective for a particular innovation. The success of a firm in reaping the fruits of its investment depends on the right choice of instruments and their efficient application. The strength of the instruments can vary depending on the circumstances. It is also possible that not all instruments are available in every case, that is, not every invention can be protected with intellectual property rights or the use of secrecy may not be possible (Hurmelinna Laukkanen/Puumalaien 2007: 99). For instance, an important differentiation has to be made between complex and discrete industries. Whereas discrete industries rely on simple technologies that are easy to copy, complex industries are based on innovations that require broad and diverse knowledge and also several patents. From this perspective, complex industries employ patent and copyrights for strategic uses like strengthening their own negotiation position for licensing agreements. In contrast, firms in discrete industries need intellectual property protection to protect their innovations from imitators.

The choice of the most effective appropriability mechanism is also likely to be affected by the underlying nature of knowledge; that is to say, is the required knowledge existent in a codified version or is it tacit (Jensen/Webster 2006: 4)? If an innovation is based on tacit knowledge, the innovator will probably choose secrecy instead of intellectual property. As tacit knowledge is based on routines and path dependencies within an organization, it not likely that a competitor will be able to imitate the invention right away. Moreover, not only the imitator but also the innovator would have to codify the knowledge before she could, for instance, apply for patent protection. In contrast, if an invention is based on already codified knowledge, the innovator will most likely use intellectual property rights to protect the invention. This can be observed, for example, in the pharmaceutical industry. Here, patents have been rated as very effective. Generally, for the reproduction of a particular drug, it is not necessary to know the routines within the original firm. For a successful imitation, it is enough to know the ingredients and their composition, which can easily be found by reverse engineering. Thus, secrecy would not effectively protect the invention, and in these cases, companies would rather rely on patenting.

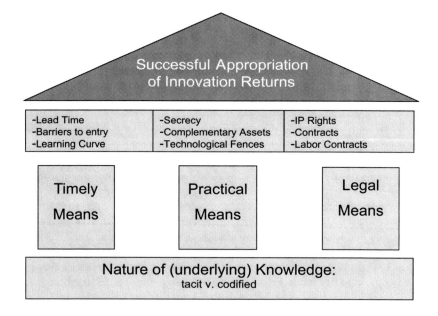

Figure 4-3: Building blocks of appropriation

However, abstaining from these extreme cases where knowledge is either tacit or codified, the challenge is to determine the influence of underlying knowledge and also routines on the effectiveness of appropriability instruments. That is to say, in a lot of cases it might be difficult to determine exactly the optimal mix of appropriability instruments. The graphic above (Figure 4-3) illustrates the different building blocks of successful appropriation.

Generally, we can say that the degree of appropriation depends on the strength of the barriers to imitation evoked by the appropriability strategies. However, the height of the imitation barriers depends not only on the appropriability strategy of the innovating firm but also on the previous investments of the imitators in R&D and complementary assets.

In sum, this section shows that firms do have more appropriability instruments than only intellectual property rights. In dependence of the characteristics of the particular innovation, the effectiveness of the different instruments differs and, hence, companies choose the appropriability mechanism from which they expect the greatest returns. In other words, possessing intellectual property rights is not automatically an indicator that a company needs them to appropriate the returns on investments. For a correct determination of intellectual property rights and also for a balancing of innovation effects, it is necessary to consider the preconditions for innovation, for instance, the absorptive capacity, and the availability of alternative appropriability mechanisms.

However, in contrast to our result from section 4.1, this section does not provide differentiated models or rules for a distinct evaluation of the effectiveness of alternative appropriation mechanisms. Even though we know that firm do not necessarily need intellectual property rights for the appropriation of their R&D returns, we do not know, for instance, at which point these alternative appropriability instruments make intellectual property rights completely obsolete. The fact that firms mostly employ appropriation strategies, that is, a mix of the different appropriability instruments, further impedes the precise evaluation of the strength and effectiveness of the single instruments. Firms may know which mechanisms they rate as the most important but the question is whether they can exactly rate how effective each instrument is in the interplay of the different instruments. Even if the firms had this precise knowledge, the question remains whether competition authorities would be able to get this information too. Against this background, it is notable that extending our analysis from the law and economic theories of intellectual property rights to insights from innovation research does again not contribute to a simplification of the analysis of the appropriate scope of intellectual property rights. Although this section demonstrates that appropriation is influenced by several other factors, such a broader analysis requires also more information and knowledge on the specific market conditions. Nevertheless, the results of this section can be useful for a qualitative analysis that abstains from a quantitative assessment of the different effects.

4.3 Innovation in Markets with Network Effects

This section now turns to the question of whether special characteristics of a market can have an influence on innovation and competition. Thus, in contrast to the previous sections, this section does not aim at providing criteria which can directly be applied in assessing whether a particular intellectual property right is welfare enhancing. Instead, this section shall analyse market conditions and product characteristics that might have an influence on competition and innovation in that market. Special attention lies at markets in which network effects occurs.

However, before turning to the latter, we will make a brief excursion to the relationship between market structure and innovation. This excursion is necessary because we saw that the Commission and also the European Courts tend to favour the theory that a low firm concentration is better for innovation than a high concentrated market structure (compare Chapter 2 and 3). Consequently, this section shall clarify on whether there is a certain market structure that fosters innovation most.

Afterwards, we will turn to industries with network effects and standards and will analyse how these features determine innovative behaviour. The results of this section can be from importance, for instance, for finding the right remedy if abusive behaviour could be testified.

4.3.1   Theoretical Digression on Innovation and Market Structure

In this section, we turn now to an issue we have already touched on several times in the previous discussion, which is the question of if and how market structure influences innovation or innovation incentives. Since the Commission in the *Microsoft* case (see Chapter 2) based its decision on the assumption that low firm concentration in any case is better than monopoly or a highly concentrated market structure, it is necessary to analyse the influence of market structure on innovation in more detail.

Generally, two views exist in regards to the relationship between innovation and market structure (Baker 2007). One view follows the theory of Joseph Schumpeter (1942), who argues that monopolies and big firms innovate more than firms in low concentrated markets.[153] According to Schumpeter, big firms dispose of more capital than smaller firms to fund R&D efforts. Moreover, big firms have less fear that (potential) rivals might be able to place a successful

---

153 This is the "late" Schumpeter position. The "early" Schumpeter demanded more competition in the sense of low firm concentration. Specifically, he stressed that competition is driven by the tension between imitation and innovation, but also by personal motives like aspiration after success and power (Schumpeter 1934).

imitation of their products on the markets (Baker 2007: 578). The other view follows the theory of Kenneth Arrow (1959). In contrast to Schumpeter, Arrow argues that low firm concentration stimulates more innovation than a highly concentrated market structure. Without innovation, the monopolist has already a steady flow of profits from its current products. Accordingly, the monopolist has fewer incentives to innovate because if it makes a significant improvement, the market share it wins is at the expense of its previous products. Introducing a better or improved good would only pull away demand from its own, already dominant, product. Tirole (1997) calls this reduced innovation incentive the "replacement effect." [154] Further, Arrow argues that if a firm in a competitive market innovates successfully, it gains market share from its competitors, albeit under the premise of exclusive intellectual property protection. To date, both theories have followers, with a slight bias towards the Arrow approach, but empirical data and theoretical models do not clearly support one particular view.

Gilbert (2006a) illustrates the difficulty of correctly observing and interpreting the relation between market structure and innovation with a short example of the telecommunications sector that is both highly innovative and competitive. According to Gilbert, many management teams in telecommunication companies trace their employment and development histories back to large companies like Bell Laboratories or IBM; in other words, these companies are led by former employees of telecommunication giants. Thus,

> "[I]s it correct to conclude that competitive markets promote innovation in this example? Perhaps a better interpretation is that competitive markets were useful only in a more limited sense to exploit innovations whose seeds were sown at Bell Labs or IBM." (Gilbert 2006a: 184)

As this example demonstrates, we need to be careful before we jump to conclusions. Generally, economic analysis can make only one statement regarding the influence of market structure on innovation: It depends. However, the results are not as inconclusive as one might assume. As such, in the following section, we identify some conclusions.[155]

In general, we can conclude that bigger firms or monopolistic firms have greater incentives to invest in process innovations (Gilbert 2006a: 161-162). Usually invented for internal uses, the benefits of a process innovation increase proportionally to the production level to which the innovation is dedicated (ibid.). In other words, bigger firms have stronger incentives to invest in process

---

154　Please note that Arrow refers to process innovations. The explanation above is therefore only a simplified depiction.

155　The following section is based in large parts on Gilbert (2006a), who gives a very broad overview of the literature concerning market structure and innovation. For a more general depiction of the influence of market structure on innovation, compare to Scherer/Ross 1990 Chapter 17 and to Kamien/Schwartz 1989.

innovation than smaller firms because they can realize economies of scale. Without intellectual property rights (and with profit-maximizing inventors), this tendency to innovate in highly concentrated markets becomes even stronger. Large or monopolistic firms are better able to capture the benefits of innovation, for instance because they have the necessary complementary assets or are able to build them up quickly, whereas smaller firms have lesser possibilities to protect their inventions (Gilbert 2006a: 164). For product innovation, we cannot prove such a correlation, instead there is only some evidence that concentrated market structure promotes incentives to innovate, however, there is some evidence that a low firm concentration has positive effects on innovation (Gilbert 2006a: 162).

Usually, we can assume that low concentration generates more incentives for product innovation if two main conditions are fulfilled: first, competition in the market for the old product is intense. This implies that competitors earn only a small profit and therefore have greater incentive to innovate in order to increase their profits. Second, the innovation replaces the old product. This condition ensures that the net gain of a new competitor exceeds the gain of a monopolist. In other words, if an invention makes an old product obsolete, a monopolist has few incentives to innovate, because she cannot earn additional benefits whereas with low firm concentration, firms take that as an advantage to increase their profits (Gilbert 2006a: 168).

However, if the innovation is non-drastic, that is, it does not replace the old product, a monopolistic firm has more incentive to invest in innovation and, thus, pre-empt R&D competition (Gilbert/Newbery 1982). In the model of Gilbert and Newbery, firms bid for an innovation. Thus, a monopolist has the incentive to overbid potential competitors to protect its monopoly rent. If a competitor won the auction for the non-drastic innovation, the competitor would not leapfrog the monopolist but rather compete with her in the same market and lessen the profit of the monopolist. Thus, the incentive of the monopolist is the difference between her monopolistic profit and a duopolistic profit if she loses the auction. The incentive of the competitor is the difference between the profit she earns if she wins the auction and the profit without it. We can assume that this incentive exceeds the expected profit, that is, the duopolistic profit, of the potential competitor (ibid.). Hence, bidding for the invention and pre-empting R&D competition maintains the monopolistic gain.[156]

---

156 However, this result rests on several assumptions. First, it is necessary that bidding firms are certain about the result of the auction. In other words, firms must know how much they have to bid to exceed their competitors, which means they have a high level of certainty. Further, the patent ensures perfect competition; that is to say, there are no other ways to enter the market besides the patented technology and besides the monopolist possessing the old technology. A new entrant cannot bargain with or license from the monopolist. And finally, in the old technology, the monopolist did not face any competitors (Gilbert 2006a: 170).

According to Reinganum (1983), the result in Gilbert and Newbery's model changes when the outcome of R&D efforts is stochastic and the innovation is drastic. This outcome is correlated to Arrow's replacement effect. Assume that the risk is low that the competitor will innovate successfully. Consequently, a monopolist has reduced incentives to innovate; her incentives to innovate are described by the difference between the monopoly profit of the old product and the monopoly profit of the new product. The difference is probably marginal. If the risk is high that the competitor will be successful with its invention, than the monopolist again has the same incentive to invest in R&D. Otherwise, she would lose all her monopoly profits. However, as the inventive process is stochastic, the monopolist earns profits from her old product during the R&D process. Although we cannot specify the length of the invention time, we can assume that this inventive period decreases with increasing R&D expenses and therewith the time the monopolist get flows from the old product (Reinganum 1983: 741). As such, when the invention is drastic, it is reasonable for the monopolist to invest less than the competitor (Reinganum 1983).

Further, Boone (2001) shows that, assuming all companies have the same cost structure, larger firms dominate in R&D in markets with strong or aggressive competition and innovate more than their smaller competitors. In contrast, in markets with weak competition, smaller or previously less successful firms invest more in R&D to catch up or leapfrog the leading companies (ibid.: 706). If competition is strong, firms that are already successful in the market can profit most from the innovation and therefore have higher incentives to innovate than weaker competitors. Consequently, Boone concludes that if policy makers decide to intensify competition in a certain industry, it is very likely that the already leading firm will increase its R&D efforts and, as a result, the industry may be more concentrated in a couple of years (ibid.: 723). However, if competition is weak, successful companies tend to rely on their previous success and reap the fruits of their efforts, while weaker competitors take the opportunity to catch up with their successful rivals (ibid.).

In sum, the economic literature does not provide any clear evidence that the Schumpeter hypothesis that large firms spur innovation because of better risk diversification, economies of scale, and better appropriability mechanisms is accurate. However, there is also no strong evidence that Arrow's approach is correct. As soon as we begin differentiating between process and product innovation and drastic and non-drastic innovation, and as soon we use varying underlying assumptions (for example, whether the firms have the same cost structure or whether they bid for innovations), then both economic theories and empirical studies[157] fail to make a universally valid statement regarding the correlation between market concentration and investments in R&D to determine an op-

---

157 Compare exemplarily to Scherer/Ross 1990.

timal degree of competition for the promotion of innovation (Gilbert 2006a: 205-206). As Dasgupta and Stiglitz (1980) put it, in the short run, market concentration may be treated as a datum and therefore it might be possible to seek a causal relation between market structure and R&D expenditures. However, in the long run, the structure of a particular industry is endogenous and the relation between market structure and innovation is influenced by more determinants like demand structure and technology of research (Dasgupta/ Stiglitz 1980: 2).

This result shows us that an assumption that a low concentrated market structure always spurs innovation better than a high concentrated market structure cannot be made. Instead it is necessary to analyse the specific circumstances. This is especially important if such a finding constitutes the basis for a analysis of competition policy like the Commission did in the *Microsoft* case. That is to say, we cannot simply deviate from the market structure if a market is highly innovative or not. Nevertheless, there might also be specific market characteristics that influence the innovative activity and competition on a certain market. The next section will analyse this correlation in more depth.

4.3.2   Markets with Network Effects

In markets with network effects and standards, innovation processes and the appropriability problem will greatly differ from those in other markets. In these markets, the access of downstream firms to technological standards represents a particular critical issue and might imply solutions that limit intellectual property rights in order to promote innovation in downstream markets. However, since their analysis requires the use of network economics and the economics of standards, I will start with an introduction on the characteristics of network industries before analysing the impact of network effects on innovation.

4.3.2.1   Characteristics of Network Industries

Network industries make up an important part of our economy. Examples of these industries include the telecommunications sector (voice and data services, including the Internet, computer hardware, and software), transportation sectors like railroads, roads, and airlines, and also the financial sector like credit card and ATM networks. We can also differentiate between so-called virtual or indirect networks. In contrast to factual networks, virtual networks are goods using the same technical platform. For instance, computers running the same operation system constitute a virtual network (Economides 2004: 96).

Generally, network industries differ from other industries due to some specific characteristics.[158] First, many network industries are related to economies

---

158   For a broader overview on network industries, *compare to* Besen/Saloner 1989; Economides 1996; Economides/Flyer 1998; Farell/Saloner 1985, 1992; Katz/Shapiro 1985, 1994; Laffont/Rey/Tirole 1998a. 1998b; Lemley/McGowan 1998. Further, Nicholas

of scales, that is, the average costs of production decline with an increase in the production number and the marginal costs for the last produced unit are insignificant (Cohen 1996). As economies of scale also occur in other industries, these features alone still do not make a typical network. Rather, besides these characteristics, networks consist of complementary nodes and links because a service within a network requires the use of not less than two components; for instance, when we want to use the train, this involves not only the railroad but also at least two stations we can get in and out of (Economides 2004: 98). That is to say that network industries often feature natural monopolies.[159] Further, network industries are characterized by increasing value for consumers with an increase in consumption. That is, with every sold unit, the value of the network grows, both for the existing consumer and for the buying consumer. This is typically illustrated with the example of telephones. The value of a telephone obviously increases the more households possess one (Katz/Shapiro 1985: 424). This may lead to the effect that, in contrast to non-network goods, the willingness to pay for the last unit increases with the number of units sold (Economides 2004: 98).[160]

Indirect or virtual network effects occur when – due to the high numbers of consumers of a certain network, for instance, a particular computer operating system – more complementary applications are developed. Besides the positive effect for the consumers, these indirect network effects, for example, in software and hardware markets, cause consumption externalities. That is, the amount and the plurality of software for a given hardware causes an increase in the selling number of hardware. Still, the value of the hardware (or whatever the underlying technology is) will not increase infinitely, as the additional positive feedback of every new complementary component will decline with the growth of the network (Economides 2004: 5).

This example illustrates again the central question for determining a network, that is to say, whether the products of different firms can be used together (Katz/Shapiro 1985: 424). For software markets, it is therefore decisive whether software produced for a certain brand also runs on hardware from another brand (ibid.: 425). Thus, the bigger the network or, in other words, the bigger the con-

---

Economides has collected dozens of articles and working papers regarding the economics of networks on his website http://www.stern.nyu.edu/networks/site.html (last visit 2009-08-10).

159 For a detailed discussion of the characteristics of natural monopolies compare to Section 5.1.2.

160 However, as Liebowitz and Margolis (1994) note there might also be some negative effects of consumption within network industries. For instance, if too many consumers join a phone network, the problem might arise that the network is overloaded and the consumer experiences negative effects in the sense that her use of the phone network is restricted (ibid.: 134).

sumer basis, the more complementary components are developed. This scale effect can lead to the problem that only one technology survives on the market, that is, the market tips towards one de facto standard (Katz/Shapiro 1994: 105 et seq.). In the case of computer software, standardization facilitates the use of computer networks or the transfer of data among users and applications and reduces training costs. Thus, new consumers have to decide whether they use a new system or benefit from the compatibility of an established standard. Mostly, they decide in favour of compatibility (Farrell 1989: 37).

As a result, an inequality exists in markets with strong network effects between the participating firms in regards to market shares and profits. Even though they are not "winner-takes-all" markets, they are often "winner-takes-most" markets (Economides 2004: 104). As long as the networks are not connected with high fix costs or entry costs, several firms will survive on the market; however, it is most likely that there will be only one or two big firms whereas the rest will have only an insignificant market share. Assuming that all firms produce homogenous products – differences in quality are possible, though – that no firm has a particular technical advantage, and that the production costs are zero, Economides and Flyer (1997) show that for pure network goods, that is, there is no use without network externalities, it is more or less intrinsic to the system that inequalities exist. In contrast to markets without externalities, network industries are marked with strong asymmetries between the participating firms in regards to output, prices, and profits. (ibid.: 31) Irrespective of free market entry, the market is dominated by one or a few firms (ibid.: 30). For instance, Economides and Flyer show that in a market with 10 firms, the leading firm sells 63,4 percent of the industry output, whereas the second firm sells only 23,2 percent, the third 8,5 percent, and the remaining six firms sell in total 5,1 percent of the industry output. If the number of firms increases the market structure does not change significantly (Economides/ Flyer 1997: 17-18). Even though the model is based on very narrow assumptions and can therefore not be transferred one-to-one to actual markets, it at least gives us an idea of the special market structure of network industries.[161] This model also illustrates that in markets with network effects a concentrated market structure is not necessarily a result of anti-competitive behaviour and that free market entry does not automatically lead to more (or perfect) competition (Economides 2004: 106-107).[162]

Furthermore, Economides and Flyer show that monopoly may even maximize total surplus in a network industry, given that the competing platforms are incompatible. With more firms, coordination is required and less (in-) direct network effects occur. With fewer firms, the positive network effects increase

---

161   For a detailed depiction of the model, compare Economides and Flyer 1997.
162   For a similar result compare to Ahlborn/Evans/Padilla 2001: 159.

and exceed the welfare loss due to monopolization. In other words, a de facto standardization is often beneficial (Economides 2004: 107).

4.3.2.2 Competition, Innovation, and Intellectual Property Rights in Networks and Standards

Having said this, we now turn to the question of how competition and innovation are affected in network industries. This analysis can be of use, for instance, for the determination of abusive conduct but also for the determination of a remedy if abusive conduct can be approved. In the following we will see that network effects can have a significant influence on competition and innovation. Due to the special characteristics of network industries, competition does not take place *in* the market but *for* the market. Still, this does not imply that competition is weaker in network industries than in a market without network externalities. As the high concentrated market structure implies that the winner "takes most," firms have strong incentives to compete or to race for the market (Farrell/Klemperer 2007: 1976).

However, as soon as a product or any other innovation is established as a standard, competition between rival products (for the standard) is eliminated. Users might refuse to change to a new, perhaps better standard, only because it has far less users and, therefore, less network benefits (Farrell 1989). Therefore, it might be much harder to replace an already existing product in network industries.[163] Besides this general problem of lock-in effects and path dependencies, interconnection within a network might constitute a bigger problem, especially if one company controls the so-called bottleneck of the network, that is, the part that is necessary to reach the consumers and provide services (Economides 2004: 110). In other words, if a (de facto) standard[164] in a network industry constitutes a bottleneck, competition issues might arise since cooperation with the

---

163 As Lopatka and Page (1999) explain, "In theory, a market may tip toward an inferior product. Consumers may initially adopt a product because it has a greater inherent benefit to them than the other products then available. Such a good may gain a first-mover advantage, which may then be reinforced by positive feedback. Another good with smaller inherent benefits may lose in such a process even if its network benefits increase at a higher rate that, and would eventually surpass, those of the winning good. Although such a good might have offered greater social benefits had it been widely adopted, the market would be 'locked in' on the good that obtained the initial advantage," ibid., p. 169.

164 Please note that I do not refer to those standards that firms jointly set to facilitate coordination and development. I only refer to those standards that developed in the course of the market process due to consumer preferences or because suppliers and producers of complementary products chose one product in a network over the other. Thus, I also ignore problems that may occur if, for instance, in negotiations on a standard, a firm keeps a patent secret and only discloses it when the standard is almost fixed (hold-up problematic).

dominant firm is essential for competitors to succeed in the market (Shapiro/Varian 1999: 227-253). A prominent example of this is a case in the telecommunications sector in the early 20th century where AT&T,[165] a telephone service provider, had a monopoly in long distance calls but had to compete with other companies in the market for local calls. Thus, AT&T excluded its competitors by refusing to connect independent providers for local calls (Weiser 2009: 274-279). Consequently, in those cases we face a typical natural monopoly situation. The de facto standard in a certain network industry constitutes the bottleneck for competition in up- and downstream markets. That is to say, access to this bottleneck is necessary to offer products in related markets. In contrast to traditional natural monopolies the reason for the bottleneck function lays not solely in physical features of the concerned good or service but in the network effects described above, that is, the market tipped already for a certain technologies. However, from a welfare perspective, it would be desirable if access to these standards would be unlimited because then competition would not be distorted and consumers could benefit from all available components within a certain network irrespective of the producer (Farrell/Klemperer 2007: 2054). For competition policy, this means that in those markets competition authorities sometimes must evaluate whether certain conduct by a dominant firm denies consumers the benefits of a new technology that a competitive market would offer (Shapiro 1999: 674).

Whereas regulation and mandatory access has been widely accepted in most sectors with natural monopolies (Economides 2004), mandatory access is disputed in the software sector because of the presence of intellectual property rights. It is an open and not clearly answered question as to whether the protection of a standard by intellectual property rights would aggravate the lock-in problem and the replacement of an inefficient standard by a superior one. Since a product within a huge network is already protected against competition through the nature of network industries in that a concentrated market structure is promoted, intellectual property rights might be generally less important for providing innovation incentives. However, intellectual property rights might be decisive for competitors because the intellectual property rights can impede the development and supply of compatible products.

The impact of intellectual property rights on a standard for innovation on downstream markets is even more important for competitors if the compatibility of these innovations is crucial, as in the software industry. If a certain operating system constitutes a de facto standard, intellectual property rights for this operating system can constitute a barrier for interoperability. If the owner of the operating system denies access to its intellectual property rights, the interoperability of competitors' applications is endangered. A computer operating system

---

165   United States v. AT&T Co., 552 F. Supp. 131 (D.D.C. 1982).

"controls the interaction between the computer system's microprocessors, and peripheral devices such as display screens, disk drives, keyboards, printers, scanners, etc, allowing those elements to work in a co-ordinated manner." (Creuss/ Agustinoy 2000: 71)

Thus, compatibility with the operating systems is essential for the whole industry. Even the right to reverse engineering, which has been set up to promote compatibility, does not necessarily impede the dominance of a certain standard and does not ensure interoperability (Marengo/ Vezzoso 2006: 12).[166] According to Menell (1987) copyright protection for software enhances the difficulties to profit from network externalities and moreover, it can discourage and impede innovation in operating systems and other complementary soft- and hardware (ibid.: 1363).

As such, the question arises as to whether interfaces and other standards should be considered essential facilities to which all firms and entrants into downstream markets should have non-discriminatory access. A facility or technology can be seen as essential if it is indispensable for competing in the downstream market, if sufficient capacity is available to provide access, and if its duplication is economically unfeasible (Creuss/Agustinoy 2000: 69). Considering (de facto) standards in modern communication technologies such as software as natural monopolies would give guidance how to deal with abusive cases in which access to the standard is denied. As already mentioned, in the economic theories of natural monopolies and essential facilities, there is broad consensus that non-discriminatory access to this essential facility (as here the IP-protected standard) might be a suitable remedy for solving the problem of impeding competition and innovation in downstream markets (compare e.g. Knieps 2008).[167]

---

166   Please note that the right to reverse engineering can itself be interpreted as a limitation of intellectual property rights, which is not undisputed within intellectual property law (e.g. Lemley/ McGowan 1998: 526). For a detailed discussion of the economics of reverse engineering compare to Samuelson/Scotchmer 2002.

167   Interestingly, there have already been some governmental steps to achieve and maintain non-discriminatory access to crucial facilities or standards in network industries. In 2002, the European Parliament decreed a directive on access to and interconnection of communications networks (Directive 2002/19/EC of the European Parliament and of the Council of 7 March 2002 on access to and interconnection of, electronic communications networks and associated facilities, OJ L108/7 [hereinafter: Access Directive]). Here, the Parliament highlighted the importance of access and compatibility to increase consumer welfare. In so doing, the Parliament establishes that national authorities may oblige operators to allow access to specific network elements and facilities if a denial impedes competition or is not in the "end-user's interest" (Access Directive: Article 12(1)). Thus, firms owning the particular network element can be forced "to grant open access to technical interfaces, protocols or other key technologies that are indispensable for the interoperability of services or virtual network services." (Access Directive: Article 12 (1)(e)) Therewith, the European Parliament (and the Commission that suggested

However, it is important to keep in mind that, taken alone, the market structure is more concentrated as in other industries. Thus, the goal of (competition) policy should not be to enhance competition in the market but to ensure competition in secondary markets, that is, for products and services relying on the standard to achieve consumers. The competition for the good/service evoking the strong network effects, that is, the potential de facto standard, is often similar to the competitive process described by Joseph Schumpeter. Firms or entrepreneurs try to develop new ideas and therewith lead to create destruction. In other words, in network industries it is most likely that an existing standard offered by a certain company is not replaced by a similar, maybe higher quality product from a competitor, but rather it is replaced by a somewhat novel good (Economides 2004: 109).

4.3.3   Intermediate Result: Considering Differences between Market Structure, Industry Features, and Innovation

This section has shown us it is impossible to make a clear prediction of the effects of a certain market structure on innovation. For instance, if economies of scale can be realized, it is more likely that large firms have incentives to invest in process innovations because they benefit more from the realized cost-saving than small firms. A competitive market structure, in contrast, promotes R&D activities for drastic innovations replacing old products, because firms want to escape the pressure of competition. For non-drastic innovations, we can again assume that monopolistic or dominant firms have slightly more incentive to innovate because they want to avoid any (further) competition. Thus, within an analysis of competition policy, we have to consider at least the type of innovation before we can take a position for or against a concentrated market structure as a driver for innovation.

The example of network industries has shown that certain product or industry features also influence the market structure. This section has demonstrated that, in these industries, a normal tendency towards concentration exists, and this tendency is also beneficial to consumer welfare. However, we still have to differentiate between the product with the network effects, for instance an operating system, and compatible applications. Whereas standardization for the first is welfare enhancing, competition for the second can still be beneficial. To put it differently, in markets with network effects natural monopolies often occur. Competition authorities should therefore aim at ensuring access to these natural monopolies in order to establish or maintain competition in the related markets.

---

the directive) acknowledges the importance of interoperability and open access in network industries.

Hence, if we want to correct anti-competitive effects, we should account for the market features and the kind of innovation involved before we impose a remedy.

4.4 Conclusion: Redefining Misallocated Intellectual Property Rights with Competition Policy

4.4.1 Summary of the Previous Results

In this chapter, we started with a review of the traditional law and economics of intellectual property rights before we turned to an analysis of the preconditions of the innovative capacity of a firm and the question of whether firms have alternative appropriability instruments. The chapter concluded with an overview of theories regarding the influence of market structure on innovation and a discussion of network industries.

At large, we have seen that the economic models of intellectual property rights suggest a better differentiation between different products. As such, we can assume that the assignment of intellectual property rights according to general rules leads, at least in some cases, to inefficiencies. Thus, from this perspective it seems rather appropriate to follow the approach outlined in Chapter 3, that is, to use competition policy to interfere with intellectual property rights and restrict them in those cases where we do not only suspect inefficiencies but where we can also prove that intellectual property rights have negative effects on welfare. However, the exploration of the literature on the law and economics of intellectual property rights has also shown that an assignment according to specific models is rather cumbersome, because we need to possess sufficient information about the detailed market conditions, such as the exact demand elasticity of consumers for a certain product, which is necessary to optimally define intellectual property rights. Besides the amount of information required another shortcoming of the economics of intellectual property rights is that the assumptions are too narrow, for instance, regarding the public good characteristics of knowledge.

Therefore, we complemented these theories with insights from innovation research concerning appropriability conditions. We started by repudiating the argument that imitation is more or less costless and an imitator does not have to fulfil certain preconditions. In other words, we analysed which capabilities a firm needs to dispose of to innovate or, alternatively, imitate. This analysis showed us that a firm's R&D activities are strongly influenced by previous efforts, specifically path dependencies and routines. Furthermore, successful firms need to have a sufficiently large, developed dynamic capability to explore and use knowledge spillovers. At the same time, these dynamic capabilities and routines form barriers to imitation as first, potential imitators need to invest in their dynamic capability as well, that is, imitation is not per se costless. Second, routines are not directly observable and, therefore, a potential imitator cannot directly copy an invention, depending on the degree the invention is based on the firm's routines and how easy these routines are to imitate. Thus, this shows us that firms have to invest first before they can either innovate or imitate and that, therefore, the imitation problem is not always as severe as it is assumed in the law and economics of intellectual property rights. This result indicates that intellectual property rights are not necessarily an indispensable means of protection and that there might also exist other possible ways to protect the fruits of R&D activities. From this perspective, a restriction of intellectual property rights must not necessarily lead to a reduction of innovation incentives.

In the next section, we focused on the question of how firms themselves evaluate the effectiveness of patents. We found two results, which were counterintuitive at first sight: first, firms do not rate patents as very effective, and they would rather rely on other appropriability mechanisms; and second, the number of patent applications is nevertheless growing. Beginning with the second result, empirical surveys show that firms often patent for strategic reasons other than only the direct appropriation of innovative efforts. That is to say, in these cases firms patent because they want to strengthen their negotiation power in mergers or in licensing agreements, to use the patents in litigation, to increase the firm's value or, simply as a threat to other competitors. Thus, the driving motivation behind acquiring patents is not necessarily the protection of the particular innovation alone. As a trend, firms in discrete industries would rather revert to intellectual property rights because of their intended value, that is, to protect the innovation, whereas firms in complex industries use intellectual property rights more often for strategic purposes.

Since firms rated other appropriability instruments as more effective than patents, we took a deeper look at the alternative appropriability mechanisms. We found that firms can rely on a broad range of instruments from which they can choose, starting with secrecy, first-mover advantages, and complementary assets. It is notable that these instruments do not only allow firms to protect their innovations from competitors; in some cases, they also create direct barriers to imitation. An example of this is complementary assets. If a competitor possesses the knowledge for a certain innovation, she still cannot realize it if she does not have the necessary equipment, lacks the distribution channels, or simply cannot compete with the reputation of the innovator. Thus, before imitating, a rival has to build up the necessary competences or acquire them on the market. In other cases, where for instance the underlying knowledge is in large parts tacit, firms tend to use secrecy as a protection mechanism or to rely on lead time and learning curve effects. Consequently, we can assume that sometimes innovators do not even need intellectual property protection for their inventions or rely on them only to a limited degree. This again supports our argument that intellectual property rights are often not efficiently defined and that therefore a correction through competition policy can lead to an increase of welfare. However, this review of alternative appropriation mechanisms does not provide us with methods how to quantify and assess the use of these instruments.

Having said this, we turned to the relationship between market structure and innovation, focusing on the question of how market structure influences innovation alone; that is to say, we did not consider the reverse. In doing so, we had two goals: first we wanted to scrutinize the Commission's assumption that more competition is always tantamount to more innovation; and second, we wanted to show how important it is to consider specific market features, that is, to consider the specifics of different industries. Within a competition policy framework, the results of this examination shall help to find a prudent remedy. We found out that so far there is neither clear proof that low firm concentration always spurs innovation, nor clear proof that low concentration is detrimental to innovation and monopoly is better. Rather, the results differ greatly in dependence of the particular circumstances, and especially the type of underlying innovation. Consequently, competition authorities should be rather careful with their estimations and the resulting recommendations for potential remedies. To put it differently, a remedy aiming at the generation of as much competition as possible is not necessarily the best remedy.

Next, we looked at markets with network effects. There, we saw that competition is possible only to a limited degree. That is to say, in these markets competition tends to be *for* the market and not *in* the market. However, as soon as a standard for something has been established, we acknowledged that although further competition for that standard is probably not successful and maybe even not desirable, competition for the related applications and complementary products is still socially preferable. In this context, we recognized that intellectual property rights might indeed constitute a problem if they impede access to the network. Still, before imposing a remedy, competition authorities should consider the features of the particular industry and their influence on the "optimal" market structure. If the anti-competitive effect occurs on the level of the good with the network effects, more competition or more firms in the market do not create innovation to the same degree.

In sum, our assumption that the general assignment of intellectual property rights leads to inefficiencies has been proven. This chapter provided us with a broad overview of the economics of intellectual property rights and of the different strategies and influence factors for the appropriability of innovation returns. We also tried to analyse the influence of market structure on innovation. Although this does not cover all effects driving innovation, this overview should still be sufficient to provide a first approach as to how to assess the necessity of intellectual property rights for appropriation in particular situations.

4.4.2   Limited Practicability of the Incentives Balance Test

Thus, we can now start to bridge the gap between the theoretical consideration that competition policy can restrict intellectual property rights in certain situations and the economic and empirical results regarding innovation. In Chapter 3, we noted that the Incentives Balance Test is a good starting point for further investigations by competition authorities in cases of abuse of intellectual property rights. Since the Commission did not provide sound economic reasoning for the Incentives Balance Test, we did not know whether it would be possible to ground the test in economics, that is, if we have the economic knowledge and the required information for a detailed balancing of the welfare effects of intellectual property rights. However, from an economic point of view, the Incentives Balance Test seems convincing since it can be interpreted as an ex post determination of the optimal intellectual property right. Should the test show that the optimal intellectual property right is smaller than the actual one, a remedy such as a compulsory license can be understood as an ex post tailoring of the involved intellectual property rights.

In this chapter, we tried to provide theoretically founded arguments that could be used in a competition policy analysis. The survey of the existing economic literature and empirical results now shows that we know a lot about innovation and appropriability that should be encroached on an analysis of refusal to license intellectual property rights cases. So what did we learn for the application of these insights within the Incentives Balance Test?

First, it is notable, that the Incentives Balance Test as depicted in Chapter 3 is not as straightforward as we might have assumed in the beginning. A balancing does not only require some rough information on all the factors listed in sections 4.1 and 4.2, but we need to quantify the information. Only if we have accurate data we can make an exact balancing of the welfare effects of intellectual property rights with or without compulsory license and decide if positive welfare effects overweigh. Making rough estimations would water the result down and hence, might lead to wrong results. In the review of the economics of intellectual property right we learned that an optimal design of intellectual property right for a specific innovation requires a lot of information. Whereas it might be possible to achieve at least some information we would most likely be unable to gain all required information such as precise data for the social value of the innovation or the consumers' costs of substitution. Reviewing all these theories gives some hints why we have a uniform assignment of intellectual property rights – because the transactions costs of (trying to) achieving all these information would probably outweigh all the benefits of an accurate designed intellectual property right. However, we do not want to design all intellectual property rights but only those that evoke impediments to competition. Nevertheless, although only necessary for few cases, I do have my doubts that we could receive all the required information and moreover, that we would be able to quantify this information. In consequence, without concrete quantification of the cost structure of the innovator, the demand elasticity, the ease of innovation, the welfare losses due to allocative inefficiencies, value of the innovation and so on we cannot conduct a balancing. Besides that, it is to note that these economic models still simplify, that is, they do not consider that knowledge does not necessarily constitute a public good and that firms have to fulfil certain preconditions before innovating. Thus, basing the Incentives Balance Test solely on economics on intellectual property rights would exclude significant influence factors on innovation.

Of course, we could now argue that we also reviewed theories and empirical results from innovation research concerning appropriability. Still, applying these insights to the Incentives Balance Test does not contribute to a simplification. The ongoing problem is the need for quantification. Although we know that firms need to invest in their adsorptive capacity and that they can rely on other appropriability mechanisms, we still do not have detailed information about that. How can we know at which point a firm's adsorptive capacity is large enough to influence its success in innovation and to which degree it contributes to the sucess? For an exact measurement of the different effects it would also be necessary to determine the optimal mixture of the different available appropriability mechanisms and, again, to quantify this mixture. However, at this point we can only determine whether there are alternatives to intellectual property rights, but not to which degree exactly they weaken the necessity of intellectual property rights. Similar to our results from economics of intellectual property rights, the theories and empirical analysis' on appropriation instruments do not tell us how to evaluate precisely the optimal extent, for example, of complementary assets. Hence, although the review of results stemming from innovation research demonstrated us that firms do not necessarily rely on intellectual property rights; although it provided us with very valuable insights about appropriation mechanisms, these insights are qualitative ones. That is to say, while we can use these insights for qualitative statements as to whether we consider intellectual property rights as important protection mechanism in a specific case, we cannot quantify this assessment and, hence, cannot conduct a balancing to a situation with more or less protection. Consequently, even though from an economic point of view the Incentives Balance Test is a convincing instrument since it decides on the basis of welfare effects, it is in my opinion not feasible. The implication of this result is that we must modify, at the very least, the concept of the Incentives Balance Test in order to gain in practicability.

5 Towards a New Test to Assess Refusal to License Intellectual Property Rights Cases

In the last chapter we established some criteria that can be applied within the framework of competition policy to analyse the abuse of dominance in regards to intellectual property rights. However, we also found out that it is almost impossible to quantify all information required for a balancing. For a correct balancing it is not sufficient to know what kind of effects may arise due to a compulsory license and due to a refusal to license, instead it is essential to quantify these effects. Against this background, in this chapter I will now develop a test that is based on the idea of the Incentives Balance Test but that is simpler in the sense that it does not require a balancing and therewith, no quantification. In doing so, I will refer to the criteria exposed in Chapter 4.

The chapter starts with a review of the criteria that had been applied previously to detect the anti-competitive effect and a discussion of whether those criteria are defensible from an economic perspective or whether they need some modification. In so doing, we will refer to the criteria outlined in Chapter 2 within the description of the European Union caselaw. While having abstained from an evaluation in Chapter 2, in this section we will scrutinize the criteria from an economic perspective. This step is necessary to assess which requirements should be applied in future cases to detect anti-competitive conduct.

Before we continue with the core of this thesis, that is, the development of a test for the specific analysis of refusal to license intellectual property rights cases, we will examine if it is also possible to refer to other tests that are related to the detection of the abuse of dominance. Only if this breakdown shows that these standards exhibit shortcomings for an application in cases that involve intellectual property rights is it reasonable to continue with the development of a new test, the Innovation Effects and Appropriability Test. Otherwise, we could build on these existing standards. However, it is my hypothesis that these standards have a more general approach and do not consider the specifics of intellectual property rights. Consequently, I try to develop a test that acknowledges these specifics and incorporates them. Basing our results on the previous chapters, the new standard will both incorporate experiences from previous caselaw that have been proven to be reasonable and appropriate and the results of Chapter 4 that consider the specifics of innovation, intellectual property rights, and market structure.

The chapter closes with a comparison of this Innovation Effects and Appropriability Test and the Incentives Balance Test and the standard suggested in the new guidance paper to Article 102 TFEU. This comparison shall show whether our approach constitutes an improvement to the previous proceeding. The comparison with the guidance paper is necessary as it depicts the requirements and the proceedings the European Commission plans to apply in future cases. From this perspective, it is interesting to see to what extent our standard deviates from the standard of the Commission and what are the advantages or shortcomings of the Innovation Effects and Appropriability Test.

5.1 Experiences from Previous Caselaw: Discussion of the Criteria for Abusive Conduct

As a short reminder, Article 102 TFEU condemns the conduct of dominant firms that aims at influencing the market structure in the sense that the maintenance or growth of the existing degree of competition is impeded. Article 102(b) TFEU in particular prohibits abuse that consists of *"limiting production, markets or technological development to the prejudice of consumers."* As illustrated in Chapter 2, for refusal to license intellectual property rights cases, the caselaw has established four criteria to examine whether certain behaviour of a dominant firm constitutes an abuse of market power:

1. Is the refused good or service indispensable to compete in the (downstream) market?
2. Is the refusal likely to eliminate competition in that (downstream) market?
3. Does it prevent the emergence of a new product for which there is a potential consumer demand?
4. Does the dominant firm have an objective justification for its refusal?

These criteria had been applied in this or in a slightly altered form in the *Magill* Test and also in the Incentives Balance Test. In the next section, we will now explore the criteria from an economic point of view and try to modify them in a way that will allow them to give guidance for prospective cases.

5.1.2   Indispensability Criterion and Elimination of Competition

In the *Bronner* decision, the ECJ established that the requested input good has to be indispensable for competition in a downstream market. Basically, this requirement of indispensability is related to the leveraging theory. The economic theory of leverage describes the (attempt at) extension of market power in an upstream market to a downstream market or vice versa (Whinston 1990). Whereas it is generally accepted that the exploitation of a legally and intrinsic growing monopoly is in line with antitrust law, the extension of a monopoly on this basis causes antitrust scrutiny (ibid).[168] Since monopolies and dominant

---

168   According to Kaplow (1985), the distinction between exploitation and extension is a distinction between static and dynamic effects or between short-term and long-term effects. While exploitation refers to immediate profits (due to higher prices), extension refers to profits and welfare losses occurring in the future (ibid.: 524).

firms are connected with allocative inefficiencies (Hicks 1935), competition authorities are rather suspicious of the extension of dominance.[169] In the European Union, intervention in cases of extension (that is, abuse) of market power is justified because the strong position of the firm allows acting *independently* from competitors and customers (Canoy et al. 2004: 222).[170] However, the basis for leveraging is that the monopoly position of the firm on the upstream (or respectively on the downstream) market is incontestable.[171] For refusal to license cases this means, that only if competitors are not able to rebuild alone or in cooperation with other competitors the concerned good or service to economically reasonable terms, the market is incontestable or, in our terminology, the required item is indispensable. Thus, the dominant firm does not need to fear market entry and can try to leverage its market power to the related market. Therefore, we now analyse when such a situation can arise.

A classical example for an incontestable monopoly is a natural monopoly. Natural monopolies are related to cost advantages and economies of scale and scope; if only one firm provides a good or service, it can do so more cheaply and efficiently than if several suppliers provide the good (Knieps 2008).[172] Even though not necessarily connected to it, natural monopolies often occur in tangi-

---

169 Of course, dominant firms and monopolies are also often connected to lower dynamic efficiency, but, as we have seen in the previous chapter, this relationship is not as straightforward as often depicted.

170 This argument has its economic roots in the ordoliberal thinking of the Freiburg School. Accordingly, monopolies are per se bad because they destroy the welfare-increasing process of competition and therefore should be prohibited. However, if the existence of several companies in one market is not possible, like in case of natural monopolies or when the monopoly position rests on intellectual property rights, the firm may maintain its monopolistic position but is supposed to act *as if* it had competitors. Consequently, any conduct of the monopolist that would not be possible if it was in a competitive environment should be prohibited (Gerber 1998: 252).

171 The theory of contestable markets goes back to Baumol, Panzar and Willig (1982). A perfectly contestable market is characterized through free market entry and costless market exit, that is, no sunk costs occur (ibid.: 3). Under such market conditions, potential competitors can enter the market regardless of an incumbent's price response (Weitzman 1983: 486).

172 In economics, this is known as subadditivity of costs (Viscusi et al. 2005). This subadditivity of costs can arise, for instance, when the provision of a certain good is connected to high fix costs but very low marginal costs for an additional unit of the good. Consider exemplarily the case of electricity cables. Whereas the construction and maintenance of the cable network requires large investments, the connection of an additional household evokes comparatively low costs (Knieps 2008: 22). Thus, with a growing consumer base, economies of scale can be realized as the fixed costs can be divided between a larger number of customers. From this perspective, it is arguable that only one supplier in this market is economically more desirable than two or more competitors (Viscusi et al. 2005).

ble network industries like rail services or electricity. In those industries, the network itself constitutes the natural monopoly. Consider, for instance, rail services. For offering transportation services, competitors need access to the track system. Obviously, competitors could rebuild the tracks, but the question is: Is it economically wise to do that? Especially due to high fix costs, this reconstructing would evoke barriers to entry because competitors would first need to recapture their investment in infrastructure before they could compete with the incumbent. Since the track system cannot be used for something other than rail services, the investments in the construction of the tracks are sunk costs that strengthen the entry barrier in that market (Kahn 1970). Thus, the incumbent has a natural monopoly for the track system. Nevertheless, competition on the up- and downstream markets, such as supply of trains and transportation, is still possible. Consequently, access to the track system is essential or – in our wording – indispensable to compete on the related market. If the incumbent impedes or rejects access she can leverage her monopoly to these markets.

As section 4.3.2 has shown, in market with network effects, monopolies can also occur when a market has tipped for a certain standard. Due to the scale effects, consumers reject to change to a competing product or service. That is to say, while a natural monopoly arises on the supply side, standards in network market often develop due to the demand structure. If the (de facto) standard is protected by intellectual property rights, the monopoly position becomes even stronger. According to Weber Waller and Tasch (2009), infrastructure based on intellectual property rights like technological standards, interconnection information, or software platforms constitute the bridges and rail roads of the 21st century (ibid.: 31). Similarly, First (2006) compares intellectual property rights with public utilities like telecommunication and railroad networks. In these cases, not physical characteristics but intellectual property rights prevent competitors from imitating the required good and therewith raise entry barriers (Sullivan/Grimes 2000). Consequently, to offer compatible products on the related market, access to the standard is essential. If the dominant firm[173] denies or impedes access, it can leverage its market power to the down- and upstream markets.

Further, a market can also be monopolized through resourced-based and legal reasons. The first simply implies that a firm has a monopoly on a certain resource. Legal monopolies are mostly manifested through intellectual property rights or are governmental in the sense that a government assigns an exclusive right for the supply of a service, for instance, the postal service, to a firm. Thus, in these cases other firms would theoretically be able to rebuild the concerned

---

173   In section 4.3.2 we have seen that it is possible that other suppliers are still on the market, however, they only have negligible market shares. Thus a firm owning the (de facto) standard is not necessarily a monopolist.

good or service but due to the legal restrictions they are not allowed to do so. Consequently, if, for example, the item is necessary as an input for another product and cannot be replaced, a refusal to suppply would prohibit competition on that related market and allow leveraging of the market power.

Basically, for refusal to license intellectual property rights cases, especially incontestable monopolies through network effects and through intellectual property rights matter. Therefore, in analysing whether a certain service or good is indispensable for competition on a related market we have to scrutinize if the dominant firm has a monopoly for the refused item or if substitutes exist. Looking at the caselaw, it did not provide a clear standard for when a certain good is indispensable. Instead, the requirements for indispensability varied: Whereas in the *Bronner* judgment the court made it clear that less efficient or more expensive alternatives cannot justify access to a more advantageous good, in the *Microsoft* case both the Commission and the court claimed that an equal footing of competitors is necessary. This inconsistency has been controversial, and it has been discussed in the literature (see, for example, Dolmans et al. 2007; Lévêque 2005; Killick 2004). Nevertheless, we must scrutinize whether it is possible from an economic perspective to have clear and general criteria determining exactly what degree of indispensability is necessary and how high the expected degree of damage on competition should be to ascertain the first requirements of abusive conduct.

Consider the *Magill* case and the *Microsoft* case: In the *Magill* case the copyright protected information was an essential input to compete in the related market, in the *Microsoft* case, the refused information did not directly constitute an input good but ensured access to the de facto standard. Thus, in the *Magill* case the indispensability arose out of a legal monopoly whereas in the *Microsoft* case network effects were the main reason for indispensability. Against this background we can argue that the standard for indispensability should depend on the involved industry characteristics and the source of market power. According to my opinion, it is reasonable to argue that in case of legal monopolies the requirements for the approval of indispensability should be higher than in case of network effects. Since with legal monopolies the refused item is only used as an input good, it seems appropriate to demand that competitors search for substitutes even though these substitutes are less advantageous. As long as substitutes can be found, the production or the supply of the service on the downstream market is not endangered. In consequence, competitors might have a disadvantage because they have, for instance, higher costs than the dominant firm. However, it is not the task of the dominant firm to support less efficient firms. Only if no substitutes are available the refused item should be considered essential. In contrast, if network markets are involved and if the refusal to license prevents access to the standard, it seems reasonable to apply a lower standard of indispensability. In this case not only price effects are involved but the access information is necessary to participate at the network. Simply put, with network effects it might be that a less advantageous solution, such as reverse engineering, is available; however, if this reduces compatibility or implies that the offered service is prone to breakdowns or disruptions in operations this cannot be compensated by the competitors by improving the own efficiency. Further, as we discussed in section 4.3.2.2 there are concerns about intellectual property rights protection for (de facto) standards. Against this background, a lower standard for indispensability in markets with network effects is in line with this objection. This does not necessarily imply that in network markets the indispensability criterion should always be equal footing like in the *Microsoft* case. Instead, it is possible to further differentiate according to the involved technologies. The easier the refused good or service can be rebuilt by competitors, that is, the simpler the underlying technology, the more codified and unspecialized the required knowledge, the higher the standard for indispensability.

From this perspective, it is only logical to allow leeway for a case-by-case analysis that considers the differences between the involved industries, the concerned products and technologies, and the necessary investments. The subsequent analysis whether a significant impediment or elimination of competition can be expected helps to clarify whether an equal footing to the dominant firm is necessary or whether less advantageous alternative are sufficient to maintain competition. Thus, the criterion of indispensability is closely related to the requirement that the refusal to license is likely to eliminate competition. It seems only natural to assume that if a certain input good exists that is necessary for being active in a downstream market competition is prevented or at least impeded when access to the concerned good or service is refused.[174] And vice versa, if a refusal to license leads to an elimination of competition we can assume that the refused item is indispensable for competition.[175] Standing alone, this requirement asks whether the conduct is likely to urge rivals to quit the market by making it impossible for them to compete. The interpretation of "likely" is disputable, according to caselaw it can mean that competition will be eliminated as a direct and immediate consequence of the refusal to license, but it can also imply that competition is reduced and maybe in the long run even eliminated. However, considering the varying standards for indispensability arising out of the economic considerations above it becomes evident that the effects on competi-

---

174 Similarly, Bartosch (2007) argues that competition (on a secondary market) can only be eliminated when the refused input good is essential for that particular market (ibid: 913).

175 Even though it might be possible to further differentiate, for instance regarding dynamic and static competition, at this point I assume that the criterion of elimination of competition is fulfilled with the proof of indispensability. According to my point of view it is more appropriate to make such a differentiation when considering the effects on consumers.

tion vary with the degree of substitutability of the refused item. Against this background, we can argue that the refusal to license of an input good that cannot be substituted has an immediate effect on competition. In markets with network effects the refusal to license does not necessarily prohibit competition directly – for instance, because reverse engineering is possible – but nevertheless leads to a significant impediment of competition that, in the long run, may end in an elimination of competition as well. Consequently, the requirement should not be that the refusal to license leads to an instant elimination of competition but should also take into account long term effects. However, due to the close interdependence with indispensability it seems appropriate to analyse both criteria together.

In sum, from an economic viewpoint, investigations regarding indispensability and likelihood of elimination of competition are both necessary and reasonable criteria for analysing the anti-competitive effects of a refusal to license intellectual property rights. Thus, prospective analyses of such cases should retain these requirements. Still, while in the previous caselaw the criteria of indispensability for competition in a downstream market and the elimination of competition had been listed as separate examination steps, our analysis shows that indispensability directly affect elimination of competition and should therefore be examined simultaneously. However, as this investigation step concentrates above all on the effects on competition in general, in the following section we will focus on the impact on consumers.

5.1.3 Defining Harm to Consumers: Prevention of a New Product or Impediment to Innovation

The next criterion in the previous analysis of refusal to license cases is the prohibition of a new product. However, caselaw has been imprecise on this criterion. While in the *Magill* case or in the *IMS Health* case the prevention of a new product was necessary to detect the abuse of dominance, in the *Microsoft* case the Commission was quite unclear about that, stating that technical development was impeded to the detriment of consumers. The Court of First Instance confirmed this estimation and declared that such broad interpretation of the new product criterion complied with the legal requirements of Article 102(b) TFEU, which lists the impediment of technological development as one abuse fact.

Taking the consumer welfare standard as the normative standard of EU competition policy as a given, I can only support this broader conception from an economic point of view. As firms are generally free to choose with whom to deal and under what conditions, an intervention of competition policy through Article 102 TFEU should only be carried out when not only are competitors impeded but when this impediment also affects consumers. Obviously, the requirement that the introduction of a new product should be prevented meets this standard. At the same time, demanding a new product means that the R&D

process is already completed and the firm is close to launching the result (the new product or service) on the market. The *Magill* case is a good example of this, since the firm had already sold the first magazine when the three television companies rejected licensing its program information. In this case, the (idea of the) product was already developed; the licensing of the information was the last step for commercializing it. Thus, in the *Magill* case, we face a relatively easy innovation for which no complicated and maybe unpredictable research process is necessary and where the realization is relatively simple as well. Using the prevention of a new good as a requirement for anti-competitive action seems appropriate in this case. Nevertheless, this is not representative of all innovations. As we have seen in the previous chapter, innovation and the underlying R&D activities can be highly complex, time consuming, and involve specialized knowledge. In these cases, intellectual property rights are not the last step in the development chain but maybe one of the first, because innovators require certain knowledge (or the permission to use certain knowledge) before they can go on in their development process. If we take the impediment of innovation or technological progress as requirement, we comply with the varying nature of R&D processes. Especially in high-technology industries, R&D activities are not only time-intense but also highly costly. Requiring the actual product or result of this process to determine anti-competitive effects would impose high uncertainty on the innovating firms, which then would have to invest without knowing whether they would ever get access to a required input good or information.

Consequently, when a dominant firm refuses to supply or to give access to its intellectual property right-protected good or information, this refusal can already impede the development process of a new product or service. As we know from evolutionary innovation economics, the outcome of R&D process is not clear or only to a limited degree predictable (Harper 1996; Knight 1971; Langlois 1984; North 2005). Due to this unpredictability of innovations, the experimental character of innovation and the influence of the consumers competition can be described as an evolutionary process of variation and selection (Kerber 2006: 458). An innovator might have a certain objective or a certain idea, though; in the end, the result might differ because, for instance, a by-product of the intended invention seems to be more promising than the invention itself. Thus, demanding that the competition authority proves that the refusal to license prevents a particular product would foreclose any innovation that is based on complex technologies and/ or requires a longer and less predictable R&D process. Even though the output of the innovative effort is not foreseeable (Metcalfe 1998; Nelson/Winter 1982), we can assume that a firm aims at an invention for which a consumer demand exists. As Hayek explains, competition can be understood as a discovery procedure whereby firms – with a lack of certainty and limited knowledge – test their inventions in trial and error processes on the market (Hayek 1978). If consumers reject a certain product, firms try to modify it accordingly and to launch a better or different product. Thus, even though we can assume that not every innovation that is based on or requires access to an intellectual property right-protected good or service will be successful, we can assume that firms will try to meet consumer demand.

The position that any impediment of the innovation process is detrimental to consumer welfare follows a clear dynamic and evolutionary perspective of competition. According to this view, competition policy should focus on the competitive process itself and should not regard competition as a static equilibrium (Linge 2008). Kerber's (1997) Competition as a Test of Hypotheses concept combines this dynamic view of both competition and innovation. Under this approach, firms are driven by rivalry to test their products (hypotheses) in parallel experimentation on the market, thereby discovering new knowledge (Kerber 1993, 1997). Yet an important characteristic of this approach is that it considers mistakes to be valuable because otherwise an economy could not exhaust its possibilities and would get stuck with old and possibly inefficient solutions (Linge 2008: 108). The possibility of losses encourages firms to continue the innovation process. As firms resort to different firm-specific routines and knowledge, the R&D activities themselves differ and the resulting products are diverse. Consequently, allowing such innovation processes increases diversity[176] and therewith consumer choices. From this perspective, we can argue that it is important to leave the innovation process as open as possible in order to increase the output and resulting consumer welfare. Even though we cannot predict what products and services will result from the R&D activities, we should take it as a presumption that this innovative process is advantageous for consumers in the long run.[177]

At the same time, with such an approach we avoid the difficult problem of determining the value of already existing products and the value of prospective

---

176   For a detailed description of the value of diversity for innovation and social welfare, compare to Linge 2008.

177   Evolutionary theories of innovation and competition would predict that competition in downstream markets through non-discriminatory access would lead to a much broader and diverse development of new products (in the *Microsoft* case: application software), then a situation in which only the owner of the IP-protected standard could develop applied software in the downstream market. Therefore, it can be expected that the access to interoperability information broadens the range of innovations and enhances the diversity of software solutions. A careful study of the Commission *Microsoft* judgment shows that this is exactly what the Commission assumes. Specifically, the Commission states that there is "ample scope for differentiation and innovation beyond the design of interface specification" (COMP Microsoft, para. 698): Furthermore, the Commission points out that in consequence to Microsoft's refusal to license "various product characteristics that are important to consumers and on which competition on the merits could unfold are currently artificially relegated to a secondary position" (ibid., para. 699).

innovations. To put it differently, if we only accept the prevention of new products as detrimental to consumers, we implicitly make a statement that we value a particular, already realized, innovation higher than any prospective innovation. Consider, for instance, the *Magill* case and the *Microsoft* case. Applying the new product criterion means that we value a weekly television guide higher than any upcoming improvement of working group server systems, which might facilitate everyday working life. Although this is a very simplifying comparison, it also shows how speculative any estimation of an innovation's value is. Therefore, competition policy should try to promote the innovative process and rely on competition to select the best results instead of making indirect assumptions over values.

To sum up, taking into account the role of innovation in economic growth and considering that the possibility of innovation also increases diversity, it is only appropriate to broaden the scope of analysis of competition policy and include the impediment of technological development (to the detriment of consumers) as a requirement for anti-competitive effects. At the same time, this eliminates the burden to make statements regarding the value of innovations.

5.1.4   Objective Justification

The discussion of the criterion of objective justification from an economic point of view is not as straightforward as the discussion of the other requirements, primarily because no clear criteria exist as to what such an objective justification may be. If physical goods are involved, one justification for the refusal to deal could be that it is technically impossible to give access or that the capacities are insufficient. However, if the refusal involves intellectual property rights, these reasons cannot be used since intellectual property rights are characterized through non-rivalry in consumption (compare Chapter 3). In the *Microsoft* case, both the Commission and the ECJ rejected the argument that the possession of intellectual property rights per se could constitute a justification for the refusal. While the court argued that Microsoft simply did not put forward any reasonable justification, the Commission balanced the effects of a compulsory license on innovation incentives; in other words, the Commission conducted the Incentives Balance Test. However, the CFI did not clarify on this. In Chapter 3, we noted that the weighing of innovation incentives seems to be an appropriate solution, especially under consideration of the common goal of intellectual property law and competition law, that is, the promotion of dynamic efficiency. Further, in Chapter 4 we proved that a precise balancing of the innovation effects is not practical. Nevertheless, the chapter also showed that economics nonetheless provide criteria that can be useful for assessing the objective justification. However, since the concrete application of these criteria constitutes the core of the new test, I will elaborate on this in detail later.

5.2 General Standards to Assess Exclusionary Conduct

Besides the *Magill* Test and the Incentives Balance Test introduced in Chapter 2, other approaches also exist as to how to analyse the abuse of dominance.[178] Nonetheless, the refusal to license intellectual property rights is a very specific form of abusive behaviour. As illustrated in Chapters 3 and 4, these specifics arise from the fact that intellectual property rights already contain static inefficiencies. These inefficiencies are consciously accepted as they are considered to be unavoidable in the promotion of innovation. According to this argument, interference by competition policy could easily undermine this goal. Therefore, not every test to assess anti-competitive conduct by a dominant firm can be applied to cases involving intellectual property rights. Instead, we must first consider the goal of intellectual property rights, that is, the enhancement of dynamic efficiency. In the following section, I will give a brief overview of the most common approaches on how to examine abusive conduct in general.[179]

5.2.1 No Economic Sense Test and Profit Sacrifice Test

One possible way to assess abuse of dominance cases is the No Economic Sense Test.[180] This test asks whether the scrutinized conduct is expected to earn any

---

178 In Chapter 2 I also referred to the Essential Facilities Doctrine (see section 2.3). Even though the European Commission has never explicitly based a decision on the doctrine, the doctrine has been associated with the criteria in *Magill, Bronner, IMS Health*, and *Microsoft* (e.g. Derclaye 2003; Gitter 2003; Lang 2008; Lévêque 2005; Müller/ Rodenhausen 2008). Nevertheless, the applications in Europe differ in some respects and are better interpreted as the *Magill* Test or the Incentives Balance Test. Therefore, I will not consider the Essential Facilities Doctrine in the following sections as a test for refusal to license cases.

179 Please note that I will not consider the Ratio Test as described by Kaplow (compare section 3.2.1). The difficulty in Kaplow's approach is that the determination of anti-competitive conduct requires knowledge about the desired reward (that is, the reward legislators deem to be appropriate) and, furthermore, a definite determination of the costs related to the anti-competitive action. Thus, from my perspective, similarly to the Incentives Balance Test, the Ratio Test is unpractical as it demands complex information that we do not possess in that detail.

180 Both the No Economic Sense Test and the Profit Sacrifice Test are modern versions of the specific intent approach, which was used at the beginning of the last century in antitrust law. According to this approach, dominant firms are immune from liability in antitrust law if the conduct has a positive pro-competitive or efficiency-enhancing effect, no matter how strong the anti-competitive effect weighed (Hylton 2008: 627-628). The No Economic Sense Test basically goes back to Melamed (2005) and Werden (2006). As such, it is notable that Melamed does not use the term "No Economic Sense Test," but

profits besides those profits earned by elimination of competition. In other words, would the conduct be profitable and make good business sense without the exclusion of rivals and the extension of dominance (Melamed 2005: 1255; Werden 2006: 415)? As long as the conduct is expected to be beneficial apart from its exclusionary effects, the conduct makes economic sense and is therefore legal (DoJ 2008: 39).

To prove that the exclusionary conduct is profitable, it is not sufficient to show that it evokes some gross benefits. Instead, it is necessary to compare the gains with the costs of the realization of the conduct.[181] The payoffs of the exclusionary effect are not considered in this calculation (Werden 2006: 416). If the costs exceed the expected revenue, the conduct fails the No Economic Sense Test, because a profit-maximizing firm would not engage in practices that are related to losses.

A precondition for the test is that the competition authority or any other plaintiff has already shown that the challenged conduct is likely to create or maintain monopoly power (Werden 2006: 417). Thus, the No Economic Sense Test consists basically of two conditions: first, there must be some evidence of exclusionary effects; and second, as described above, the challenged conduct must not be expected to evoke any profits besides the elimination of rivals.

A similar approach to assess the abuse of dominance is the Profit Sacrifice Test. This test analyses whether the conduct in question is more profitable in the short-term than any other conduct in which the dominant company could have engaged. If the conduct is less profitable, then the company sacrifices short-term profits.[182] This proves the assumption that the company only undertook the conduct to exclude its competitors and to strengthen or extend its dominant position. If the company is successful with its exclusionary conduct, it will recoup its short-term losses later (DoJ 2008: 39). Thus, the firm sacrifices short-term profits in order to gain even greater profits in the long run (Werden 2006: 424).

Even though this sounds quite similar to the No Economic Sense Test, the Profit Sacrifice Test is more flawed. Obviously, almost every investment consti-

---

rather "Sacrifice Test." As Melamed's test complies with the No Economic Sense Test, I attribute his approach to the former.

181 Therefore, it is inevitable that the antitrust authorities use the expected revenues of the conduct and not the factual ones after realization to calculate. Due to unforeseeable developments in the economic environment, misfortune, or infeasibility, business decisions often turn out to be unprofitable. Deeming unprofitable decisions to be exclusionary and thus anti-competitive would have negative effects on investments and therefore is inappropriate (Werden 2006: 416).

182 Generally, the test compares the conduct of the dominant firm with the so-called "but for" market. This is a hypothetical market in which it is not possible to raise prices as a result of the exclusionary conduct. If the challenged conduct is profitable on the "but for" market, the test evaluates it as pro-competitive (Salop 2006: 319).

tutes the sacrifice of short-term profits with the aim of recouping them in the future. Applying the Profit Sacrifice Test to those cases would deem most investments to be anti-competitive. In contrast, the No Economic Sense Test would consider that these investments will probably create returns in the long run apart from the exclusionary effect and therefore would acknowledge them as competitive (Werden 2006: 424). The Profit Sacrifice Test is also deficient when the company already possesses a monopoly. In such a situation, the costs of the exclusionary conduct might be compensated immediately (ibid.). Thus, we can conclude that the No Economic Sense Test generally creates less false positives (antitrust authorities condemn pro-competitive behaviour as anti-competitive)[183] than the Profit Sacrifice Test. However, the application of the No Economic Sense Test is also not without problems. For instance, exclusionary conduct is not necessarily costly for the dominant firm as in the case of failing to disclose important information. Further, exclusionary conduct might be profitable even without the exclusionary effect (Hovenkamp 2007: 411). As a result, the No Economic Sense Test is prone to false negatives (antitrust authorities gauge anti-competitive conduct as competitive) (Lao 2007: 445).[184]

However, from our perspective, the interesting question is whether the No Economic Sense Test is a good approach to deal with refusal to license intellectual property right cases. According to Melamed (2005), the test is not only applicable in raising rivals' costs cases like predatory pricing but also in refusal to deal cases. He illustrates this with the help of an example.[185] Assume firm X is a monopolist in the market for the production of product A. A is not an alone-standing product but input for product B. X sells A separately for a price of 25€ but is also active on the market for B, that is, X produces B and sells it for 100€. Firm Y is a rival of X on the market for B but buys A from X. After buying A for 25€ from X, Y is able to produce B for 90€. Obviously, consumers are better off buying B from Y. If X refuses to deal with Y, it diminishes consumer welfare. For the application of the No Economic Sense Test, Melamed suggests treating the refusal to deal with Y as a make or buy decision regarding the other inputs needed for the production of B. If X is more efficient in producing the other required inputs, it will refuse to deal with Y. Because this decision is efficient, competition law should allow the refusal to deal. However, if X is less efficient than Y in producing the other inputs, it should not produce them itself but

---

183 This understanding of false positive follows Besanko/Spulber (1993). However, other labeling can be found in Christiansen/Kerber (2006).

184 Melamed admits that this criticism is right. However, Melamed justifies the No Economic Sense Test with the explanation that other tests, in particular balancing tests (which will be discussed next), that could theoretically condemn all welfare-reducing conduct are too complex and difficult to apply and therewith create legal uncertainty (Melamed 2005: 1258).

185 For the following, compare to Melamed 2005: 1263 et seqq.

instead buy them from Y. Or, the more practicable solution, X should sell A to Y and stop producing B. In this situation, X would maximize its profit by demanding the monopoly price for A, which might be higher than 25€. As this would still be an efficient decision, the No Economic Sense Test would let this pass. But if X refuses to deal with Y, even though Y is obviously more efficient in producing B, the application of the No Economic Sense Test would lead to the result that X is only refusing to deal because it expects to profit from the exclusion of Y. Thus, the No Economic Sense Test would deem the refusal to deal to be anti-competitive.

Still, in this case, the No Economic Sense Test would only consider static efficiency and would ignore dynamic aspects. It is difficult to imagine how an application of the test to cases in which the interests of the intellectual property holder and the promotion of innovation are at stake should look. Even if we apply the framework provided by Melamed, difficulties remain, as the dominant firm does not necessarily know if the competitor is more efficient because the result of the innovation process is not clear yet. Moreover, in an evolutionary economics framework, it is also uncertain whether the dominant firm and the competitor will develop the same products or whether the result will differ at least in the occurrence of certain features. Thus, the dominant firm cannot necessarily undertake such an efficiency balancing approach as described above. But even if the dominant firm decides to license, we arrive at a problem we already know from cumulative innovation. Assuming that its intellectual property right-protected good is an essential input for the innovation, the dominant firm would try to demand a licensing fee equal to the reward for the second innovation, which would diminish the incentive of the competitor to innovate at all. As the dominant firm is capable of conducting the innovation itself, it seems reasonable that it refuses to deal and thereby maximize its revenues. As already discussed in Chapter 2, it is almost impossible to solve the incentives problem for cumulative innovation. From this perspective, it is rather questionable whether the application of the No Economic Sense Test to refusal to license intellectual property rights evokes clear results.

5.2.2   Equally Efficient Competitor Test

The Equally Efficient Competitor Test focuses on the effects of the exclusionary conduct on the dominant firm's rivals. Accordingly, if the practice or conduct in question probably leads to an exclusion of an equally or even more efficient competitor, it is anti-competitive (Posner 2001: 194-95). If, in contrast, the dominant firm can prove that despite its market power and the exclusionary effect, its practice is efficient, it would be found to be legal (Posner 2001: 195). The underlying principle of this test is that a company should not be punished only because it has lower costs than its rivals and acts accordingly (Hovenkamp 2005: 153-54).

Generally the test aims at the detection of predatory pricing. In detail this means that a price level below the prices of the competitors is anti-competitive if an equally efficient competitor could not offer the same price. In this scenario the presumption is that the dominant firm does not offer this low price because it is more efficient than its competitors but because it has the financial strength to do so. An equally efficient competitor could therefore not compete with that low price and would be excluded from the market. The advantage of such approach is that it enables companies to fully avail themselves of their efficiency. At the same time the test protects competition by efficient rivals (DoJ 2008: 44). It prevents an external regulation of prices; the companies are able to determine their conduct according to their cost structure. (ibid.).

However, this exclusive focus on equally efficient competitors also raises problems. First, in most cases the dominant firm will be more efficient than its competitors. As far dominance is decisively defined with the help of market shares, the high market share of the dominant firm provides it with scale economies and other cost advantages (Lao 2007: 446-47). Critics further argue that the existence or the entry of a less efficient rival can likewise lead to a stimulation of competition and a reduction of prices (Hovenkamp 2005: 154-55). For example, if the exclusionary conduct or the predatory pricing leads to the elimination of competition in a market, the dominant company would now be able to set monopoly prices. Even if a less efficient competitor might have higher costs than the dominant company, it would probably still price below the monopoly price. Thus, keeping a less efficient rival in the market would prevent the dominant firm from demanding monopoly prices that are high above its marginal costs and create inefficiencies.

Furthermore, the test is only to a very limited degree applicable to exclusionary conduct other than predatory pricing or discounts. In applying this test to the refusal to license an intellectual property right-protected service or product that is necessary to compete in a downstream market, the question arises as to in which regard a competitor should be equally efficient. Since intellectual property rights protect the concerned item, even if a competitor were efficient enough to produce the item herself, she would not be able to rebuild it due to the legal protection. Thus, in this case, the Equally Efficient Competitor Test is the wrong standard as it does not consider the particular characteristics of refusal to license cases.[186]

---

186 Hovenkamp (2005) also illustrates the problem of applying the equally efficient rival standard to intellectual property rights. In his example, Hovenkamp deals with the filing of fraudulent patent infringement suits. Properly applied, the test would come to the conclusion that less efficient competitors have unequal abilities to bear the litigation costs whereas an efficient rival is able to defend and win the case (ibid.: 154).

5.2.3   Consumer Welfare Test and Disproportionality Test

The Effects Balancing Test or the Consumer Welfare Test as Salop (2006) calls it, focuses on the overall effect of the scrutinized conduct on consumer welfare. This test condemns every conduct (of dominant firms) that harms consumers as anti-competitive (DoJ 2008: 36).[187] That is to say, the test asks whether the company's conduct

> "reduces competition without creating a sufficient improvement in performance to fully offset these potential adverse effect on prices and thereby prevent consumer harm." (Salop 2006: 330)

Therewith, the test can also be interpreted as a normative standard as it solely addresses consumer welfare (Lao 2007: 434).

In applying the test, competition authorities quantify and compare the pro- and anti-competitive effects in order to estimate the impact on consumers (ibid.). The test is comprised of two steps: first, the plaintiff has to prove the likely anti-competitive effect of the conduct; and second, the defendant (the dominant firm) must show the likely positive effects (Salop 2006: 334). In evaluating the effects, two possibilities exist. One possible approach is to quantify the different effects and compare them on this basis. However, the antitrust authorities might decide not to formally compare the effects of an increase in market power. Instead, the antitrust authorities would set the pro-competitive standard higher, the greater the harmful effects of the conduct. That is, the higher the anti-competitive effects of the dominant company, the higher the requirements to prove the positive effects (Salop 2006: 332). It is important to note that the balancing of the pro- and anti-competitive effects does not compare harm to consumers against the benefits to the company. The comparison is only focused on the impact on the consumer, be it positive or negative (Salop 2006: 331). Even though the test is meant to focus also on quality aspects, it is likely that those effects are treated in a subordinated manner. As the determination of dynamic effects is normally highly complex, courts might tend to focus only on static, short-term effects like prices (DoJ 2006: 38). Obviously, the idea is similar to the Commission's Incentives Balance Test, although the big distinction with the Incentives Balance Test is that it focuses on the effects on innovation whereas the Effects Balancing Test comprises also price effects.

According to Salop, the Consumer Welfare Test has the advantage that it detects anti-competitive conduct that would evade the other tests. Salop illustrates this point with the example of the improvement of a design ("incompatible de-

---

187 Because of this orientation on consumer harm, Salop (2006) points out that it suits the test better to be called the Consumer Harm Standard Test (ibid.: 331).

sign change").[188] In this example, a dominant firm makes an improvement in the quality, which consumers value at 5€. At the same time, this improvement makes the product incompatible with its rivals' products. This incompatibility leads to an exclusion of existing competitors and creates entry barriers for potential competitors. Consequently, the dominant firm will raise the price high above the value of the improvement, which was 5€. Instead, the dominant firm raises its price by 50€. Even though this conduct would lead to significant harm to consumers, it would still be pro-competitive under the No Economic Sense Test, for example, because the improvement of the product would be profitable beyond the exclusionary effect. In contrast, under the Consumer Welfare Test, this conduct would be deemed anti-competitive because of its negative effects on consumers.

Still, there are some disadvantages connected to the Consumer Welfare Test. First, the exclusive concentration on consumer harm is too restrictive. As we have seen in Chapter 2, alone with the guidance paper on Article 102 TFEU the Commission pursues several goals: consumer welfare, protection of the competitive process, and fostering competition on the merits (or in other words, preventing dominant firms from excluding rivals by anti-competitive effects). In the U.S., antitrust laws pursue not only consumer welfare as well. As Werden (2006) explains, section 1 of the *Sherman Act* stresses that besides harm to the consumers, harm to the competitive process also causes conflicts with antitrust laws (ibid.: 429).[189]. Thus, the Consumer Welfare Test might in fact be detrimental to other goals. When an invention that makes the products of competitors incompatible is deemed to be anti-competitive, this might diminish the incentive to innovate and compete on the merits.

Another important problem that occurs in refusal to license cases (and already occurs in the context of other standards) is that it is extremely difficult to determine the value of an innovation or the improvement of a certain conduct when the consumer response to it cannot be observed yet (Werden 2006: 431). When a dominant firm rejects licensing or dealing its improved good or service to its rivals, it is a highly complex task trying to assess the value of the improvement to the consumer and whether the costs of the rival's exclusion outweigh this value. A similar problem occurs when the refusal to license prohibits innovations. In certain cases, the estimation of the effects can be straightfor-

---

188   For the following, compare to Salop 2006: 323-326; 338-339.

189   As Farrell and Katz (2006) point out, American antitrust law has evolved toward judging conduct as anti-competitive that both 1) harms competition and 2) hurts efficiency and/or consumer welfare (ibid.: 7). In other words, competition policy does not only focus on consequences but the action must clearly affect competition. As we have seen in Chapter 2 and at the beginning of this chapter, European courts and the Commission follow this approach as well since the detection of the anti-competitive effect comprises the elimination of competition *and* harm to consumers.

ward. Take the *Magill* case as an example again. *Magill* wanted to offer a comprehensive weekly television guide, which did not exist thus far and which the three television companies did not intend to offer. In this scenario, the comparison of effects on consumers is simple; one guide containing all information is better than three guides. However, the earlier in the innovation process the refusal to license occurs, the more difficult it is to estimate the value of an invention. As the innovation process is also connected to some uncertainty, that is, we cannot predict with certainty the outcome of R&D processes, the estimation of the value to consumers is quite ambitious. From this perspective, the Consumer Welfare Test is more appropriate for the evaluation of short-term effects (Werden 2006: 431).

A variant of the Consumer Welfare Test is the Disproportionality Test (Areeda/Hovenkamp 2008). This test is based on the assumption that a balancing of consumer welfare and competitive harms cannot be open-ended because no company has the duty to sacrifice its own benefits to enhance public welfare. Instead, the questions is whether the harm to the competition due to the challenged conduct is

"disproportionate to consumer benefits (by providing a superior products, for example) and to the economic benefits of the defendant (aside from benefits that accrue from diminished competition)." (DoJ/ FTC 2004: 14) [190]

Similarly to the Consumer Welfare Test, the Disproportionality Test examines whether the negative anti-competitive effects substantially outweigh the benefits. In contrast to the Consumer Welfare Test, though, the emphasis lies on the "substantially." That means that a precise quantification and balancing of the different effects is not required. Instead, significant harm to consumers and competition is needed (DoJ 2008: 45). Therewith, the test tries to focus indeed on harm to the competitive process and not only harm to single competitors. This has the advantage that companies can compete intensely without fearing that ex post small negative static effects will mark their conduct as anti-competitive (ibid.).

However, a balancing of significant effects already has its difficulties. The first question that has to be answered before applying the test is: At what degree is a conduct disproportionate? How should competition authorities decide if there is significant harm and smaller, but still significant, benefits and vice versa? Is a 45 to 55 percent relation sufficient to be disproportionate or is a 35 to 65 percent relation necessary? This definition is crucial and depends on how close the disproportionate test comes to the Consumer Welfare Test, and it also de-

---

190   Brief for the United States & the Federal Trade Commission as Amici Curare Supporting Petitioner at 14, *Verzion Commc'ns Inc. v. Law Offices of Curtis V. Trinko, LLP*, [hereinafter DoJ/FTC 2004] 540 U.S. 398 (2004) (No. 02-682), available online at http://www.usdoj.gov/atr/cases/f201000/201048.htm.

termines how precise the determination of the different effects has to be. Obviously, not every small benefit should acquit the dominant firm of antitrust liability (DoJ 2008: 46). However, the problem of the appropriate standard for proof is already inherent to the Consumer Welfare Test. According to Salop (2006), consumer harm could be determined by plausibility, tendency, significant likelihood, and so forth, to the point of absolute certainty (ibid.: 333). Therefore, it is a smooth transition from the Consumer Welfare Test to the Disproportionality Test. The biggest conceptual difference probably lies in the burden of proof. In contrast to the Consumer Welfare Test, under the Disproportionality Test the plaintiff, that is, the competition authority, has to prove that the harm substantially outweighs the benefits of the challenged conduct (DoJ 2008: 46). From this perspective, both the Consumer Welfare Test and the Disproportionality Test exhibit the same shortcoming as the Incentives Balance Test: they are only to a limited degree feasible since they require too much information.

5.3 Introduction of the Innovation Effects and Appropriability Test

5.3.1 Basic Idea

As we have seen, several tests and proposals already exist as to how to assess abuse of dominance. Still, so far none of them seems to be perfectly suited to deal with refusal to license intellectual property-protected goods or services. As our investigations in Chapter 4 have shown, trying to adapt the Incentives Balance Test for use fails because of the complexity and the amount of required information. Thus, the Incentives Balance Test does not seem to be a practical solution either. Nevertheless, besides the limited practicability the concept of the Incentives Balance Test has the advantage that is considers effects on innovation and aims at the enhancement of welfare. Therewith, it goes directly at the heart of intellectual property rights. From this perspective, it should be the goal for a new test to maintain this advantage but to avoid the difficulty of quantifying and balancing. Drawing on this and the results of the foregoing sections, I will now develop a test, the Innovation Effects and Appropriability Test, that I consider appropriate to solve the (potential) conflict between intellectual property rights and competition policy in refusal to license cases.

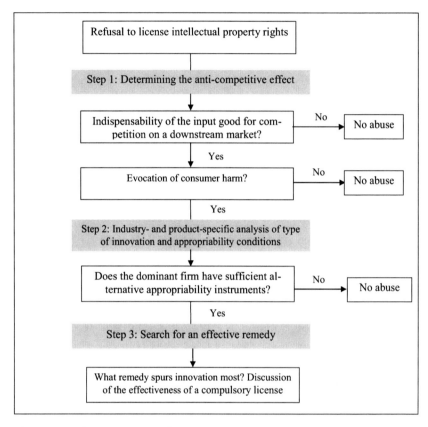

Figure 5-1: The Innovation Effects and Appropriability Test at a Glance

Basically, the test can be divided into three parts. First, after a claim that a dominant firm refuses to license its intellectual property right-protected good, service, or information, the competition authority has to detect the anti-competitive effect. This means that it must be established that the concerned good is indispensable for competition in a secondary or downstream market and that this refusal does not only affect competitors negatively but also causes harm to consumers. These conditions have to be fulfilled cumulatively. Second, in an industry-specific analysis, the authority has to scrutinize the underlying technology of the good; in other words, the authority must differentiate between simple and complex technologies. Based on this, the authority must examine whether the dominant firm relies or could rely on appropriability mechanisms other than intellectual property rights. This can be accomplished by employing empirical data or by comparison with similar industries or appropriability instruments customary in that industry. If this examination shows that the dominant firm could very well employ other appropriability instruments to protect its innovation, the authority can assume that the company did not refuse to license to appropriate the returns of its investments and to prevent imitation, but rather to impede competition and innovation in the downstream market. Third, the competition authority has to search for an appropriate remedy. So far it has not been discussed what constitutes an appropriate remedy for abuse of intellectual property rights. Imposing a compulsory license seems to be the most usual practice; however, it is questionable whether alternative or better-suited remedies can be considered. Consequently, the third step of the test closes the gap by demanding a detailed analysis of the specifics of the concerned case and how effective competition can be restored in that market.

5.3.2 Design and Structure of the Test in Detail

Having sketched the broad framework and underlying idea of the new test, this section will illustrate the single investigations step in detail. In so doing, we will use the knowledge gained in the previous chapters.

5.3.2.1 Detecting the Anti-Competitive Effects

After a suspicion has been raised that a dominant firm's refusal to license an intellectual property rights-protected item constitutes an abuse of dominance, the essential first step in the investigation is to prove an anti-competitive effect. For the identification of the anti-competitive effects of the refusal to license, it is not sufficient that the refusal impedes or even eliminates only a single competitor. It is rather decisive that the conduct affects overall competition in the market and leads to consumer harm as described in section 5.1.3. Consequently, the detection of the anti-competitive effects has a clear focus on dynamic efficiency, that is, on innovation effects. This approach is reasonable as, first, it is inherent to intellectual property rights and their enforcement that they evoke some short-term losses in order to create more long-term dynamic efficiency. Second, dynamic efficiency is assumed to create more welfare than static efficiency (Hovenkamp 2008: 253-54). As we do not know with certainty what actually drives innovation, we should avoid unduly cutting back innovation incentives when no other innovation is at stake but (only) reason to fear increased prices. According to our results in section 5.1, the examination of the anti-competitive effect can be further subdivided into the analysis of: a) the indispensability for being active in a downstream market; and b) whether the refusal harms consumers.

5.3.2.1.1   *Indispensability for Competition in a Secondary Market*

In determining indispensability, we should scrutinize whether an alternative to the refused item exists and, if so, whether this alternative is sufficient to maintain competition in the downstream market. Only if it is clear that effective competition in this market is not possible, that is, that the protected service or good either has a bottleneck function from the upstream to the downstream market or constitute a non-substitutable input for a related market can indispensability be confirmed. Only if the indispensability criterion is fulfilled can we proceed to the second level of determining the anti-competitive effect, that is, we analyse whether the refusal to license has a negative effect on consumers.

The differentiation between upstream and downstream markets is important because we consider it as a first proxy for dynamic efficiency. If competition in a secondary market is not involved, the market constrained by the refusal to license is the market for the intellectual property right-protected good itself. In this case, it is important to consider that generally with the assignment of intellectual property rights the legislator consciously puts up with some static inefficiencies in order to provide incentives to innovation. Declaring that the refusal to license an intellectual property right on which the dominant firm actually bases its dominant position is abusive counteracts the intent of intellectual property rights and therewith diminishes not only innovation incentives but also legal certainty. Moreover, if only one market, that is, the market for the intellectual property right-protected good, is involved, we cannot reasonably expect an increase of dynamic efficiency on that market. Instead, it is more probable that competition will be focused on prices. Even though one might argue that price competition is also advantageous for consumers, this view is most likely to be myopic because it does not consider the long-term effects on dynamic efficiency. Innovation is generally an important engine for economic welfare and growth.[191] Therefore, in case of doubt, we should rather decide pro dynamic efficiency and against static efficiency.

Still, legislators and/or competition authorities may believe that the static inefficiencies arising through the exercise of intellectual property rights are too large; however, this is not a task for competition policy but rather for intellectual property law. From my point of view, competition policy can only interfere if the application of intellectual property rights goes beyond the legal scope of intellectual property rights, that is, when firms try to leverage their dominance based inter alia on these particular rights on another market and when the mutual goal of promoting dynamic efficiency is counteracted. Thus, in cases in which intellectual property rights lead to immoderate static inefficiencies, this problem should be solved within intellectual property law.[192] Nonetheless, examples of

---

191 For a detailed discussion of the welfare effects of innovation compare to Solow 1957; Bernstein/ Nadiri 1988, 1991; Denison 1985; Griliches 1992; Mansfield et al. 1977.

192 From a Schumpeterian view, we would further argue that it is exactly this monopoly that should motivate (potential) competitors to innovate in order to replace the current product and therewith to inherit the position of the market leader (compare to Chapters 3 and 4).

these types of cases can be found on both sides of the Atlantic. In Europe, an example is the *IMS Health* case where the competitor wanted to offer the same product as IMS Health, that is, sales data based on the copyright-protected brick structure. In the U.S., an example is the *Data General* case where independent service providers wanted to use new diagnostic software to compete with Data General in the market for servicing hardware (from Data General) (compare to Chapter 2). However, in both cases the claimants wanted to compete with the innovating firm in the market for which the intellectual property right was requisite. Neither NDC in the *IMS Health* case nor Grumman in the *Data General* case claimed that the refusal to license impeded anything other than the production or the service for the product itself. In other words, dynamic competition was not involved. However, it is to note that while in the U.S. the decision was in line with the argumentation above, that is, the court found that Data General only exercised its rights, the *IMS Health* case has been decided rather differently. In *IMS Health*, the courts found IMS Health guilty of abuse of dominance and based their decision on an artificial differentiation of the involved markets, that is, they differentiated between a market for the intellectual property right itself and a market for the services provided on the basis of the copyright. However, from my point of view, this differentiation did not reflect the reality as the service provided from NDS did not differ significantly from that of IMS Health. Therefore, the separation of an input market and a downstream market is, in my opinion, only of pretextual nature in order to limit static inefficiencies.

Consequently, the decisive criterion is whether access to the intellectual property right-protected good is necessary for competition in a downstream market. As already described in section 5.1.1, for determination of indispensability, the investigating competition authority has to analyse whether substitutes for the concerned good or service exist or whether the item is the only economically feasible access to compete in the downstream market. A helpful indicator of whether the refused item constitutes a bottleneck to the secondary market is if it is part of a network industry and constitutes a standard in this particular network. Due to the economics of network industries and standardization as described in Chapter 4, we can assume that in those cases no reasonable alternative to the protected good exist. However, the analysis should further determine the nature of the underlying technology. According to our discussion in section 5.1.1, the more complex the underlying technology and the more specialized the necessary knowledge, the lower the degree of required indispensability. In other words, if the underlying technology is highly complex and the good already constitutes a de facto standard in the concerned industry, it seems appropriate to deem the intellectual property right to be indispensable for competition in the downstream market, even though it might be possible to reverse engineer the product. From this perspective, we can argue that both the Commission and the court were right in applying a lower degree of indispensability in the *Microsoft* case. While it was appropriate in the *Bronner* case to consider less advantageous distribution possibilities as reasonable (an equal footing was not required) since the distribution system obviously has no influence on the content and quality of the newspaper. In other words, even a less advantageous distribution system would not endanger the existence of the newspaper or impede any further developments. In contrast, in the *Microsoft* case where the underlying technologies are highly complex, it is reasonable to argue that the standard for indispensability is an equal footing of the competitors with Microsoft. Only then would competitors be able to develop and offer products that are 100 percent compatible with Microsoft's product and that can unfold their full value to the consumers. That is to say, the more complex and the more challenging an innovation, the more information is necessary to compete in the downstream market. At the same time, it should be clear that innovation processes often require a long time period. Thus, the criterion cannot be immediate elimination of competition. Instead, the decisive criterion must be whether the refusal to license impedes competition and hence, is likely to eliminate competition in the long run.

However, if our investigations show that the refusal to license concerns a market with network effects this leads us to two conclusions. The first conclusion is that if the refusal directly concerns the good or service that is considered the de facto standard, competition policy should not interfere. This is a result of the discussion in Chapter 4, which showed that there is a kind of natural tendency towards a concentrated market structure with one firm getting the biggest part of the pie and the other firms sharing the rest. Thus, efforts to open the market to competition would probably not make a signification difference.[193] The second conclusion is that if the refusal to license concerns not the standard but downstream markets or applications, more competition is welfare enhancing. The refusal to license intellectual property rights can therefore be judged to be anti-competitive, especially as they are often not necessary to protect the innovation because the network effects of tipping and switching costs make it difficult to imitate them at all.

5.3.2.1.2   Harm to Consumers

Having proven that the refusal to license impedes competition in a downstream market, the question is now whether this impediment is detrimental to consumer

---

193   However, we can assume that in most cases access to the standard to produce in a downstream market is the issue and not the other way around. Otherwise, the claim of abuse would probably already not pass the requirement that a secondary market is involved. In such a case, competitors would likewise aim only at a simple imitation of the standard, that is, dynamic efficiency would not be involved.

welfare.[194] As discussed in section 5.1.2, consumer harm can be proven if the refusal is capable of impeding technological development. Depending on the underlying technology, this criterion can be interpreted strictly or generously. If the underlying technology is simple and the innovation predictable, like for instance in the *Magill* case, the concerned competitor has to prove in more detail that her innovation or new product is impeded. This may mean that it is necessary to describe in detail the purpose and functioning of the product. In contrast, with more complex technologies, the competition authority will acknowledge that those R&D processes are only predictable to a limited extent. In these cases, the authority will analyse to what extent the intellectual property right-protected good is necessary for the development process.

Depending on the nature of the innovation, it might be possible that the access to the intellectual property right-protected good is only necessary shortly before the introduction of a certain product or at the very end of an innovation process. Consequently, the competition authority has to consider whether the complaint is only pretextual nature or whether there is indeed an actual need for the refused item. To make a clear distinction: While – besides the requirement that a down- or upstream market be involved - the analysis of indispensability for competition does not differentiate between dynamic and static competition, that is, between price effects and innovation effects, in the analysis of consumer harm we explicitly focus on the question whether the refusal to license impedes dynamic efficiency, that is, innovation.[195] In detail, consumer harm is not fulfilled when the competitors only intend to offer the same product or service as the dominant firm. Only if harm to consumers in the form of technological impediment or prevention of a new product can be shown, the investigation proceeds to the next step.

Moreover, the identification of consumer harm demands that not only is the theoretical possibility of innovation impeded but also that innovation is factually prevented. To put it differently, the question is whether without the abusive conduct, competitors would undertake innovations. That is, it is also necessary that the competition authority consider the innovative capacity of the complainants

---

194 Please note that by mentioning consumer harm, I do not refer to a full balancing of all effects of the conduct on the consumer, like, for instance, the balancing test described in section 4.2.2 does.

195 Of course, it is also possible to consider dynamic aspects already in the previous step; we could ask if the refusal to license is likely to eliminate dynamic efficiency. However, I prefer to first analyse generally the indispensability for competition since in my opinion it is easier or less complex to make a general estimation whether the refused item is necessary to compete in the downstream market. Analysing the effects on dynamic efficiency is more differentiated and, hence, more difficult. Thus, according to my point of view it is appropriate to start with the simpler part of the analysis and only if we prove indispensability, proceed to the more challenging investigation step.

or the competitors in general. As we have seen in Chapter 4, successful innovation requires the fulfilment of some preconditions. Thus, for a better estimation of the potentially prevented innovation(s), it is helpful to analyse whether the competitors face internal barriers to imitation; for instance, we can scrutinize whether they are already equipped with specialized knowledge. Hence, for the analysis of the competition authority this means that access to the refused item does not necessarily imply that competitors conduct more innovation but that it is also possible that the dominant firm has the biggest incentives to innovate because it is the only firm that has the necessary capabilities.

Of course, in detecting the anti-competitive effect there will also be cases in which the indispensability is not as clear and in which competition might be impeded but still possible in some niches. In these cases, the affect on the innovation process is not as distinct as described above. However, if we accept that the evolutionary notion of competition comprises the outcome that innovation processes are not as predictable as described in section 5.1.2, the requirement of the impediment of technological processes leads more or less to a rebuttable presumption that whenever a dominant firm impedes the innovation process on the downstream market, this can be judged as harm to consumers and is therefore anti-competitive. This presumption can only be rebutted if an objective justification can be found.

5.3.2.2   Are Intellectual Property Rights Necessary to Protect the Innovation?

5.3.2.2.1   Methodological Approach

The second step, which is the question of whether the dominant firm disposes of alternative appropriability instruments, replaces the previous criterion of an "objective justification." Instead of asking whether the refusal to license generates efficiencies or is necessary to protect the firm's investments, we look at the alternatives the firm could have chosen. The advantage of this proceeding is that the availability of appropriability instruments is easier to measure and more reliable than the determination of prospective efficiencies and effects on innovation incentives. At the same time, looking at the appropriability conditions in the concerned industry deals with the intent of both competition policy and intellectual property law that innovation incentives shall be maintained in the sense that the innovator can cover her costs and earns a just reward for her efforts. Thus, Step 2 can be interpreted as a kind of simplified inquiry into whether the intellectual property rights of the dominant firm are assigned correctly. Simply put, the underlying idea is to analyse whether the dominant firm would have received the intellectual property rights in a case-by-case assignment.

As we have seen in the previous chapter, it is not a straightforward task to determine which market form most promotes innovation. Consequently, a balancing like the Commission used in the *Microsoft* case that is solely based on the assumption that lower firm concentration is tantamount to more innovation whereas less competition, that is, concentration, leads to less innovation misses a distinct economic justification. Thus, it is necessary to consider other criteria to evaluate the effects of the refusal to license on the innovation level in a certain industry. Since the previous chapter has shown that a balancing of the innovation effects with and without refusal to license fails because of practicability reasons, we have to search for an alternative approach.

From this perspective, it is a good compromise to use the available appropriability mechanisms as a means analysing whether the intellectual property rights offer an overbroad protection of the investments or whether they display an adequate safeguard for the innovator. If the dominant firm can choose between a broad range of alternative mechanisms, we can assume that the intellectual property protection is too broad. In this case, the dominant firm cannot argue that it only refuses to license to protect its innovations and that an intervention of competition policy would therefore diminish its incentives to innovate. Instead, it is arguable that the innovation incentives of the dominant firm would not be affected by a restriction of the intellectual property rights because the firm can protect its investments in other ways.

Specifically, we assume that the firm is, of course, well aware of its strategic opportunities and employs them accordingly. If the firm does not need to rely on intellectual property rights to protect its innovation and could instead apply other strategies like using complementary capabilities, the refusal to license does not make sense from an economic point of view because the dominant firm abandons license revenues. This strategy only makes sense when it aims at a long-term recumbent of these short-term losses through an impediment or elimination of competition. Consequently, we would interpret the use of intellectual property rights as a pretext to cover anti-competitive conduct. The reference to intellectual property rights would not constitute an objective justification for the refusal to license. In contrast, if the inquiry shows that intellectual property rights are highly important in this industry and other appropriability instruments are insufficient, we would accept these signs as indicators that the intellectual property rights are assigned correctly. Therefore, we would assume that the dominant firm only refuses to license in order to recoup its investment in this particular innovation. This result would supersede the anti-competitive effects diagnosed in Step 1.

To put it differently, Step 2 of the investigation has a similar function to the efficiency defence in merger cases. After the detection of the anti-competitive effect, we acknowledge that the dominant firm possesses intellectual property rights that normally give the right holder the authority to exclude others from the use of its innovation. However, as we have seen in Chapter 4, the general assignment of intellectual property rights is prone to social inefficiency in the sense that in some cases they are too narrow and in other cases too broad. As the economic intention of intellectual property rights is the warranty that the innovator can reap the fruits of her efforts, which would result in the maintenance of innovation incentives, we take this as the starting point for our examination. If we find that the dominant firm does not necessarily need to rely on its intellectual property rights and instead can choose between various alternative appropriability instruments, we take this as a proxy for overbroad intellectual property rights. Thus, the leading question of our analysis is whether the firm refused to license in order to reap the fruits of its own investments and thereby maintained dynamic efficiency in the sense that it would have the incentive to innovate, now and in the future, without fearing that competition policy would divide the benefits between other competitors. The latter is an important goal to maintain, especially since, from an economic perspective, the purpose of intellectual property rights is to stimulate innovation and correct market failures. This goal is also preserved by determining whether other instruments for recouping the investment are available. Of course, certain strategies may fail, but, especially in the case of big firms with large market shares, we can presuppose that firms themselves are more successful in realizing their appropriation strategies simply because they have the financial strength to do so. Since we assume that each firm knows the possibilities it can apply to protect its innovation, a dominant firm can assess whether or not its refusal to license would be deemed to be anticompetitive. Thus, this approach would also be qualified to give firms at least some legal certainty.[196] An estimation of the proper scope of intellectual property rights based on the availability of alternative appropriation mechanisms is easier, more predictable, and more precise in every case than an assessment based on a rough balancing of potential innovation incentives. The same is true of comparing the exact determination of the optimal scope of intellectual property rights and the alternative appropriability instruments; it is not only easier for competition authorities to identify alternative mechanisms than to get the information for the calculation of the optimal patent, for example, but also for the dominant firm. However, it is to note that this proceeding simplifies: Instead of conducting a precise ex post analysis of the dominant firm's intellectual property rights as the Incentives Balance Test as described in section 3.3.3 would do, we only focus on the question whether the dominant firm has alternative appropriation mechanisms and whether we consider them as sufficient. Simply put,

---

196   Although it is not a central issue in our analysis, it should be noted that legal certainty is a worthwhile economic goal. Walter Eucken (1952), a German Ordoliberal, and Friedrich A. von Hayek (1960), one of the most influential economists of the Austrian School, emphasized the importance of legal certainty in the form of clear rules that limit the governmental sphere of influence. Furthermore, empirical studies show that discretional state action has a negative impact on economic growth (Heinisz 2000; Klump/Reichel 1994; Mahoney 2001; Scully 1997). In a reverse conclusion, this result proves the importance of legal certainty (Christiansen 2006: 33).

we are testing the appropriability conditions and mechanisms. While this proceeding is not as precise as the Incentives Balance Test since it abstains from quantifying the effectiveness of the alternatives, it has the advantage that it requires solely information we can get and, therefore, gains in practicability.

Having said this, in the next subsection we will turn to the question of specifically what criteria we can employ in these investigation steps.

5.3.2.2.2   The Criteria in Detail

In analysing the availability of appropriability instruments, we will refer to the results developed in Chapter 4. First, it is necessary to identify the type of underlying technology. As the results of several surveys have demonstrated, the use of appropriability mechanisms differs in dependence of the nature of the technology. This is particularly evident in the application of intellectual property rights. Whereas in discrete or simple industries patents are indeed employed to protect the innovation itself and to impede competitors from inventing close substitutes, in complex industries patents have a more strategic use in the sense that they strengthen the negotiation position of the firm in cross-licensing agreements or firms intend to create or to amplify patent thickets. Thus, consolidated findings of the nature of the industry or the specific product provide a first impression as to the importance of intellectual property rights. To achieve such findings, one possibility is to mandate experts to analyse the complexity of the involved knowledge, the composition of the products (are they comprised of several components or are they rather simple?), and other factors that can be decisive for the characterization of the industry. Further, it is possible to refer to already existing empirical studies or economic models that discuss the nature of the industry or, for instance, to survey the concerned industry or industries with comparable products asking for the motivation and reasons to patent. If such an inquiry shows that most firms in that industry or in closely related industries only use intellectual property rights for strategic purposes such as licensing agreements and instead rely on other appropriability mechanisms, this could be a preliminary hint that the dominant firm does not need intellectual property rights to protect its innovation either.

A further indication of the importance of intellectual property rights for the appropriation of the returns of the investment is the nature of the underlying knowledge. As mentioned in the previous chapter, we can differentiate between tacit and codified knowledge and also between organizational and individual knowledge. The more codified the information and knowledge, the easier the imitation and, therefore, the more important the role of intellectual property rights. Similarly, if information is not or only to a limited extent incorporated in organizational knowledge in the sense that firm-specific routines play a limited or no role in the development and understanding of the knowledge, imitation is easier than in cases where the knowledge is based on firm-specific capabilities.

In contrast, the more "firm-inherent" and tacit the knowledge and information, the less important the intellectual property rights, because competitors first need to imitate firm-specific capabilities and routines and codify the knowledge. Experts would also be useful in analysing the nature of the necessary knowledge. In a simplified situation, we can conclude that if any expert in the field of the concerned technology is able to understand and apply the particular information, the involved knowledge is largely codified and not firm-specific. The more research and diverse knowledge is required to interpret the information, the more tacit and firm-specific it is, that is, the underlying knowledge is organizational. In this case, we can again assume that intellectual property rights are not necessarily decisive for the protection of the innovation.

Moreover, the type of the underlying knowledge also gives some hints as to the availability of alternative appropriability mechanisms. For instance, when the manufacturing process is only obvious or traceable to a limited degree because it requires a great amount of organizational and tacit knowledge, a firm could also rely on secrecy to protect its innovation. However, from my point of view, the possibility of using secrecy plays only a minor role in our investigations. Even though secrecy might have been a workable alternative in the specific case, the fact that we are dealing with refusal to license intellectual property rights-protected goods or services indicates that the firm decided against secrecy in favour of patents and/or copyrights. Although, with complex products, some parts of the concerned item might be protected through secrecy, we cannot consider it an appropriate alternative after the dominant firm has already disclosed at least parts of the required knowledge.

Still, the degree of tacit knowledge also gives some leads as to whether the dominant firm can exploit first-mover advantages. If a competitor requires time to understand and apply the knowledge necessary for a certain product or process, the innovator can use this lead time to march down the learning curve and learn from mistakes, improve features of the product, amend production processes, or establish service and repair units. Thus, if the competitor enters the market with its imitation, the innovator can already offer higher quality or lower prices. Further, the innovator can use this lead time to differentiate its product from subsequent products in the sense that it builds up a reputation for the concerned product. A good example of the successful exploitation of first-mover advantages is Apple with the introduction of its iPod. Whereas Apple launched the first version of its music player in 2001, the rival product from Microsoft and Toshiba, Zune, was first introduced in 2006. During this imitation lag, Apple set up an Internet platform for music downloads, improved the design and features of its product, and established its product as a brand. Therewith, it successfully differentiated its product from all subsequent products, like the Zune from Microsoft, and Apple can now, to a certain extent, set its prices independently of its competitors.

In addition to scrutinizing these advantages in relation to lead time, the investigating competition authority can also analyse whether the dominant firm can realize economies of scale or has absolute cost advantages compared to its competitor to further develop its first-mover advantage. Cost advantages, for instance, can arise if the dominant firm has already developed advance production technologies or invested in the specialization of its employees. Another possibility for creating cost advantages is to close contract with suppliers of rare resources. Because of the first-mover advantage, the dominant firm might have been able to bargain better conditions than competitors would now receive.

Furthermore, the competition authority should examine whether the dominant firm has complementary capabilities and assets. As illustrated in Chapter 4, the advantage of complementarities is twofold. First, the company can realize economies of scope by exploiting already existing resources, technologies, and structures for the production and marketing of the innovation. That is, if the concerned item is a successor product or if the firm offers a wide choice of products, it can refer to already existing structures and knowledge. Therewith, it facilitates the introduction of the new product and avoids cost in the sense that it does not have to establish, for instance, a distribution system or invest in new production machines. Second, by establishing specialized and co-specialized compatibilities, the dominant firm makes it more difficult to get copied. That is to say, when the complementary capabilities are closely intertwined with the product and the product characteristics, the likelihood of acquiring such skills on the market is further diminished. Instead, rivals have to invest and rebuild this capability or asset. An example of this can be a service unit that customers can contact if they face problems with their products. Consumers tend to consider the highly experienced and specialized customer service of the dominant firm to be a part of the product, and they would expect that rivalling products offer the same service. Another example of complementary capabilities can be found in the *IMS Health* case. The mutual development of the brick structure together with potential customers and suppliers constituted a strong complementary asset for IMS Health because it was almost impossible for rivals to develop a product that met the needs of consumers as precisely as did the IMS Health product. From this perspective, we can consider this cooperation for the design of the brick structure to be a very distinctive specialized capability. Thus, specialized complementary assets also create time and cost advantages for the innovating firm. First, competitors have to rebuild the complementary assets and second, because of their time lag, they have to invest more than the innovating firm to develop the required assets.

In order to assess whether the dominant firm has certain (specialized) complementary capabilities and/ or assets, the competition authority must scrutinize which competences or technologies are necessary to launch the product successfully on the market. Specifically, the competition authority must analyse whether the dominant firm reverted to already existing manufacturing capabilities, knowledge resources, service and distribution units, and so forth. Further, it must examine whether certain capabilities are required to sell a product. For instance, we can ask if consumers expect customer service or compatible applications for the product. For such an analysis, the competition authority can inter alia survey customers to determine what they consider to be important. In addition, it is possible to make a questionnaire for competitors, asking what they deem to be decisive capabilities or assets for successfully marketing a new product or service or to evaluate what they regard as the strategic strength or competence of the dominant firm. With such information, the investigating authority should be able to analyse whether the dominant firm can rely on complementary assets and capabilities to protect its innovation.

In general, surveys among competitors or among firms within markets with similar or related products can always be conducted in order to estimate whether it would be possible for the dominant firm to employ alternative appropriation strategies to intellectual property rights. Besides that, the competition authority can employ experts with wide knowledge in this particular industry. Moreover, the competition authority could refer to economic literature regarding innovation strategies or to already conducted sector analyses to gain knowledge about the appropriability conditions. While this section should not be understood as a comprehensive and complete overview of how to assess the availability of alternative appropriation instruments, it does give an idea as to what competition authorities should focus on for an analysis of refusal to license intellectual property rights. If the examination suggests that the dominant firm does not need to rely on intellectual property rights but could resorts to other appropriability instruments, that gives evidence that the dominant firm did not refuse to license to protect its innovation. Instead, we can assume that the dominant firm intended to impede competition and to leverage its dominant position in the upstream market to the downstream market. In this case, an intervention of competition policy would not diminish the incentive to innovate, because the investigation has shown that the dominant firm can appropriate a sufficient reward for its innovation in other ways, for instance through first-mover advantage or through the exploitation of complementary assets. Based on this, the resort to intellectual property rights to justify the refusal to license can be judged as pretextual. Consequently, the refusal would be deemed as abusive.

5.3.2.3   Imposing the Remedy

Having determined that the refusal to license constitutes an abuse of dominance, the third step aims at the imposition of an effective remedy that is capable of restoring competition in the downstream market. Depending on the involved goods and technologies, the standards for the remedy might very well vary. In examining whether a remedy is appropriate, it is also necessary to identify distinct goals to be achieved. It is only possible to evaluate the effectiveness of a remedy and to gain further insights for other prospective abuse of intellectual property rights cases if its purpose is clear. Consequently, in the next sections we analyse the question of the right remedy in more depth.

5.3.2.3.1   Choosing the Right Remedy

Having demonstrated the anti-competitive effect and the lack of a plausible defence, we turn now to the question of how to change this situation. In other words, we are searching for an effective but also efficient remedy. From an economic perspective, a remedy should pursue two goals: first, it should restore competition in the concerned market; and second, it should prevent prospective anti-competitive behaviour (Bresnahan 2002: 1). An efficient remedy also implies that it does not prevent firms from engaging in lawful and innovative actions in the future. A remedy should correct the dominant firm's behaviour in the past, but it should not choke prospective investments in innovation (Barnett 2009: 35; similar: Werden 2009).197 Thus, an effective and efficient remedy for anti-competitive behaviour varies depending on the type of market distortion evoked by the behaviour. Based on an examination of the caselaw and previous explanations for refusal to license intellectual property, we can assume that competition in a secondary market is restricted if not prohibited in most refusal to license cases. Access to the intellectual property right is decisive for competition. In other words, we have to look for a remedy that enables access to the denied intellectual properties in order to restore competition. At the same time, we have to consider whether that remedy also has a prohibitive character for prospective – similar – anti-competitive actions.

Generally, we can differentiate between pecuniary, behavioural, and structural remedies. Pecuniary sanctions can either be compensation payments aiming at the reparation of the damages caused or simply fines of a prohibitive nature for prospective infringers (Montagnani 2007: 633).198 Behavioural remedies aim at changing the dominant firm's actions and therewith also the competitors' actions in the concerned market, but they do not change the structure of the market (Shelanski/Sidak 2001: 15). Structural remedies, in contrast, modify the property rights of a firm, which may imply the disposal of certain parts of the

---

197 For the further purposes of remedies, compare to Melamed 2009.
198 European Union Article 7 of Council Regulation (EC) no. 1/2003, 2003 O.J. L 1, 1 empowers the European Commission to detect anti-competitive actions and to require the (dominant) firm to suspend that action. Under this reasoning, a remedy leads to a reestablishment of competition. Thus, according to European law, a monetary fine or any other form of sanction is not a remedy as it usually does not bring the anti-competitive conduct to an end (Hellström/Maier-Rigaud/Bulst 2009: 44). According to Hellström et al., fines have a preventative character that shall distract the infringing firm as well as its competitors from prospective anti-competitive actions (ibid.: 45).

dominant firm or even a divestiture (Motta 2004: 69). According to Shelanski and Sidak (2001), a structural remedy comprises every sanction aiming at a redistribution of the competitive assets, which implies also mandatory access or compulsory licenses (ibid.: 15). However, following the prevailing opinion (Bresnahan 2002; Lenard 2000; Levinson/Romaine/Salop 2001; Motta 2004; Picker 2002), we will consider the obligation to access or a compulsory license as behavioural structure.[199] With regards to intellectual property rights, this interpretation can easily be justified, because with a compulsory license, the dominant firm (or the intellectual property right holder in general) will still get a fee for the usage. The property right for the concerned item is maintained and the compulsory license alone unbundles the right to exclude (Gwartney 2009: 1421).

From an economic perspective, instead of differentiating between pecuniary, behavioural, and structural remedies, it is also reasonable to differentiate according to the effect, that is, to differentiate between an "incentives based remedy" or a "command-and-control remedy" (Lévêque 2000). The first type of remedy aims at changing a firm's conduct by giving incentives to adopt socially desirable conduct. The second type of remedy functions more like a regulation in that the government or competition authority instructs the firm how to behave (ibid.).

In the context of intellectual property rights, two remedies have been discussed thus far: divestiture and compulsory licensing (Montagnani 2007: 637). According to the differentiation noted above, a divestiture provides incentives for "new" firms to act competitively whereas a compulsory license functions like a command-and-control remedy as the competition authority sets requirements for the licensing conditions (Lévêque 2000). The discussion about a structural remedy, that is, divestiture, stems mainly from the U.S. *Microsoft* case. Even though the court did not execute this option, it seriously considered it.[200] This idea was broadly discussed in the literature and found both advocates and opponents.[201] Even though divestiture might have been appropriate in this specific case,[202] we should be rather careful in considering this structural remedy as

---

199 According to Motta (2004), even though it is a conduct remedy, a compulsory license or mandatory access to an essential facility can be viewed as a quasi-structural remedy as it has a similar effect as a redistribution of resources (ibid.: 268).

200 (United States v. Microsoft, 253 F.3f 34 (D.C. Cir. June 28, 2001). For a detailed discussion of the eventually imposed remedy compare to Page/Childers 2009.

201 For an overview compare examplarily to Bresnahan 2002; Comanor 2001, Elzinga/Evans/Nichols 2001; Lenard 2001; Levinson/Romaine/Salop 2001; Liebowitz 2001; Lopatka/Page 2001; Picker 2002.

202 Defender of the divestiture of Microsoft inter alia argued that Microsoft's anticompetitive behaviour was not limited to one or two cases but rather constituted a strategy of exclusionary conduct. For a detailed explanation of this *compare to* Lenard 2001.

a conventional remedy in refusal to license cases, especially as we do not know its effects on innovation incentives for prospective companies.[203] This issue is further demonstrated by the fact that the rescission and correction of structural remedies causes grave difficulties (Sullivan 2002: 612). Moreover, in markets where innovation can be originated from synergies with downstream (complementary) markets, structural remedies are unlikely to evoke more innovations. Since, for instance, a divestiture can prevent a firm from exploiting the innovative potentials arising from combining functions of products from neighbouring markets, a structural remedy can indeed also restrict innovation (Montagnani 2007: 635). The second remedy discussed and exercised is compulsory licensing. The effect is quite clear: With a compulsory license, the dominant intellectual property holder is forced to share its protected assets and therewith, competition can be reinstalled. The advantage of a compulsory license is twofold. First, it is also used in competitive markets; and second, it is already anchored in most intellectual property laws.

According to Evans (2005), it is useful when estimating the effects of certain practices to examine practices on both competitive and concentrated markets. As Evans explains, if a certain practice, for instance, licensing, is common in competitive markets, we can assume that this is an efficiency-enhancing practice (Evans 2005: 98). If it did not contribute to efficiency, it would not persist in the long run (ibid.). If, in contrast, another practice is rarely used in competitive markets, we can assume that only dominant firms can use this practice profitably (ibid.). Using this assumption with our example, we can conclude that licensing intellectual property is probably an efficient solution because it is a widely accepted practice in a lot of markets (aside from markets where innovations are mainly discrete and therefore rely on intellectual property rights to protect these innovations; compare to Chapter 4). From this perspective, we can justify compulsory licensing as a remedy for refusal to license intellectual property rights cases.[204]

---

203   Consequently, in the American *Microsoft* case, the court argued that a divestiture should be applied with great caution, especially if the concerned firm grew by its own strength making it almost impossible to split into equal parts. Thus, a divestiture should only be applied when "tailored to fit the wrong creating the occasion for the remedy." *United States v. Microsoft*, 253 F.3f 34, 106 (D.C. Cir. June 28, 2001).

204   As we saw in the discussion at Chapter 4.3, a compulsory license is supposed to be successful since it allows the development and production of applications independently of the standard owner especially if the refused intellectual property rights constitute a standard in a network industry (Scotchmer 2004: 303). Hence, in the U.S. compulsory licensing of intellectual property rights, especially patents, is a common practice to remove the effects of the unlawful conduct (Crandall 2001: 116). According to Weber Wallace (2009), the imposition of a compulsory licenses comprised 20.5 percent of relief granted in reported civil monopolization cases through 1996 (ibid.: 18).

Moreover, most national intellectual property laws, for instance the German Patent Law, recognize the compulsory license as an instrument with which intellectual property rights can be restrained under certain circumstances. In Germany, paragraph 24 of the Patent Law regulates the imposition of mandatory licensing. To name two examples, according to paragraph 24(1), a compulsory license can be imposed if the potential licensee unavailingly tried to get a license and at the same time a public interest in the license exists. Nevertheless, in paragraph 24(6), the legislator emphasizes that both scope and period have to be adjusted according to the special purpose of the license (that is, the license is not unlimited) and the patent holder is entitled to demand a fee for the usage of her patent.

But also supranational regulations acknowledge the possibility of mandatory access to intellectual property rights. For example, The Agreement on Trade-Related Aspects of Intellectual Property Rights (TRIPS)[205] dedicates Article 31 to "Other Uses Without Authorization of the Right Holder," in other words, compulsory licenses. This article also mentions that a compulsory license can be imposed as a remedy for anti-competitive usage of the concerned intellectual property right (Article 31 No. 7 TRIPS Agreement). Thus, as the intellectual property laws themselves use compulsory licenses as an instrument to solve problems arising when an intellectual property owner rejects dealing a protected good that is either important for further innovation or necessary for viable competition in the market, it seems appropriate that competition policy also employs this instrument.

A weaker remedy, for instance, is the obligation to disclose the information (Montagani 2007: 637). However, the appropriateness of disclosure varies from case to case. Since disclosure does not authorize the usage or reproduction of the intellectual property rights, it is not effective in restoring competition in every case. Thus, the decision as to whether to impose a compulsory license or demand disclosure also depends on the requirements of the market, that is, whether the disclosure of information is sufficient to renew competition.[206] Nevertheless, disclosure can be highly important in complex industries like the software industry. For instance, to achieve interoperability, it is not only necessary to get access to the protocols. Instead, it is essential that the dominant firm also disclose

---

205 The Agreement on Trade-Related Aspects of Intellectual Property Rights (TRIPS Agreement), adopted in Marrakesh, Annex 1C, Agreement Establishing the World Trade Organization, 1869 U.N.T.S. 299, 33 I.L.M. 1197 (1994).

206 It is notable that a compulsory license certainly requires the disclosure of information as well. As Weber Wallace (2009) argues, in intellectual property-driven industries a compulsory license can be interpreted as a "divestiture by disclosure" since it would create non-discriminatory access and a more competitive environment for alternative solutions (ibid: 26-27).

the architectural overviews so that competitors can understand the interaction of the different protocols (Dolmans 2009).

5.3.2.3.2   Enforcement and Supervision

However, the imposition of the right remedy remains a complex and controversial task. The reason for this lies, first, in the uncertainty over the effectiveness of the remedy and, second, in the information asymmetry between the dominant firm and the competition authority (First 2008). The intricacy of high technology and information sectors evokes complex remedies that demand innovative monitoring and compliance obligations. Hence, competition authorities and courts will require more external support, for instance specialists and compliance committees, to enforce the remedy (Weber Waller 2009: 26). Especially when both intellectual property rights and trade secrets are involved, only the dominant firm knows whether it discloses or licenses all relevant information (First 2008). Even though independent experts or monitoring trustees can reappraise whether the supplied information is sufficient to compete on equal footing, this review process takes time and, therewith, creates another advantage for the dominant firm. Another problem is the efficient enforcement of the remedy. In the European *Microsoft* case, the Commission obliged Microsoft to license the necessary interface information to "reasonable and non-discriminatory terms."[207] However, it took one and half years after the imposition of the remedy for Microsoft to supply licensing information that complied with the requirements in regards to its content and its price.[208] Moreover, the Commission reported that Microsoft's market share of working group server operating systems grew within this time.

This leads to another requirement connected to remedies, that is, the formulation of goals. Since the success of a remedy is only predictable to a limited degree, it is important to scrutinize its effectiveness in regards to its target achievement. According to First (2008), competition authorities tend to lose

---

207   This also leads to the question of what an appropriate royalty for a compulsory license should be, which constitutes an important part of the effectiveness of the remedy. If the fee is set too high, this would still impede access to the intellectual property rights. However, the question is whether every competitor should be able to get access to the intellectual property right. An alternative solution is, for instance, an auction system. In a bidding process, only the most efficient competitor will get access to the concerned intellectual property rights (Montagnani 2007: 640). However, I will not deal with this problem any further here. For a more detailed discussion, *compare to* Geradin 2009 and *to* Dolmans/O'Donoghue/Loewenthal 2007.

208   Commission Decision of 27 February 2008, Case COMP/C-3/37.792 Microsoft, available at http://ec.europa.eu/competition/antitrust/cases/decisions/37792/decision2008.pdf (last visit 2009-09-07). For a comprehensive discussion of the effectiveness of the remedies in the EU Microsoft case compare to Economides/Lianos 2009.

track of their goals because they focus on the supervision of compliance to the remedy instead of on the effectiveness of the remedy itself. Although ensuring compliance is important for the deterrent effect of the remedy, it is also necessary to question whether the chosen remedy was effective in achieving its goal, for instance, renewing competition in the market (ibid). Especially as it is a difficult and complex process to foresee further market development, it is necessary to make some assumptions and review the success after a certain period. Such a limited remedy is also in line with those intellectual property laws where the obligation to license is only valid for a certain time.[209] If the revision shows that the remedy, for instance a compulsory license, did not lead to more innovations in the concerned industry, this requires a careful analysis of the reasons. One possibility is that the licensed information was not sufficient to render access to the downstream market. Thus, the compulsory license needs to be redefined. As Hellström et al. (2009) note, remedies often mirror the infringement, that is, if access was denied, the remedy requires access. Depending on how successful the dominant firm already was with its anti-competitive strategy, it might be necessary to go beyond mirroring the abuse. In detail, it might be necessary not to put the competitors on equal footing but in a better position. In the case of a compulsory license, the competition authority could, for instance, require a firm to license for free within a limited period (Hellström/Maier-Rigaud/Bulst 2009: 59). The other possibility is that in this particular case a compulsory license was simply not an effective remedy. In this situation, the compulsory license should be nullified. If, in contrast, dynamic efficiency in the downstream market is enhanced, new products and services had been introduced, and the market records new entrants, it is nevertheless necessary to review whether a compulsory license is still necessary or if the market developed substitutes for the refused item. Such a proceeding creates incentives for both competitors and the dominant firm to innovate. The competitors know that if they do not prove any success in regards to dynamic efficiency, the competition authority will withdraw the license. The dominant firm can defend its status quo and prove its leadership in innovation in the hopes that it might get released from the mandatory licensing.[210] Moreover, such a proceeding provides the possibility of drawing further knowledge on the effectiveness of compulsory licenses, which can be used for prospective cases.

---

209 Besides this, Werden argues that a remedy that is left in place too long could become unduly regulatory and thereby restrict further market developments (Werden 2009: 77).

210 Further, this creates incentives for the dominant firm to include all necessary information in the license agreement right away, because otherwise it has to expect stricter, additional requirements and conditions in the review phase.

5.4 Critical Acclaim

Having outlined the basic ideas and the constitutive criteria and elements of the Innovation Effects and Appropriability Test, this section explores why the test is appropriate as a means of dealing with the abuse of intellectual property rights and in what regards it differs from existing standards. As the Incentives Balance Test is state of the art and the starting point of this thesis, in the following we will compare the Innovation Effects and Appropriability Test with the Incentives Balance Test as applied in the *Microsoft* case. However, with the publication of the Article 102 TFEU guidance paper, the Commission also provides some insights into how it intends to analyse prospective cases of abuse of dominance, including refusal to license intellectual property rights. Therefore, we will extend our comparison to the principles laid out in the guidelines and examine whether the Innovation Effects and Appropriability Test fits into the new standard of the Commission. This analysis is completed with a critical discussion of the advantages and shortcomings of the Innovation Effects and Appropriability Test in comparison to the principle of the guidance paper and the Incentives Balance Test.

5.4.1 Analysis of the Anti-Competitive Effects

5.4.1.1 Indispensability Criterion and Elimination of Competition

Generally, the criteria of indispensability and elimination of competition stemming from the previous caselaw and applied in the Incentives Balance Test basically remain unchanged in the guidance paper and also in our Innovation Effects and Appropriability Test. The differences are only slight in nature: Whereas in both the Incentives Balance Test in the *Microsoft* case and the Article 102 TFEU guidance paper, the indispensability criterion and the requirement of the likelihood of elimination of competition are listed as separate criteria, the Innovation Effects and Appropriability Test examines them as one criterion. As we have seen in section 5.1, the indispensability of a certain good or intellectual property right for being active in a downstream market and the likelihood of impeding or eliminating competition in that downstream market are so closely intertwined that a separate analysis is rarely possible.

However, this interrelation is not new to the Commission, but in fact became evident in previous decisions of the Commission. As already discussed in section 2.3.1, for instance, the Commission concluded in the *Microsoft* case that

> "Microsoft's behaviour risks eliminating competition in the work group server operating system market, due to the indispensability of the input that it refuses to supply to its competitors." (*COMP Microsoft*: para. 692)

This statement makes it apparent that the Commission is very well aware of the difficulties of analysing both criteria independently from each other. Consequently, the Commission states in the guidance paper that it considers the likelihood of eliminating competition as a given if indispensability has been proven (European Commission 2009: para. 85). From this perspective, the combination of indispensability and elimination of competition into one criterion, that is, the indispensability of competition in a downstream market, does not constitute a break with previous caselaw or with the Commission's guidance paper. Rather, this new singular criterion aims only at the simplification of the examination and the avoidance of the likely confusion that would occur when basically the same arguments are discussed twice – once for the detection of indispensability and once for the detection of the likelihood of competition. Nevertheless, we can conclude that, in regards to these requirements, the Innovation Effects and Appropriability Test is in line with the present criteria.

5.4.1.2   Consumer Harm

The harmony with previous caselaw and the guidance paper is not so clear-cut in terms of the detection of consumer harm. As outlined in Chapter 2 and in section 5.2.4, the previous caselaw, that is, the New Product Test and Incentives Balancing Test, required proof that the refusal to supply prevented the introduction of a new product for which there is potential consumer demand. In the *Microsoft* judgment, the CFI extended this criterion to include the impediment of technological development. Thus, the Innovation Effects and Appropriability Test diverges only slightly from the Incentives Balance Test by putting a stronger emphasis on dynamic efficiency.

In the guidance paper to Article 102 TFEU, the Commission goes further as it already conducts a balancing of the different effects of the refusal to license. Strictly speaking, a refusal to supply evokes consumer harm when the anticompetitive effects on the consumers outweigh the negative effects of an obligation to supply (European Commission 2009: 86). Thus, in the guidance paper the Commission already questions what negative consequences for the consumer may arise from mandatory licensing or supply. Whereas the Commission gives some examples of what can be classified as anti-competitive effects, it does not give any guidance as to what it might consider to be negative effects of the obligation to supply. The negative consequences of the refusal to supply on consumers, though, can be either of static or dynamic nature. Regarding the dynamic effects, the Commission considers, for example, the prevention of new goods or services and the impediment of follow-on innovation as harm to consumers. Nevertheless, even if dynamic efficiency is not impeded, consumer harm can be evoked when the refusal to supply leads to higher prices in the affected downstream market.

Hence, the differences of the Innovation Effects and Appropriability Test to the standard put forward in the guidance paper are significant in two respects. First, while the guidance paper also takes into account effects on static efficiency, the Innovation Effects and Appropriability Test focuses explicitly and also exclusively on obstructions of dynamic efficiency. Consequently, competitors or claimants in the abuse action have to prove that they do not only intend to copy the service or product of the dominant firm but that they need the intellectual property right to conduct innovation and/or to place a new product or service on the market. This focus on dynamic efficiency is important as the promotion of innovation is the mutual goal of intellectual property law and competition law. Interference when solely static efficiency is impeded is likely to counteract this common goal since it diminishes prospective innovation incentives. Nonetheless, we do not know for sure if the Commission will indeed consider static efficiency when analysing refusal to license intellectual property cases as the guidance paper addresses refusal to supply cases in general. Although the Commission points out that refusal to license intellectual property rights and interface information constitutes a case group of refusals to supply, it does not differentiate within the description of the examination criteria. Thus, it might be possible, that the Commission will also focus exclusively on dynamic efficiencies in prospective intellectual property rights cases. Nevertheless, by mentioning the price effects as anti-competitive effects, the Commission opens the door for cases in which an argument based on innovation effects might evoke problems, but in which allocative efficiency is impeded.[211]

Second, in contrast to the guidance paper, the Innovation Effects and Appropriability Test does not weigh the different effects. To put it differently, similar to the approach in the Incentives Balance Test, the Innovation Effects and Appropriability Test completes the establishment of consumer harm with the identification of the anti-competitive effects. In contrast, the guidance paper goes further as it weighs these anti-competitive effects against the negative consequences of the obligation to supply. The difference is twofold. First, the proceeding in the guidance paper implies that the competition authority must undertake a further inquiry at this investigation step, that is, it must analyse the effects of, for instance, a compulsory license. Second, a balancing requires a quantification of the different effects. In my view, this puts a high burden on the competition authority because it not only has to detect the effects on the consumer, but it

---

211 It is questionable whether the *IMS Health* case is an example for such a situation. As at the time of its investigation the requirement for anti-competitive effects was the impediment of a new product in a downstream market, the Commission differentiated between a hypothetical market, which is the market for the intellectual property right itself, and the downstream market, which is the market for the service offered. Proponents of a compulsory license for the involved copyright inter alia argued that even though innovations from the competing firm NDS Health were questionable, a compulsory license would at least restore allocative efficiency in the market (Drexl 2004). Thus, extending consumer harm to static inefficiencies would prevent the Commission from making all kind of efforts to prove impediment of dynamic efficiency.

must also evaluate them. This becomes especially difficult when it comes to the assessment of dynamic efficiency. As already mentioned, one aspect of consumer harm is the impediment of follow-on innovation. Thus, the innovation is not yet realized, but the investigating authority still has to appraise the potential value for or the potential willingness to pay of the consumers of this prospective innovation. As we already discussed in this chapter, the outcome of innovation processes is only to a limited degree predictable and may also lead to results different from what was expected. Thus, any evaluation of the negative effects on dynamic efficiency is highly speculative, especially when the research process is still in an early phase. From this perspective, a requirement to quantify the effects again gives incentives to focus the analysis on static effects, that is, price effects. The same problem arises for the quantification of the likely negative consequences of the obligation to supply. As the formulation already shows, it is not possible to make definite statements but only presumptions regarding the consequences of an obligation to supply. This may contain an educated guess about innovations or product improvements the dominant firm might otherwise conduct or the prevention of the realization of economies of scale. Thus, an evaluation of these effects is probably even more challenging than the quantification of the anti-competitive effects, because for the latter, in the best case scenario, we have at least a relatively precise knowledge of what is suppressed by the refusal to supply, for instance, like in the *Magill* case, whereas for the effects of a compulsory license, we do not have any factual knowledge.

Consequently, the approach of the Innovation Effects and Appropriability Test is advantageous because it avoids such a difficult quantification and balancing and it only considers the prevention or reduction of dynamic efficiency as negative for consumers. As already pointed out previously, this focusing is reasonable because it turns the attention to the mutual goal of competition policy and intellectual property rights policy and therewith should not lead to a reduction in innovation incentives.

5.4.2   Objective Justification

The last criterion is the objective justification. Since this criterion constitutes the core of the new test, we will discuss the differences to the Incentives Balance Test and to the guidance paper separately.

5.4.2.1   Incentives Balancing v. Appropriability Test

While the differences between the Innovation Effects and Appropriability Test and the Incentives Balance Test are only marginal in regards to the detection of the anti-competitive effect, this changes in regards to the objective justification. In its application in the *Microsoft* case, the Commission conducted a balancing of the different effects on the innovation incentives. If the innovation incentives of the dominant firm resulting from the refusal to license outvalued any other innovation incentive arising from a compulsory license, this would have counted as an objective justification of the refusal. In contrast, if the overall innovation incentives, that is, the long- and short-term innovation incentives of both the competitors and the dominant firm, evoked by a compulsory license outweighed, the refusal to supply was not justified. As already discussed in Chapter 2, the Commission did not give any guidance as to what should be considered in such a balancing. The balancing conducted in the *Microsoft* case seemed to be rather vague and primarily based on the assumption that less firm concentration can always be equalized with more innovation. However, taking the test literally, a comprehensive balancing of the innovation incentives includes inter alia an analysis of the appropriation possibilities, the influence of the market structure on the innovation incentives, demands of consumers, immaterial motivations for innovation, and every other factor that might affect a firm's incentive to innovate. As a balancing demands the consideration of opposing effects, estimations need to be made for the situation where the refusal to license continues and for the situation where a compulsory license is obliged. While such an approach seems to be an almost optimal solution for refusal to license intellectual property rights cases as it considers all possible effects, it faces the problem that it requires too much information we do not have, for instance, information about consumer demand for an undeveloped product. Thus, as we outlined in Chapter 4, due to this information problem, such an "advanced" Incentives Balance Test is not practical.

In contrast, the Innovation Effects and Appropriability Test builds upon the analysis of the availability of appropriation mechanisms. Having the advantage of referring to "observable" information, the Innovation Effects and Appropriability Test follows a reduced version of an optimal Incentives Balance Test. While the Incentives Balance Test aims at a comprehensive evaluation of innovation incentives, the Innovation Effects and Appropriability Test restricts itself to the analysis of whether the dominant firm could use appropriability instruments other than intellectual property rights to protect its innovation. As such, the Innovation Effects and Appropriability Test is more rule-orientated,[212] since it stops the investigations after detecting of the availability of alternative appropriability instruments. The underlying idea is simple: Generally, firms have several appropriation mechanisms from which they can choose. Depending on specific circumstances, firms will decide in favour of a certain appropriation strategy; for instance, they use intellectual property rights to protect their innovation or rely on complementary capability and lead time to recoup their investments.

---

212 As Kerber (2006) points out, rules can shape a firm's incentives. Thus, a rule as described by the Innovation Effects and Appropriability Test may provide incentives to search for more or new mechanisms of appropriation because it restricts the intellectual property rights of a dominant firm.

As a result, if the analysis shows that the nature of the intellectual property pro-
tected-item allows the employment of alternative appropriability instruments,
this can be regarded as an indicator that intellectual property rights are only to a
limited degree necessary. As illustrated in our discussion in section 3.3.3, we
can argue that in this case the intellectual property rights are not optimally assigned; in particular, they should at least be smaller. In some cases, we might
also argue that they are not necessary at all. However, if our analysis shows that
the dominant firm could rely on other appropriation mechanism, we can assume
that it uses its intellectual property rights only for strategic uses, that is, for the
foreclosure of its competitors and the leveraging of its market power.

From this perspective, we can argue that the Innovation Effects and Appropriability Test is a simplified analysis of whether the intellectual property rights
of the dominant firm are too broadly assigned. Instead of examining the optimal
scope of intellectual property rights in detail, though, the test takes the availability of alternative appropriation instruments as a proxy for the necessity of intellectual property rights. The advantage of this is that we can obtain information
about the disposability and usage of appropriability instruments whereas the re-
ceipt of the information for the determination of the optimal scope of intellectual
property rights is only to a limited extend possible. Further, this proceeding still
maintains the goal of promoting innovation: If the analysis finds that the dominant firm relies on the intellectual property rights to protect its investments, this
would be valid as an objective justification of the refusal to supply. Thus, the
Innovation Effects and Appropriability Test allows the dominant firm to use the
intellectual property rights for its legislator-intended purpose, that is, to gain a
reward for its innovative efforts.

The differences to the Incentives Balance Test rest in a one-sided focus on
the appropriability mechanism, which can also be interpreted as an analysis of
the innovation incentives. Another important distinction – which is also the reason why we can say that the Innovation Effects and Appropriability Test is a
simplified test, is that we do neither quantify nor do we weigh different effects
against each other. That is to say, while an optimal Incentives Balance Test
would also assess how a compulsory license or any other remedy would affect
the innovation incentives of the dominant firm, in the Innovation Effects and
Appropriability Test the detection of the abusive conduct basically closes with
the determination of whether the dominant firm could use alternatives strategies
to recoup its investments in innovation or whether it relies on intellectual property rights. The disadvantage of this proceeding is that we only analyse whether
alternative appropriability instruments are available, but we cannot quantify the
degree of protection they offer and if they are sufficient to replace intellectual
property rights. Instead, we can only make a rough estimation. Against this
background, the application of the Innovation Effects and Appropriability Test
can lead to mistakes in the sense that we under- or overestimate the influence of

alternative appropriability instruments. Still, it is this surrender of quantification (and balancing) that makes the test practicable. Compared to the Incentives Balance Test, the big advantage of the Innovation Effects and Appropriability Test is that it is based on information that is not only available for the competition authorities but also for the dominant firm. Therewith, dominant firms can predict whether their conduct would be deemed as abusive or not.[213] At the same time, competition authorities have clear criteria they can use in their examinations. However, the most important distinction is that the test refers to sound economic theories and, therefore, its result will be better traceable and less vulnerable.

5.4.2.2 Efficiency Defense v. Appropriability Test

The distinctions between the Innovation Effects and Appropriability Test and the standard suggested in the guidance paper are already apparent in the determination of the consumer standard and continue with the requirements for the objective justification. With the publication of the guidance paper, the Commission officially introduced for the first time an efficiency defence for abuse of dominance cases. However, as already indicated in Chapter 2, its barriers are quite high. First of all, it is notable that proof of the efficiencies generated by the abusive conduct is incumbent upon the dominant firm (European Commission 2009: para. 28). Accordingly, the dominant firm can bring forward objections that the refusal to license is necessary to recoup its investments for the concerned intellectual property rights. Considering the risk that not every R&D activity leads to a success, such an objection aims at the maintenance of future incentives to innovate (European Commission 2009: para. 89). Further, the Commission will regard pleas that the structural change evoked by an obligation to license could diminish the innovations of the dominant firm (ibid.). At first glance, this wording is reminiscent of the Incentives Balance Test, since the starting point for the Incentives Balance Test was the objection of Microsoft that a compulsory license would diminish all future incentives to innovate (COMP Microsoft: 709). However, taking a deeper look we see that the similarity is only limited, as the guidance paper also points out, to the general requirements of the efficiencies defence described in the introductory part of the guidelines: first, the efficiencies realized by the conduct must outweigh any likely negative effects on competition and consumer harm; and second, the conduct must not eliminate all

---

213 In contrast, the Incentives Balance Test evokes great uncertainties in this regard: "Considering the complex effects of IPRs on innovation incentives and competition, and the acknowledged difficulties of defining and delimiting IPRs generally, this endeavour appears overambitious. Dominant firms will not be able to discern ex ante whether they are under a duty to license, or whether they enjoy full freedom of trade." (Schweitzer 2007: 24)

effective competition in the concerned market (European Commission 2009: para. 30).

Already the latter evokes confusion because the Commission tests exactly this requirement with the indispensability criterion and the criterion of elimination of effective competition. Therefore, one might argue that an efficiency defence in refusal to supply cases is more or less impossible. Reverting to the criterion of the elimination of competition, this requirement leaves room for a broader interpretation; here, the Commission mentions the likelihood of eliminating competition. Against this background, it is possible to argue that the requirement of the efficiency defence refers to the immediate elimination of competition whereas the requirement for the anti-competitive conduct considers potential long-term effects as well. Nevertheless, the guidance paper does not provide a clear answer and how the Commission plans to interpret and apply these criteria remains open to interpretation.

The requirement that the efficiencies must prevail over the negatives effects on consumers for the acceptance of the defence is similarly nebulous. Again, the question arises as to what constitutes harm to consumers. In its analysis of consumer harm, the Commission stated that the (direct) negative effects on consumers have to outweigh the likely negative effects of the remedy on the consumers. As already discussed in section 5.4.1.2, it is unclear what the negative effects on consumers of, for example a compulsory license, are. According to my point of view, these negative effects are the prevented efficiencies of the abusive conduct. In other words, if the dominant firm refuses to license because it plans to innovate or because it considers the refusal as necessary for the appropriation of its returns, a compulsory license would frustrate these intentions and therewith harm consumers. Consequently, in my opinion, the detection of consumer harms already implies a balancing of efficiencies. From this perspective, the requirement that the efficiencies evoked by the abusive conduct shall outweigh the negatives effects on consumers is an oxymoron. It seems very unlikely, that a strict application of the guidance paper will ever accept the objection of an efficiency defence.

Thus, although it seems as if the introduction of the efficiency defence for refusal to deal cases is pretextual in nature, the analysis of the requirements of consumer harm (and the discussion above) has shown that the Commission also continues including likely efficiencies arising from the abusive conduct.[214]

---

214 Since it is the underlying presumption of Article 102 TFEU that dominant firms are free to choose with whom to deal and under which conditions, the reverse onus of proof introduced with the efficiency defence is questionable. The competition authority must consider the efficiencies in the analysis of the anti-competitive effects (Schweitzer 2007: 22). From this perspective, the weighing of the efficiencies within the detection of

Therewith, like in the Incentives Balance Test, the Commission pursues a rule of reason approach. Instead of separating the detection of the anti-competitive effect and the analysis of efficiencies, though, the Commission combines them.

Therefore, in comparing this proceeding to the Innovation Effects and Appropriability Test, we need to step back and consider the requirements for the detection of consumer harm. As with the comparison to the Incentives Balance Test, two differences exist. First, the Innovation Effects and Appropriability Test does not balance pro- and anti-competitive effects. Second, the Innovation Effects and Appropriablity Test does not consider the overall effects on innovation, but rather restricts itself to the assessment of whether the dominant firm has sufficient possibilities other than intellectual property rights to protect its investment in innovation. If so, the test assumes that an interference of competition policy with intellectual property law would not reduce innovation incentives. The advantage of this is that the test considers only aspects we can measure and assess. In contrast, an assessment of all the effects on innovation and innovation incentives arising with and without a refusal to license is, at least in my opinion, almost impossible because, in a lot of regards, we still do not know enough about what actually drives innovation. In the previous chapter, we saw that monopoly profits can be a source for innovation, competitive pressure can promote innovation, financial strength can influence innovation, and so forth. However, despite this information, we are not certain in which situation which influence factor acts as either a stimulant or deterrent. From this perspective, the Innovation Effects and Appropriability Test cannot claim completeness, but rather must take a simplified approach to gain in practicability.

5.4.3   Problems related to the Innovation Effects and Appropriability Test

Even though the Innovation Effects and Appropriability Test offers the advantages that 1) it is based on available and reliable information and 2) it maintains the goal of promoting innovation, some difficulties remain. For instance, it is questionable how much intellectual property right protection a dominant firm requires. To put it differently, does the dominant firm need the intellectual property rights at all? Or does it use the intellectual property rights in combination with other appropriability instruments?[215] Since we do not (and probably cannot)

---

consumer harm is welcome. Still, the explicit introduction of the efficiency defence and its requirements against the dominant firm is irritating.

215   Another related problem concerns our limited knowledge about innovation incentives. Even if it is possible to argue that the innovator does not necessarily need the intellectual property right, this argument does not tell anything about whether the additional profit through the intellectual property right is nevertheless a desirable spur to innovation (Epstein 2009: 208).

quantify the effectiveness of the alternative instruments, we cannot differentiate. The dominant firm may, in fact, need the intellectual property rights to protect its innovation, but it still may use these rights to leverage its market power in the downstream market. That is, if we were to assign intellectual property rights, we would define a right that still allows a certain element of exploitation but does not cover a refusal to license. From this perspective, the Commission is at least not wrong when it says in the guidance paper that the interruption of a previous supply gives some evidence of an abusive behaviour (European Commission 2009: para. 84). If the firm previously licensed the intellectual property rights to competitors in the downstream market, this can serve as an indicator that the intellectual property right protection was obviously sufficient to appropriate the returns on the upstream market. However, market conditions might change and thus we should be careful in judging too soon.

Another problem related to the Innovation Effects and Appropriability Test is that the test is prone to false negatives in the sense that even though the dominant firm actually needs intellectual property rights, important and socially desirable innovation is nevertheless impeded. That is to say, the value of the protected good is lower than the value of the prevented innovation, for instance when the refusal prohibits the development of an important drug.[216] Due to the missing quantification and balancing of the different effects, the Innovation Effects and Appropriability Test would not capture such a case. At this point, the test does not offer a solution as to how competition authorities should act if they are confronted with that scenario. Because of the missing evaluation of the anticompetitive effects, it is likely that the competition authority is not even aware of the value of the follow-on innovation. But even if its significance becomes obvious, the question remains whether this can change the proceeding of the test. The problem of how to deal with follow-on innovation and how to find the right balance between the interests of first and follow-on innovators is not precisely answered in intellectual property law either. In her paper on cumulative innovation, Scotchmer shows that it is (ex ante) not possible to define intellectual property rights in a way that preserves the interests and provides sufficient incentives for innovators (Scotchmer 1991: 35). It might be arguable that the competition problem occurs ex post, and therefore we are able to (re-)define the concerned intellectual property right ex post as well. Still, I have doubts that this would not affect the innovation incentives of firms.

One might also argue in favour of an exemption; if a socially desirable innovation is impeded, a compulsory license should be imposed independently of

---

216   As Gilbert and Weinschel (2007) point out, the optimal degree of intellectual property protection is not only influenced by the cost of innovation and the ability to protect the innovation apart from intellectual property rights but also by the importance of follow-on innovation (ibid.: 42).

the detection of abusive behaviour by the dominant firm. However, I would be rather careful regarding such exemptions because they may give the competition authorities leeway to interpretation. As already discussed in this chapter, the value of an innovation is only difficult to determine (compare Section 5.1). From this perspective, we do not have reliable instruments to assess and compare the values of innovation while maintaining sufficient innovation incentives for all involved parties. Moreover, the decision as to when an innovation is socially mandatory is not a purely economic question but rather a political issue. Hence, in my opinion, it is adequate to demand from a company an assessment of whether it really relies on intellectual property rights or whether it uses other appropriability instruments. In contrast, demanding the estimation of incentives of follow-on innovation ex ante would increase legal uncertainty and therefore negatively affect innovation. Thus, although the Innovation Effects and Appropriability Test is not free from defects, its benefits outweigh its disadvantages.

5.5 Intermediate Result

In general, this chapter has shown that the previous caselaw developed economically reasonable criteria like the requirements for indispensability, elimination of competition, and prevention of a new product. While the indispensability and elimination of competition requirements basically remained unchanged, we extended the new product criterion to the new criterion "consumer harm" which analyses whether the conduct has negative effects on dynamic efficiency. Moreover, we have seen that already-existing standards for the examination of abuse of dominance cases are not geared to the analysis of refusal to license intellectual property rights. This result confirms our hypothesis from Chapters 2 and 3, where we saw that previous decisions involving refusal to license and intellectual property rights were highly disputed and no consistent standard of analysis existed in these cases.

This led us to the development of a new framework, the Innovation Effects and Appropriability Test. The goal of this test is to provide a standard that considers the specifics of intellectual property rights and relies on economically reasonable theories and criteria. The analysis in Chapter 4 demonstrated that innovation research commands a broad range of theories that are helpful in analysing the effectiveness of intellectual property rights and the availability of other appropriability instruments. These insights constitute the basis of the Innovation Effects and Appropriability Test. After the detection of the anti-competitive effects, our argument is that whenever the dominant firm could easily refer to alternative appropriability instruments, the use of intellectual property rights serves a rather strategic purpose or is simply a pretext for anti-competitive behaviour. Consequently, if the analysis suggests that the dominant firm can choose from a broad range of appropriation strategies, we would deem the refusal to license to be anti-competitive. If, in contrast, the examination shows that the firm acts in an industry in which intellectual property rights are essential for the protection of innovation, the refusal to license is justified. Therewith, we take the availability of other appropriation mechanisms as means in determining whether a firm's intellectual property rights are optimally defined. If the firm has sufficient other mechanisms to appropriate the returns of its innovative efforts, we presume that in a case-by-case assignment of the intellectual property rights the firm would have gained only a very narrow or even no intellectual property right. From this perspective, the interference of competition policy through intellectual property law would not diminish incentives to innovate. This proceeding is in line with the basic idea of the Incentives Balance that was meant to be an ex post definition of intellectual property. However, an ex post definition comprises always a balancing of the welfare effects and hence, a quantification of these effects. The Innovation Effects and Appropriability Test overcomes this hurdle of quantification by focussing solely on the availability of alternative appropriability mechanisms. With the approach set out in the Innovation Effects and Appropriability Test, it is ensured that the dominant firm can always benefit from its innovation. Competition policy would only interfere when the firm tries to exploit the right beyond its designated purpose. As such, the intervention of competition policy through the Innovation Effects and Appropriability Test can be understood as an ex post investigation into whether the intellectual property rights are appropriate or whether they should be redefined through the imposition of a remedy. In case of establishing that the dominant firm could refer to other appropriability mechanisms, the test closes with the determination of the right remedy. In doing so, we highlighted the importance of a monitoring process that analyses whether the remedy is effective. Such monitoring first ensures that competition is reinstalled and second, gives valuable insights for future cases.

Compared to the Incentives Balance Test but also to the standard suggested in the guidance paper, the Innovation Effects and Appropriability Test abstains from balancing the differing welfare effects. While this implies a simplified approach, it has the advantage that the Innovation Effects and Appropriability Test refers only to information we can actually obtain. Consequently, besides the focus on innovation, practicability is a big plus of the test.

6 Lessons Learned and Open Questions

Having outlined our new test to assess refusals to license intellectual property rights, this chapter now briefly recalls the course of the investigations and summarizes the main results of this thesis. However, it should be clear that the results presented do not offer a comprehensive solution for all kinds of cases; instead, they are a starting point for further research. Consequently, the chapter closes with a brief forecast as to in which areas further research is essential.

6.1 Summary of the Results

In Chapter 2, we saw that the approach of the Commission to abuse cases in which dominant firms refused to supply intellectual property rights has evolved over the years. In the *Magill* case, for the first time the Commission applied structured criteria, which were then valid in subsequent cases. According to the so-called *Magill* Test, a refusal to license intellectual property rights is anti-competitive when: 1) the concerned intellectual property right is indispensable for competition in a downstream market; 2) the refusal is likely to eliminate competition in that market; 3) the production of a new product is prohibited; and 4) the refusal cannot be objectively justified. Considering the criteria of indispensability for a downstream market and the requirement of a new product, it seems as if the Commission already aimed at an enhancement of dynamic efficiency. Nevertheless, in some cases, in particular the *IMS Health* case, the Commission tried to circumvent this goal by artificially separating a market for the intellectual property right itself and a market in which the intellectual property right is used. To put it differently, in this case, the Commission basically aimed at an enhancement of static efficiency. Thus, although the Commission tried to stick to criteria from the *Magill* Test, there was also leeway for interpretation, that is, the Commission as well as the European courts adjusted the criteria to the specific circumstances of individual cases.

In the European *Microsoft* case, the strict application of the *Magill* Test became even more challenging. The Commission not only interpreted the criteria from the *Magill* Test very broadly, but it also added a new test: the Incentives Balance Test. The Incentives Balance Test is used in the fourth step of the investigation, that is, as part of the objective justification, and compares the overall innovation incentives when the dominant firm does not license and when it does license. If the innovation incentives are stronger in license situations, the refusal is anti-competitive.

In general, this proceeding seems convincing, as the Commission strongly focuses on innovation. However, the Commission did not further elaborate on what it will consider in weighing innovation incentives. At this point, it rather seems as if the Commission did not undertake a sound economic assessment and evaluation of the assumed incentives on innovation, but instead based its decision on the presumption that lower firm concentration always goes along with more innovation. Although the criteria of the Incentives Balance Test found their way into the new guidance paper to Article 102 TFEU, the Commission still did not clarify on which economic theories it would base future proceedings. From this perspective, it became evident that in regards of an economically founded test for the assessment of refusal to license intellectual property rights, the approach of the Commission was still not convincing.

However, before we proceeded to the analysis of which criteria should be considered in such an economically founded test, Chapter 3 took a step backwards and examined the general relationship between competition policy and intellectual property law. This step was necessary to overcome the perpetual claim that it is the inherent entitlement of intellectual property holders to exclude others from the usage of this right and, hence, an interference of competition policy would unduly constrain that right. Thereby, it is to note that the underlying assumption of intellectual property law is that intellectual property has quasi-public good characteristics; that is, without the protection through the intellectual property right, the innovator could not profit from her efforts but would immediately be copied. However, the comparison of goals proved our initial assumption that competition law and intellectual property law pursue a common goal, which is the promotion of innovation. On this basis, we came to the conclusion that competition law and intellectual property law can be considered to be complementary laws. In detail, this implies that only the interplay of the two can lead to an innovation-enhancing environment. If the exercise of a certain intellectual property right leads to a decline of innovation incentives, for instance because a dominant firm uses its property right together with its market strength to extend its power to another market, competition policy ought to step in and cut the intellectual property right back to an optimal degree of protection. From this perspective, the Commission's proceeding in the *Microsoft* case can be interpreted as a first attempt to use competition policy to tailor intellectual property rights in those cases in which they do not fulfil their goal of enhancing dynamic efficiency. However, even though this interpretation gives a justification for the basic idea of the Incentives Balance Test, it does not put the test on a solid economic grounding.

Consequently, in Chapter 4 we started with a literature survey on the law and economics of intellectual property rights in order to analyse how an optimal right should indeed look and whether these theories can be applied in a competition political analysis. This survey showed that plenty of theories and approaches exist as to how to determine the optimal length and scope of both patents and copyrights. However, at the same time it became obvious that these theories are only applicable in practice to a small extent. The application of these theories is related to two main problems: 1) the theories do not consider alternative appropriation mechanisms, that is, they treat intellectual property rights as the only possibility to protect innovation from imitation; and 2) the determination of optimal (welfare enhancing) intellectual property rights demands comprehensive information, which we do not have in reality.

Hence, in the next step in Chapter 4 we focused on the insights of general innovation economics, especially evolutionary economic theories and the resourced-based view of the firm. Thereby, we yielded two essential results. First, we learned that the basic assumption of intellectual property law, which is that without protection competitors would be able to freely and immediately imitate the innovation, is only convincing in the world of perfection competition. Considering that innovation is the outcome of a long learning process that requires different capabilities, potential imitators first need to achieve certain capabilities before they can copy the imitation. Moreover, routines and firm-specific knowledge complicate the imitation process because they are not observable from outside the firm. Thus, the public good problematic of intellectual property is not as severe as described in the neoclassic economics of intellectual property rights. Second, the literature survey shows that firms have more possibilities of appropriating the returns of their innovations. Depending on the type of innovation, specifically the distinction between complex and discrete technologies, firms have appropriability instruments like lead time and complementary assets to protect their innovation from (immediate) imitation and to earn a sufficient reward for their investments. Empirical studies prove that intellectual property rights play only a minor role in the protection of innovation. Instead, those firms with alternative appropriability mechanisms often use intellectual property rights for strategic purposes, for instance to strengthen their negotiating positions in cross-licensing agreements or simply to impede rivals. From this perspective, we can argue that in those cases in which firms have sufficient alternative appropriability instruments, intellectual property rights are not essential for innovation.

In the last part of Chapter 4, we analysed the relationship between market structure and innovation as well as the influence of certain market features on innovation. With regards to the relationship between market structure and innovation, we came to the conclusion that a clear statement such as "low firm concentration always spurs innovation" is not possible. Instead, it is necessary to differentiate and analyse the particular conditions in the concerned market. As such, we proved that it is not possible to determine anti-competitive effects simply by market structure. Turning to markets with network effects we saw that specific market characteristics influence market structure and have an impact on conditions for complementary or follow-on innovation. Accordingly, in markets with network effects, it is necessary to differentiate between products constituting the standard and products that are applications or features of the standards. While there is a natural tendency for a highly concentrated market structure for the standard, for example, a software platform, competition is normally possible in the related markets. Since the standard is regulated by few firms, it constitutes a bottleneck for competition in the downstream markets, as the applications offered by other firms need to be compatible with the standard. Therefore, barrier-free access to the standard is essential for competing and innovating in that downstream market. Thus, while any effort of competition authorities to bring more competition into the market for the network good itself will probably fail, competition authorities should pay attention to the question of whether other firms have access to the network good and are therefore able to offer compatible products. Again, this result shows that it is necessary to differentiate before making a certain judgement.

The chapter closes with an assessment as to whether the criteria outlined throughout the chapter can be applied within the Incentives Balance Test. Thereby we noted that a balancing always requires a quantification of the different effects since otherwise a comparison of the effects is not possible. Although this chapter provided us with valuable insights, we can use these results only for a qualitative analysis. Due to a lack of comprehensive information and due to the complexity of the required information, we are not able to quantify the different effects. Against this background, we concluded that the Incentives Balance Test is not practical and that we have to search for an alternative instrument to analyse refusal to license intellectual property rights cases.

Consequently, in the last chapter we turned to the question of how such an alternative instrument of competition policy should look. Therefore, we first established criteria for the determination of the anti-competitive effects of a refusal to license. After reviewing the previous criteria – that the intellectual property be indispensable for competition in the downstream market and that there be a new product – for the detection of anti-competitive effects, the examination showed that these criteria can be justified from an economic perspective. However, the analysis also showed that the new product requirement is probably too narrow because it does not consider innovations that are on an earlier development level. Such proceedings would not cope with the complexity of innovation processes. Consequently, while upholding the requirement of indispensability, we extended the new product criterion to "consumer harm," defining consumer harm as the impediment of innovation and technological progress.

Before we turned to the development of a new framework for the assessment of refusal to license intellectual property rights cases, we reviewed already-existing standards to assess abuse of dominance cases. However, this review proved that, to date, no test exists that is appropriate to consider the specifics of cases involving intellectual property rights. The shortcoming of most approaches is that they focus mainly on static effects. From my point of view, such a focus is not appropriate in the case of intellectual property rights as it is the special intent of intellectual property law to promote innovation. Concentrating on static effects would therefore undercut this goal. Thus, it became evident that it is necessary to develop an alternative test that embraces the specific goal of intellectual property law (and competition policy as well).

Eventually, this led us to the development of the Innovation Effects and Appropriability Test, which shall close the aforementioned gap. Based on our results from Chapter 4, the basic idea of the Innovation Effects and Appropriability Test is to scrutinize whether the dominant firm has appropriability instruments other than intellectual property rights to protect its innovation. If the dominant firm has sufficient alternatives and uses the intellectual property rights more or less only for strategic purposes, the refusal to license is not necessary to protect the innovation. Thus, the conduct can be deemed as anti-competitive.

In detail, the Innovation Effects and Appropriability Test starts with the detection of the anti-competitive effect. As such, it equals the proceedings in previous case law. Only if the refused intellectual property right is indispensable for competition in the downstream market and only if it is necessary for further innovation, the conduct has anti-competitive effects. These criteria shall guarantee that solely those refusals to supply that indeed affect dynamic efficiency can be deemed to be detrimental to competition. The underlying idea is that certain static inefficiencies are already part of the intellectual property right. Forcing firms to license when static efficiency is impeded would undercut the goal of intellectual property rights as it would open the door for simple copying. Having detected the anti-competitive effect, the Innovation Effects and Appropriability Test examines whether the dominant firm has alternative appropriability mechanisms besides intellectual property rights. In doing so, the test recognizes that intellectual property rights are assigned to ensure a certain reward to the inventor. As we saw in Chapter 4, it is almost impossible to determine the optimal scope of intellectual property rights. Consequently, we use the existence of alternative appropriability mechanisms as a proxy for the necessity of intellectual property rights. In those cases in which (dominant) firms have multiple other appropriability mechanisms, I argue that those intellectual property rights are assigned too broad or maybe not even necessary at all, because the firm has enough incentive to innovate. In those cases, firms would also innovate absent intellectual property rights because they have alternatives to appropriate a reward for their investments. Thus, the reasoning that a dominant firm refuses to license because it needs to protect its innovation would fail. In contrast, if the analysis shows that the dominant firm must rely on its intellectual property rights and has no workable alternative possibility to protect its innovation, the Innovation Effects and Appropriability Test would acknowledge the intellectual property right and would decide that the refusal to license is not an anti-competitive attempt to extend the dominant position but a legal enforcement of its rights.

Hence, a decision based on the Innovation Effects and Appropriability Test focuses on the promotion of dynamic efficiency and at the same time upholds the rights and the purpose of intellectual property. Such a proceeding has the advantage that an interference of competition policy would both enhance competition and maintain innovation incentives for firms. In comparison to the test conducted in the *Microsoft* case and the criteria outlined in the Article 102 TFEU guidance paper, the Innovation Effects and Appropriability Test has the further advantage that it is relatively simple to apply. While it is a very difficult and complex, if not impossible, undertaking to analyse and quantity the effects on innovation, it is comparatively to assess whether a company has alternative appropriability instruments. This fact does not only facilitate the analysis of the competition authorities but also enhances the legal certainty of firms. Since the Innovation Effects and Appropriability Test sets out very clear criteria, each firm should be able to assess whether its conduct would be in line with the law or whether it would be judged to be anti-competitive under Article 102 TFEU.

6.2 Fields of Further Research

Besides these benefits, it should be clear that the Innovation Effects and Appropriability Test can only be a starting point for further research. While giving some indication as to how a test to examine refusal to license intellectual property rights cases should look, the test introduced here has at least two shortcomings: 1) it restricts the broad concept of dynamic efficiency to appropriability; and 2) it generalizes between intellectual property rights. In the following section, I will briefly outline why it is worthwhile to undertake further research in this regard.

6.2.1   Implementing a Dynamic Perspective

Looking at current legal practice in competition policy, we can observe that there is a bias towards static efficiencies (e.g. Ahlborn/Evans/Padilla 2001: 161). In detail, the focus of analysis seems to lie mostly on price effects and fails to consider dynamic efficiency. For instance, the experience in merger control has shown that since the introduction of the "more economic approach," effects on quantities and prices have grown in importance.[217] Even though we established in Chapter 3 that competition law and intellectual property law are complementary, this was based on the assumption that the two types of law promote the same goal: dynamic efficiency. From this perspective, in order to maintain this common goal, it is necessary to focus the analysis of competition policy on the effects on innovation as well. In contrast, if competition policy concentrates on static effects, this withdraws the foundation of complementarity since in a static

---

217 Examples for this are cases no. COMP/M.3333 – *Sony/BMG*, Commission Decision 19/07/2007 and COMP/M.3216 – *Oracle/Peoplesoft*, Commission Decision 26/10/2004. For a detailed discussion of these cases, compare Christiansen 2010; Budzinki/Christiansen 2006; Aigner/Budzinksi/Christiansen 2006.

world, competition law promotes lower prices whereas intellectual property law promotes higher prices (compare section 3.2.3). Hence, the question arises as to why competition authorities and courts tend to base their decisions on static effects – despite the general acknowledgment of the role of innovation in economic growth. As Evans (2005) points out, courts (and competition authorities) rely in their decision-making process on insights and knowledge provided by economists:

> "So what do these customers of economic insight need? They [the courts] would be delighted if we [the economists] could give them necessary and sufficient conditions for a practice to be anti-competitive or pro-competitive – provided, of course, that those conditions could be verified with accessible evidence. While that is a laudable goal, I doubt that many economists believe that the discipline will yield such robust results. The fault lies less with the state of economic science and more with the complexity of the world we study." (Evans 2005: 97)

In other words, implementing the goal of dynamic efficiency is connected with at least some uncertainty as it is simply not possible to predict reliably future developments. Further, as we already observed in the course of this thesis, it is difficult to assess the value of technological development whereas price effects are comparatively easy to measure. Although drivers and sources of technological development and innovation in many regards still constitute a "black box,"[218] a lot of research has been undertaken to light up this box, especially in evolutionary economics. According to Dosi (1997), the analysis of technological progress can be divided into four research objects: 1) innovative opportunities; 2) incentives to exploit these opportunities; 3) the capabilities of the agents to realize such exploitation, and; 4) organizational arrangements and mechanisms for the search and realization of the innovative opportunities (ibid.: 1532). In the course of this thesis, we discussed primarily the second object and also the third object (compare Chapter 4.2). However, by discussing the incentives to innovate, we concentrated exclusively on the possibilities of appropriation. Even though this approach is in line with the state of the art in evolutionary economics, it is notable that the question of appropriation is not a comprehensive depiction of the incentives problem (Dosi 1997: 1533). Thus, further research is mandatory in this area. Only when economics can provide results regarding the analysis of effects on innovation and on innovation incentives can competition authorities and courts consider dynamic efficiency in their decisions.

Apart from the implementation of dynamic efficiency in the analysis of the anti-competitive conduct itself, it is actually necessary to incorporate this dynamic perspective one step earlier at the level of the determination of market power. At present, competition authorities almost exclusively use models focus-

---

218 *Inside the Black Box* is a famous book by Nathan Rosenberg (1982) discussing the relationship between technology and economics.

ing on price effects to establish market share. For instance, the competition authority analyses whether a hypothetical monopolist could increase prices profitably (hypothetical monopolist or Small but Significant Non-transitory Increase in Prices (SSNIP) test) or whether substitutes for the product of the dominant firm exist in regards to the product characteristics, price, application possibilities, and so on (Kerber/Schwalbe 2008: 264). Thus, in the determination of the relevant market and therewith in the establishment of the dominant position, the competition authorities merely include already-existing products but do not include the competitive threat by potential new products. However, in the guidance paper to Article 102 TFEU, the Commission states that it will not only account for the current market share but, where necessary, also consider the dynamics of the market (European Commission 2009: para. 13). Yet it remains questionable how the Commission plans to do so or whether it is only paying lip service to dynamic efficiency. Further research is needed as to whether an analysis of the anti-competitive effects based on a static definition of the market does not already suppress some dynamic effects and how a market definition considering dynamic efficiency should look.

6.2.2   Differentiation between the Various Types of Intellectual Property Rights (One Size Cannot Fit All)

Another area of further research lies in the field of intellectual property rights. In Chapter 4, we saw that the justifications for patents and copyrights differs and also that the models for the determination of their optimal scope differs. Whereas copyright only prohibits the copying of a certain expression in that it is still possible to copy the idea and bring a similar product to the market, patent protection is generally broader in that the innovator gets an exclusive right that prevents competitors from practising the invention (Farrell/Shapiro 2004). The legal differentiation between copyrights and patents aims at different needs of the varying industries and their developments.

Hence, one can argue that because of the different definitions and determinations of patents and copyrights, one must also differentiate in an analysis through competition policy as well. However, I have my doubts regarding this line of argument. From an economic point of view, both competition law and intellectual property rights law aim at the creation of innovation incentives by offering a certain reward. Thus, in those cases in which scepticism exists that the way the concerned right is exercised is really necessary for the appropriation of a reward but instead aims at the impediment of competition, it seems only reasonable to analyse whether the intellectual property right holder (in our case, a dominant firm) indeed needs the intellectual property right or whether it has alternative ways to protect its innovation. In my opinion, this analysis does not necessarily have to differentiate between copyrights and patents; in the course of this thesis, we saw that it is necessary to differentiate according to industries, involved technologies, and so on. Thus, with such an approach it should be possible to meet the requirements of the varying industries without differentiating according to copyrights and patents.

Instead, it should be an ongoing discussion as to whether some of the problems intellectual property law has with competition law are not intrinsic. For instance, in the *Magill* case, one might question whether the television programs are indeed worth a copyright. We have also seen that the economic literature on patents is much more developed and advanced than the economic literature on copyrights. Thus, it is also necessary to undertake some more research in this regard. From this perspective, lawyers, legal scholars, and also economic scholars concerned with intellectual property right law should not rely on competition policy to solve all the problems on the interface between intellectual property rights and competition, but rather they should try to think about a more differentiated assignment of intellectual property rights.

6.3 Conclusion

To conclude, even though there are still plenty of unanswered questions, the Innovation Effects and Appropriability Test builds an economically founded basis for the interference of competition law with intellectual property rights in refusal to license cases. By focusing on the availability of alternative appropriation mechanisms, the Innovation Effects and Appropriability Test creates a balance between the promotion of innovation on the one hand and the maintenance of competition on the other.

Bibliography

Agarwal. Rajshree/ Gort, Michael (1999): First Mover Advantage and the Speed of Competitive Entry, 1887-1986. Working Paper. Online available at http://papers.ssrn.com/sol3/papers.cfm?abstract_id=167330 (last visiti 2009-11-16).

Ahlborn, Christian/ Evans, David S. (2008): The Microsoft Judgment and its Implications for Competition Policy towards Dominant Firms in Europe. Working Paper. Online available at http://ssrn.com/abstract=1115867 (last visit 2009-02-20).

Ahlborn, Christian/ Evans, David S./ Padilla, Atilana Jorge (2001): Competition Policy in the New Economy: Is European Competition Law Up to the Challenge? In: European Competition Law Review, Vol. 22, pp. 156-167.

Aigner, Gisela/ Budzinski, Oliver/ Christiansen, Arndt (2006): The Analysis of Coordinated Effects in EU Merger Control: Where Do We Stand after Sony/BMG and Impala? Working Paper. Online available at http://ssrn.com/abstract=933548 (last visit 2009-10-29).

Akerlof, George A./ Arrow, Kenneth J./ Breshnahan, Timothy F./ Buchanan, James M./ Coase, Ronald H./ Cohen, Linda R./ Friedman, Milton/ Green, Jerry R./ Hahn, Robert H./ Hazlett, Thomas W./ Hemphill, C. Scott/ Litan, Robert E./ Noll, Robert G./ Schmalensee, Richard/ Shavell, Steven/ Varian, Hal R./ Zeckhauser, Richard J. (2002): Amici Curiae in Support of Petitioners in the Supreme Court of the United States, Eldred versus Ashcroft.

Albers, Michael (2006): Der „more economic approach" bei Verdrängungsmissbräuchen: Zum Stand der Überlegungen der Europäischen Kommission. Discussion Paper, online available at http://ec.europa.eu/competition/antitrust/art82/albers.pdf (last visit 2010-01-06).

Alchian, Armen A./ Demsetz, Harold (1973): The Property Rights Paradigm. In: The Journal of Economic History, Vol. 33, pp. 16-27.

Allison, John R./ Lemley, Mark A. (2000): Who's Patenting What? An Empirical Exploration of Patent Prosecution. In: Vanderbilt Law Review, Vol. 53, pp- 2099-2174.

Altmann, Jörg (2000): Wirtschaftspolitik. 7th edition, Stuttgart: Lucius & Lucius.

Anderman, Steven D. (1998): EC Competition Law and Intellectual Property Rights: The Regulation of Innovation. New York/ Oxford: Clarendon press.

Anton, James J./ Yao, Dennis, A. (2004): Little Patents and Big Secrets: Managing Intellectual Property. In: RAND Journal of Economics, Vol. 35, pp. 1-22.

Areeda, Phillip/ Hovenkamp, Herbert (2008): Antitrust Law, Vol. 3. 3rd ed., New York, NY: Aspen Law & Business.

Arrow, Kenneth J. (1959): Economic Welfare and the Allocation of Resources for Invention. In: Rand Cooperation, Discussion Paper No. P 1856RC, Santa Monica.

Arora, Ashish/ Ceccagnoli, Marco (2004): Patent Protection, Complementary Assets, and Firms' Incentives for Technology Licensing. Working Paper, Carnegie Mellon University, Pittsburgh. Online available at http://www.heinz.cmu.edu/research/170full.pdf (last visit 2009-06-22).

Arundel, Anthony (2001): The relative effectiveness of patents and secrecy for appropriation. In: Research Policy, Vol. 30, pp. 611-624.

Audretsch, David B. (1988): Divergent Views in Antitrust Economics. In: The Antitrust Bulletin, Vol. 33, pp. 135-160.

Bain, Joe S. (1956): Barriers to New Competition. Cambridge, Massachusetts: Harvard University Press.

Baker, Jonathan B. (2007): Beyond Schumpeter v. Arrow: How Antitrust Fosters Innovation. In: Antitrust Law Journal, Vol. 74, pp. 575-602.

Baldwin, John/ Hanel, Petr/ Sabourin, David (2002): Determinants of Innovative Activity in Canadian Manufacturing Firms: The Role of Intellectual Property Rights. In: Kleinkrecht, Alfred / Mohnen, Pierre (eds.), Innovation and Firm Performance – Economic Explorations of Survey Data, London, UK; pp. 86-111.

Banasevic, Nicholas/ Huby, Jean/ Pena Castellot, Miguel/Sitar, Oliver/ Piffaut, Henri (2004): Commission Adopts Decision in the Microsoft Case. In: Competition Policy Newsletter 2004, No. 2, pp. 44-48.

Barnett, Thomas O. (2009): Section 2 Remedies: What to Do After Catching the Tiger by the Tail. In: Antitrust Law Journal, Vol. 76, pp. 31-41.

Barney, Jay B. (1991): Firm Resources and Sustained Competitive Advantage. In: Journal of Management, Vol. 17, pp. 99-120.

Barney, Jay B. (1986): Strategic Factor Markets: Expectations, Luck and Business Strategy. In: Management Science, Vol. 32, pp. 1231-1241.

Bartosch, Andreas (2007): Das Urteil des Europäischen Gerichts erster Instanz in der Rechtssache Microsoft. In: Recht der Internationalen Wirtschaft, Vol. 53, pp. 908-919.

Baumol, William J./ Panzar, John C./ Willig, Robert D. (1982): Contestable Markets and the Theory of Industry Structure. New York: Harcourt Brace Jovanovich.

Becker, Lawrence C. (1993): Deserving to Own Intellectual Property. In: Chicago-Kent Law Review, Vol. 68, pp. 609-629.

Besanko, David/ Spulber, Daniel F. (1993): Contested Mergers and Equilibrium Antitrust Policy. In: Journal of Law, Economics, and Organization, Vol. 9, pp. 1-29.

Besen, Stanley M./ Saloner, Garth (1989): Compatibility Standards and The Market for Telecommunications Services. In: Crandall, Robert/ Flamm, Kenneth (eds.): Changing Rules: Technological Change, International Competition, and Regulation in Telecommunications. Washington: The Brookings Institution, pp. 177-220.

Bergin, James (2008): Optimal Patent Length. Working Paper, University College Dublin. Online available at http://ideas.repec.org/p/ucd/wpaper/200808.html (last visit 2009-10-28).

Bernstein, Jeffrey I./ Nadiri, M. Ishaq (1991): Product Demand, Cost of Production, Spillovers, and the Social Rate of Return to R&D. NBER Working Paper 3625. Stanford, CA.

Boldrin, Michele/ Levine, David (2005): IP and Market Size. Levine's Working Paper Archive 618897000000000836, UCLA Department of Economics. Online available at http://ideas.repec.org/s/cla/levarc.html (last visit 2008-02-25).

Boone, Jan (2001): Intensity of Competition and the Incentive to Innovate. In: International Journal of Industrial Organization, Vol. 19, pp. 705-726.

Bork, Robert H. (1978): The Antitrust Paradox: A Policy at War With Itself. Reprinted 1993, New York: The Free Press.

Botteman, Yves/ Ewing, Kenneth P. (2009): Guidance on Enforcement Priorities Regarding Exclusionary Abuses: A Comparative Overview. In: Global Competition Policy, February 2009.

Bowman, Ward S. Jr. (1957): Tying Arrangements and the Leverage Problem. In: Yale Law Journal, Vol. 67, pp. 19-37.

Bresnahan, Timothy F. (2002): The Right Remedy. John M. Olin Program in Law and Economics Working Paper No. 233, Stanford, California. Online available at http://ssrn.com/abstract_id=304702 (last visit 2009-08-05).

Breyer, Stephen (1970): The Uneasy Case for Copyright: A Study of Copyright in Books, Photocopies, and Computer Programs. In: Harvard Law Review, Vol. 84, pp. 281-351.

Brodley, Joseph F. (1987): The Economic Goals of Antitrust: Efficiency, Consumer Welfare, and Technological Progress. In: New York University Law Review, Vol. 62, pp. 1020-1053.

Budzinski, Oliver (2008): Monoculture versus Diversity in Competition Economics. In: Cambridge Journal of Economics, Vol. 32, pp. 295-324.

Budzinski, Oliver (2004): An Evolutionary Theory of Competition, Working Paper, online available at http://www.uni-marburg.de/fb02/wipol/team/wiss-ma/budz/public (last visit 2007-08-14).

Budzinski, Oliver/ Christiansen, Arndt (2006): Simulating the (Unilateral) Effects on Mergers: Implications of the Oracle/PeopleSoft Case. Working

Paper, Marburg. Online available at http://ssrn.com/abstract=924375 (last visit 2009-10-12).

Burr, Wolfgang/ Musil, Antje/ Stephan, Michael/ Werkmeister, Clemens (2005): Unternehmensführung. München: Verlag Vahlen.

Burr, Wolfgang/ Stephan, Michael/ Soppe, Birthe/ Weisheit, Steffen (2007): Patentmangement: Strategischer Einsatz und ökonomische Bewertung von technologischen Schutzrechten. Stuttgart: Schäffer-Poeschel.

Byrne, David (2006): Compulsory Licensing of IP Rights: Has EC Competition Law Reached a Clear and Rational Analysis Following the IMS Judgment and the Microsoft Decision? In: Journal of Intellectual Property Law and Practice, Vol. 2, pp. 1-14.

Canoy, Marcel/ Rey, Patrick/ van Damme, Eric (2004): Dominance and Monopolization. In: Neuman, Manfred/ Weigand, Jürgen (eds.): International Handbook of Competition. Cheltenham, UK: Edward Elgar, pp. 210-289.

Carlton, Dennis W. (2007): Does Antitrust Need to Be Modernized? In: Journal of Economic Perspectives, Vol. 21 pp. 155–176.

Caves, Richard E./ Porter, Michael E. (1977): From Entry Barriers to Mobility Barriers: Conjectural Decision and Contrived Deterrence to Competition. In: Quarterly Journal of Economics, Vol. 91, pp. 241-262.

Chang, Howard F. (1995): Patent Scope, Antitrust Policy, and Cumulative Innovation. In: The RAND Journal of Economics, Vol. 26, pp. 34-57.

Chou, Teyu/ Haller, Hans (1995): The Division of Profit in Sequential Innovation Reconsidered. Department of Economics Working Paper no. E95-02, Virginia Polytechnic Institute and State University.

Christiansen, Arndt (2010): Der „More Economic Approach" in der EU-Fusionskontrolle: Entwicklung, konzeptionelle Grundlagen und kritische Analyse. Frankfurt a. M.: Peter Lang.

Christiansen, Arndt (2006): The Reform of EU Merger Control – Fundamental Reversal or Mere Refinement? Forthcoming in: Columbus, Frank H. (ed.): Antitrust Policy Issues. Hauppage, NY: Nova Science Publication. Online available at http://papers.ssrn.com/sol3/papers.cfm?abstract_id=898845 (last visit 2009-10-20).

Christiansen, Arndt/ Kerber, Wolfgang (2006): Competition Policy with Optimally Differentiated Rules Instead of "Per Se Rules vs Rule of Reason." In: Journal of Competition Law and Economics, Vol. 2, pp. 215-244.

Coase, Ronald H. (1960): The Problem of Social Cost. In: Journal of Law and Economics, Vol. 3, pp. 1-44.

Coase, Ronald H. (1937): The Nature of the Firm. In: Economica, Vol. 4, pp. 386-405.

Cohen, Julie E. (1998): *Lochner* in Cyberspace: The New Economic Orthodoxy of "Rights Management." In: Michigan Law Review, Vol. 97, pp. 462-563.

Cohen, William E. (1996): Competition and Foreclosure in the Context of In-
stalled Base and Compatibility Effects. In: Antitrust Law Journal, Vol. 64,
pp. 535-569.

Cohen, Wesley W./ Levinthal, Daniel A. (1990): Absorptive Capacity: A New
Perspective on Learning and Innovation. In: Administrative Science Quarterly, Vol. 35, pp. 128-152.

Cohen, Wesley W./ Levinthal, Daniel A. (1989): Innovation and Learning: The
Two Faces of R&D. In: The Economic Journal, Vol. 99, pp. 569-596.

Cohen, Wesley W./ Nelson, Richard R./ Walsh, John P. (2000): Protecting their
Intellectual Assets: Appropriability Conditions and Why U.S Manufacturing Firms Patent (or Not). Working Paper, online available at
http://www.nber.org/papers/w7552 (last visit 2007-08-17)

Comanor, William S. (2001): The Problem of Remedy in Monopolization Cases:
The Microsoft Case as an Example. In: Antitrust Bulletin, Vol. 46, pp.
115-133.

Comanor, William S./ Wilson, Thomas A. (1979): Advertising and Competition:
A Survey. In: Journal of Economic Literature, Vol. 17, pp. 453-476.

Cotter, Thomas F. (2008): Reflections on the Antitrust Modernization Commission's Report and Recommendations Relating to the Antitrust/IP Interface. In: The Antitrust Bulletin, Vol. 53, pp. 745-801.

Craig, Carys J. (2002): Locke, Labour and Limiting the Author's Right: A
Warning Against a Lockean Appproach to Copyright Law. In: Queen's
Law Journal, Vol. 28, pp. 1-60.

Crampton, Paul S. (1994): Consumers' Surplus, Total Surplus, Total Welfare
and Non-Efficiency Goals. In: World Competition, Vol. 17, pp. 55-86.

Crandall, Robert W. (2001): The Failure of Structural Remedies in Sherman Act
Monopolization Cases. In: Oregon Law Review, Vol. 80, pp. 109-197.

Creuss, Antonio/ Augustinoy, Albert (2000): The Operative System as an Essential Facility: An Open Door to Windows? In: World Competition, Vol. 23,
pp. 57–78.

Cseres, Katalin (2007): The Controversies of the Consumer Welfare Standard.
In: The Competition Law Review, Vol. 3, pp. 121-173.

Damstedt, Benjamin G. (2003): Limiting Locke: A Natural Law Justification for
the Fair Use Doctrine. In: Yale Law Journal, Vol. 112, pp. 1179-1221.

Dasgupta, Partha/ Stiglitz, Joseph (1980): Uncertainty, Industrial Structure and
the Speed of R&D. In: The Bell Journal of Economics, Vol. 11, pp. 1-28.

David, Paul A. (1985): Clio and the Economics of QWERTY. In: The American
Economic Review, Vol. 75, pp. 332-337.

Demsetz, Harold (1982): Barriers to Entry. In: The American Economic Review, Vol. 72, pp. 47-57.

Demsetz, Harold (1979): Accounting for Advertising as a Barrier to Entry. In:
The Journal of Business, Vol. 52, pp. 345-360.

Demsetz, Harold (1967): Towards a Theory of Property Rights. In: The American Economic Review, Vol. 57, pp. 347-359

Denicolò, Vincenzo (1996): Patent Races and Optimal Patent Breadth and Length. In: The Journal of Industrial Economics, Vol. 54, pp. 249-265.

Denison, Edward F. (1985): Trends in American Economic Growth, 1929-1982. Washington D.C.: The Brookings Institution.

Department of Justice [DoJ] (2008): Competition and Monopoly: Single Firm Conduct under Section 2 of the Sherman Act. Washington D.C., online available at http://www.usdoj.gov/atr/public/reports/236681.htm (last visit 2009-03-20).

Department of Justice [DoJ] (2007): Assistant Attorney General for Antitrust, Thomas o. Barnett, Issues Statement on European Microsoft Decision. Press Release Monday September 17, 2007, Washington D.C. Online available at http://www.usdoj.gov/atr/public/press_releases/2007/226070.pdf   (last visit 2009-10-22).

Department of Justice/ Federal Trade Commission [DoJ/ FTC] (1995): Antitrust Guidelines for Licensing of Intellectual Property. Online available at http://www.ftc.gov/bc/0558.pdf (last visit 2010-01-22).

Derclaye, Estelle (2003): Abuses of dominant position and intellectual property rights: a suggestion to reconcile the community courts case law. In: World Competition, Vol. 26, pp. 685-705.

Dierickx, Ingemar/ Cool, Karel (1989): Asset Stock Accumulation and Sustainability of Competitive Advantage. In: Management Science, Vol. 35, pp. 1504-1511.

Director, Aaron/ Levi, Edward (1956): Law and the Future: Trade Regulation. In: Northwestern University Law Review, Vol. 51, pp. 281-296.

Doherty, Barry (2001): Just what are Essential Facilities? In: Common Market Law Review, Vol. 38, pp. 397-436.

Dolmans, Maurits (2009): Interoperability Remedy Proposal. Speech at the European Committee for Interoperable Systems (ECIS) Workshop, 23.09.2009, Brussels.

Dolmans, Maurits/ Graf, Thomas (2004): Analysis of Tying under Article 82 EC: The European Commission's Microsoft Decision in Perspective. In: World Competition, Vol. 27, pp. 225-244.

Dolmans, Maurits/ O'Donoghue, Robert/ Loewenthal, Paul-John (2007): Are Article 82 EC and Intellectual Property Interoperable? The State of the Law Pending the Judgement in Microsoft v. Commision. In: Competition Policy International, Vol. 3, pp. 107-144.

Dosi, Giovanni (1997): Opportunities, Incentives, and the Collective Patterns of Technological Change. In: The Economic Journal, Vol. 107, pp. 1530-1547.

Dosi, Giovanni (1988): The nature of the innovative process. In: Dosi, Giovanni et al. (eds): Technical Change and Economic Theory. London, pp. 221-238.

Dosi, Giovanni/ Malerba, Franco/ Ramello, Giovanni B./ Silva, Francesco (2006): Information, appropriability, and the generation of innovative knowledge four decades after Arrow and Nelson: an introduction. In: Industrial and Corporate Change, Vol. 15, pp. 891-901.

Dosi, Giovanni/ Marengo, Luigi/ Pasquali, Corrado (2006): Knowledge, competition and appropriability: Is strong IPR protection always needed for more and better innovations? Unpublished Working Paper, Pisa.

Drahos, Peter (1996): A philosophy of intellectual property. Brookfield, Vermont: Dartmouth.

Dreyfuss, Rochelle (2005): Unique Works/ Unique Challenges at the Intellectual Property/ Competition Law Interface. In: Ehlermann, Claus-Dieter/ Atanasiu, Isabela (eds.): European Competition Law Annual 2005: The Interaction between Competition Law and Intellectual Property Law. Oxford: Hart Publishing. Online available at http://ssrn.com/abstract=763688 (last visit: 2008-10-27).

Drexl, Josef (2004): Intellectual Property and Antitrust law – IMS Health and Trinko – Antitrust Placebo for Consumer Instead of Sound Economics in Refusal-to-Deal Cases. In: International Review of Intellectual Property and Competition Law, Vol. 2004, pp. 788-808.

Economides, Nicholas (2005): Vertical Leverage and the Sacrifice Principle: Why the Supreme Court Got Trinko Wrong. NET Institute Working Paper No. 05-05, online available at http://papers.ssrn.com/sol3/papers.cfm?abstract_id=797142 (last visit 2008-10-18).

Economides, Nicholas (2004): Competition Policy in Network Industries: An Introduction. In: Jansen, Dennis (ed.): The New Economy and Beyond: Past, Present and Future, Edward Elgar, pp. 96-121.

Economides, Nicholas (1996): The Economics of Networks. In: International Journal of Industrial Organization, Vol. 14, pp. 673-699.

Economides, Nicholas (1988): The Economics of Trademarks. In: Trademark Reporter, Vol. 78, pp. 523-539.

Economides, Nicholas/ Flyer, Fredrick (1998): Compatibility and Market Structure for Network Goods. Discussion Paper EC-98-02, Stern School of Business, New York. Online available at http://www.stern.nyu.edu/networks/98-02.pdf (last visit 2009-07-20)

Economides, Nicholas/ Lianos, Ioannis (2009): The Quest for Appropriate Remedies in the Microsoft Antitrust EU cases: A comparative Appraisal. NET Institute Working No. 09-05, online available at http://ssrn.com/abstract=1464505 (last visit 2009-10-28).

Eilmansberger, Thomas (2003): Abschlusszwang und Essential Facility Doktrin nach Art. 82 EG: Überlegungen aus Anlass der Entscheidung „IMS Health". In: Europäisches Wirtschafts- und Steuerrecht, Vol. 2003, pp. 12-23.

Elzinga, Kenneth G./ Evans, David S./ Nichols, Albert L. (2001): United States v. Microsoft: Remedy or Malady? In: George Mason Law Review, Vol. 9, pp. 633-690.

Epstein, Richard A. (2009): Monopolization Follies: The Dangers of Structural Remedies under Section 2 of the Sherman Act. In: Antitrust Law Journal, Vol. 76, pp. 205-237.

Eucken, Walter (1952): Grundsätze der Wirtschaftspolitik. Ed. by Edit Eucken and Karl Paul Hensel, Tübingen: Mohr Siebeck.

European Advisory Group of Competition Policy (2005): An economic approach to Article 82. Online available at http://ec.europa.eu/comm/competition/publications/studies/eagcp_july_21_05.pdf (last visit 2008-10-08).

European Commission (2009): Guidance on the Commission's Enforcement Priorities in Applying Article 82 EC Treaty to Abusive Exclusionary Conduct by Dominant Undertakings. Official Journal C 45/02, pp. 7- 20.

European Commission (2004): Guidelines on the assessment of horizontal mergers under the Council Regulation on the control of concentrations between undertakings. OJ C 31, 5.2.2004, pp. 5–18.

European Commission (2001): Innobarometer 2001. Innovation Papers No. 22, online available at http://cordis.europa.eu/innovation/en/policy/innobarometer2001.htm (last visit 2009-06-22).

European Commission (1999): XXIXth Report on Competition Policy 1999. Brussels. Online available at http://ec.europa.eu/competition/annual_reports/1999/en.pdf (last visit 2009-01-21).

Evans, David S. (2005): How Economists Can Help Courts Design Competition Rules: An EU and US Perspective. In: World Competition, Vol. 28, pp. 93-99.

Evans, David S./ Padilla, A. Jorge (2004): Tying under Article 82 EC and the Microsoft Decision: A Comment on Dolmans and Graf. In: World Competition, Vol. 27, pp. 503-512.

Farrell, Joseph (1989): Standardization and Intellectual Property. In: Jurimetrics Journal, Vol. 30, pp. 35-50.

Farrell, Joseph/ Katz, Michael L. (2006): The Economics of Welfare Standards in Antitrust. In: Competition Policy International, Vol. 2, Autumn 2006.

Farrell, Joseph/Klemperer, Paul (2007): Coordination and Lock-In: Competition with Switching Costs and Network Effects. In: Armstrong, Mark/ Porter,

Robert H. (eds.): Handbook of Industrial Organization, Vol. 3, Amsterdam et al.: Elsevier, pp. 1970-2072.

Farrell, Joseph/ Saloner, Garth (1992): Converters, Compatibility, and the Control of Interfaces. In: Journal of Industrial Economics, Vol. 40, pp. 9-36.

Farrell, Joseph/ Saloner, Garth (1985): Standardization, Compatibility, and Innovation. In: The RAND Journal of Economics, Vol. 16, pp. 70-83.

Farrell, Joseph/ Shapiro, Carl (2007): Improving Critical Loss Analysis. University of California at Berkeley, Competition Policy Center, Paper CPC07-079, online available at http://repositories.cdlib.org/iber/cpc/CPC07-079 (last visit 2009-10-22).

Farrell, Joseph/ Shapiro, Carl (2004): Intellectual Property, Competition, and Information Technology. Working Paper No. CPC04-45, University of California, Berkely, CA. Online available at http://iber.berkeley.edu/cpc/pubs/Publications.html (last visit 2009-10-11).

Farrell, Joseph und Carl Shapiro (1990): Horizontal Mergers: An Equilibrium Analysis. In: American Economic Review, Vol. 80, pp. 107-126.

First, Harry (2008): Netscape is Dead: Remedy Lessons from the Microsoft Litigation. Law & Economics Research Paper Series, Working Paper No. 08-49, New York. Online available at http://ssrn.com/abstract=1260803 (last visit 2009-09-07).

First, Harry (2007): Controlling the Intellectual Property Grab: Protect Innovation, Not Innovators. In: Rutgers Law Journal, Vol. 38, pp.365-398.

First, Harry (2006): Microsoft and the Evolution of the Intellectual Property Concept. In: Wisconsin Law Review, Vol. 2006, pp. 1369-1432.

Fox, Eleanor (2008): Microsoft (EC) and Duty to Deal: Exceptionality and the Transatlantic Divide. In: Competition Policy International, Vol. 4, pp. 25-32.

Fox, Eleanor (2005): Is there Life in Aspen after Trinko? The Silent Revolution of Section 2 of the Sherman Act. In: Antitrust Law Journal, Vol 73, pp. 153-169.

Friedman, David D./ Landes, William M./ Posner, Richard A. (1991): Some Economics of Trade Secret Law. In: Journal of Economic Perspectives, Vol. 5, pp. 61-72.

Frischmann, Brett (2007): Evaluating the Demsetzian Trend in Copyright Law. In: Review of Law and Economics, Vol. 3, pp. 649-677. Online available at http://www.bepress.com/rle/vol3/iss3/art2/ (last visit 2009-10-01).

Furubotn, Eirik G./ Pejovich, Svetozar (1972): Property Rights and Economic Theory: A Survey of Recent Literature. In: Journal of Economic Literature, Vol. 10, pp. 1137-1162.

Gallini, Nancy T. (1992): Patent Policy and Costly Imitation. In: The RAND Journal of Economics, Vol. 23, pp. 52-63.

Gallini, Nancy T./ Scotchmer, Suzanne (2002): Intellectual Property: When is the Best Incentive System. In: Jaffe, Adam/ Lerner, Joshua/ Stern, Scott (eds): Innovation Policy and the Economy, Vol. 2. Cambridge, Mass.: MIT Press, pp. 51-78.

Gallini, Nancy T./ Trebilcock Michael J. (1998): Intellectual Property Rights and Competition Policy: A Framework for the Analysis of Economic and Legal Issues. In: Anderson, Robert D./ Gallini, Nancy T. (eds.): Competition Policy and Intellectual Property Rights in the Knowledge-Based Economy, Calgary, Canada: University of Calgary Press, pp. 17-61.

Garud, Raghu/ Kumaraswamy, Arun (1993): Changing Competitive Dynamics in Network Industries: An Exploration of Sun Microsystems' Open System Strategy. In: Strategic Management Journal, Vol. 5, pp. 351-369.

Geradin, Damien (2009): Pricing Abuses by Essential Patent Holders in a Standard-Setting Context: A View from Europe. In: Antitrust Law Journal, Vol. 76, pp. 329-357.

Gerber, David J. (1998): Law and Competition in Twentieth Century Europe: Protecting Prometheus. Clarendon, Oxford: Oxford University Press.

Geroski, Paul (1998): Markets for Technology: Knowledge, Innovation and Appropriability. In: Stoneman, Paul (ed.): Handbook of the Economics of Innovation and Technological Change. Reprinted edition, Oxford, UK: Blackwell Publishers, pp. 90-131.

Gifford, Daniel (2003): Antitrust's Troubled Relations with Intellectual Property. In: Minnesota Law Review, Vol. 87, pp. 1695-1718.

Gilbert, Richard J. (2007): Holding Innovation to an Antitrust Standard. In: Competition Policy International, Vol. 3, pp. 47-77.

Gilbert, Richard J. (2006a): Looking Mr. Schumpeter: Where Are We in the Competition-Innovation Debate? In: Jaffe, Adam B./ Lerner, Josh/ Stern, Scott (eds.): Innovation Policy and the Economy, Vol. 6, Cambridge, Mass.: MIT Press, pp. 159-215.

Gilbert, Richard J. (2006b): Competition and Innovation. In: Journal of Industrial Organization Education, Vol. 1, Article 1.

Gilbert, Richard J./ Newbery, David M.G. (1982): Preemptive Patenting and the Persistence of Monopoly. In: The American Economic Review, Vol. 72, pp. 514-526.

Gilbert, Richard J./ Shapiro, Carl (1996): An Economic Analysis of Unilateral Refusals to License Intellectual Property. In: Proceedings of the National Academy of Sciences of the United States of America, Vol.93, pp. 12749-12755.

Gilbert, Richard J./ Shapiro, Carl (1990): Optimal Patent Length and Breadth. In: The RAND Journal of Economics, Vol. 21, pp. 106-112.

Gilbert, Richard J./Weinschel, Alan J. (2007): Competition Policy for Intellectual Property Rights: Balancing Competition and Reward. Working Paper, Berkely, CA. Online available at http://iber.berkeley.edu/cpc/pubs/Publications.html (last visit 2009-10-18).

Gitter, Donna M. (2003): The Conflict in the European Community between Competition Law and Intellectual Property Rights: A Call for Legislative Clarification of the Essential Facilities Doctrine. In: American Business Law Journal, Vol. 40, pp. 217-300.

Goyder, Daniel G. (2003): EC Competition Law. 4th edition, Oxford, UK: University Press.

Gordon, Wendy J. (1993): A Property Right in Self-Expression: Equality and Individualism in the Natural Law of Intellectual Property. In: The Yale Law Journal, Vol. 102, pp. 1533-1609.

Gordon, Wendy J. (1992): Of Harms and Benefits: Torts, Restitution and Intellectual Property. In: Journal of Legal Studies, Vol. 21, pp. 449-482.

Gordon, Wendy J. (1989): An Inquiry into the Merits of Copyright: The Challenges of Consistency, Consent, and Encouragement Theory. In: Stanford Law Review, Vol. 41, pp. 1343-1469.

Grant, Robert M. (1991): The Resourced-based Theory of Competitive Advantage: Implications for Strategy Formulation. In: California Management Review, Vol 33, pp. 114-135.

Green, Jerry R./ Scotchmer, Suzanne (1995): On the Division of Profit in Sequential Innovation. In: The RAND Journal of Economics, Vol. 26, pp. 20-33.

Greenstein, Shane/ Ramey, Garey (1998): Market Structure, Innovation and Vertical Product Differentiation. In: International Journal of Industrial Organization, Vol. 16, pp. 285-311.

Griliches, Zvi (1992): The Search for R&D Spillovers. In: Scandinavian Journal of Economics, Vol. 94, Supplement, pp. 29-47.

Gutermuth, Axel (2009): Article 82 Guidance: A Closer Look at the Analytical Framework and the Paper's likely Impact on European Enforcement Practice. In: Global Competition Policy, February 2009.

Gwartney, Troy L. (2009): Harmonzing the Exclusionary Right of Patents with Compulsory Licensing. In: William & Mary Law Review, Vol. 50, pp. 1395-1438.

Harabi, Najib (1995): Appropriability of technical innovation – an empirical analysis. In: Research Policy, Vol. 24, pp. 981-992.

Harhoff, Dietmar/ Hall, Bronwyn H./ Graevenitz, Georg von/ Hoisl, Karin/ Wagner, Stefan/ Gambardella, Alfonso/ Giuri, Paola (2007): The strategic use of patents and its implications for enterprise and competition policies.

Report ENTR/05/82 for DG Enterprise, European Commission. Online available at http://www.en.inno-tec.bwl.uni-muenchen.de/research/proj/ laufendeprojekte/patents/stratpat2007.pdf (last visit 2010-08-03).

Harper, David A. (1996): Entrepreneurship and the Market Process: An Enquiry into the Growth of Knowledge. London: Routledge.

Hayek, Friedrich A. von (1978): Competition as a Discovery Procedure. In: Hayek, Friedrich A.: New Studies in Philosophy, Politics, Economics and the History of Ideas. London: Routledge & Kegan Paul, pp. 179-190.

Hayek, Friedrich A. von (1960): The Constitution of Liberty. London: Routledge & Kegan Paul.

Heinemann, Andreas (2001): Immaterialgüterschutz in der Wettbewerbsordnung: Eine grundlagenorientierte Untersuchung zum Kartellrecht des geistigen Eigentums. Tübingen: Mohr Siebeck.

Heller, Micheal A./ Eisenberg, Rebecca S. (1998): Can Patents Deter Innovation? The Anticommons in Biomedical Research. In: Science, Vol. 280, pp. 698-701.

Hellström, Per/ Maier-Rigaud, Frank/ Bulst, Friedrich Wenzel (2009): Remedies in European Antitrust Law. In: Antitrust Law Journal, Vol. 76, pp. 43-63.

Henisz, Witold J. (2000): The Institutional Environment for Economic Growth. In: Economics and Politics, Vol. 12, pp. 1-31.

Heyer, Kenneth (2006): Welfare Standards and Merger Analysis: Why not the Best? Discussion Paper EAG 06-8. Online available at http://ssrn.com/abstract=959454 (last visit 2008-12-05)

Hicks, John R. (1935): Annual Survey of Economic Theory: The Theory of Monopoly. In: Econometrica, Vol. 3, pp. 1-20.

Horowitz, Steven J. (2005): Rethinking Lockean Copyright and Fair Use. In: Deakin Law Review, Vol. 10, pp. 209-232.

Horstman, Ignatius/ MacDonald, Glenn M./ Slivinski, Alan (1985): Patents as Information Transfer Mechanisms: To Patent or (Maybe) Not to Patent. In: The Journal of Political Economy, Vol. 93, pp. 837-858.

Hovenkamp, Herbert (2008): Restraints on Innovation. In: Cardozo Law Review, Vol. 29, pp. 247-260.

Hovenkamp, Herbert (2007): Signposts of Anticompetitive Exclusion: Restraints on Innovation and Economics of Scale. In: Hawk, Barry E. (ed.): Annual Proceedings of the Fordham Competition Law Institute: International Antitrust Law & Policy 2006. New York: Juris Publishing, pp. 409-431.

Hovenkamp, Herbert (2005): Exclusion and the Sherman Act. In: The University of Chicago Law Review, Vol. 72, pp. 147-164.

Hovenkamp, Herbert/ Janis, Mark D./ Lemley Mark A. (2005): Unilateral Refusals to License in the U.S.. Working Paper No. 303, Stanford.

Howarth, David/ McMahon (2008): "Windows has Performed an Illegal Operation": the Court of First Instance's Judgement in Microsoft v Commission. In: European Competition Law Review, Vol. 29, pp. 117-134.

Hughes, Justin (1988): The Philosophy of Intellectual Property. In: Georgetown Law Journal, Vol. 77, pp. 287-366.

Hurmelinna-Laukkanen, Pia/ Puumalainen, Kaisu (2007): Nature and Dynamics of Appropriability: Strategies for Appropriating Returns on Innovation. In: R&D Management, Vol. 37, pp. 95-112.

Hurt, Robert M./ Schuchman, Robert M. (1966): The Economic Rationale of Copyright. In: The American Economic Review, Vol. 56, pp. 421-432.

Hussinger, Katrin (2006): Is Silence Golden? Patents versus Secrecy at the Firm Level. In: Economics of Innovation and New Technology, Vol. 15, pp. 735-752.

Hylton, Keith N. (2008): Unilateral Refusals to Deal and the Antitrust Modernization Commission Report. In: The Antitrust Bulletin, Vol. 53, pp. 623-641.

Janssens, Thomas (2009): The Commission Guidance on Predation: A Cautious Step in the Right Direction? In: Global Competition Policy, February 2009.

Jefferson, Thomas (1854): Letter from Thomas Jefferson to Isaac McPherson, August 13, 1831. In: Writings from Thomas Jefferson, Vol. 6, Washington D.C. 1853-1854.

Jensen, Paul H./ Webster, Elizabeth (2006): Managing Knowledge Flows through Appropriation and Learning Strategies. Melbourne Institute Working Paper No. 6/06. Melbourne. Online available at http://papers.ssrn.com/sol3/papers.cfm?abstract_id=900757 (last visit 2009-11-16).

Jones, Alison/ Sufrin, Brenda (2004): EC Competition Law: Text, Cases, and Materials. 2nd edition, Oxford, UK; New York: Oxford University Press.

Kaestner, Jan (2005): Missbrauch von Immaterialgüterrechten – Europäische Rechtsprechung von Magill bis IMS Health. Munich: C.H. Beck.

Kahn, Alfred E. (1970): The Economics of Regulation: Principles and Institutions, Vol. 1: Economic Principles. New York: John Wiley & Sons.

Kamien, Morton I./ Schwartz, Nancy L. (1989): Market Structure and Innovation. Cambrigde: Cambrigde University Press.

Kant, Immanuel (1895): Fundamental Principles of the Metaphysic of Ethics. London. Cited edition: http://www.netlibrary.com/Details.aspx (last visit 2009-10-01).

Kantzenbach, Erhard (1967): Die Funktionsfähigkeit des Wettbewerbs. 2nd edition, Göttingen: Vandehoeck & Ruprecht.

Kaplow, Louis (1985): Extension of Monopoly Power Through Leverage. In: Columbia Law Review, Vol. 85, pp. 515-556.

Kaplow, Louis (1984): The Patent-Antitrust Intersection: A Reappraisal. In: Harvard Law Review, Vol. 97, pp. 1813-1892.

Kaplow, Louis/ Shapiro, Carl (2007): Antitrust. In: Polinsky, A. Mitchell/ Shavell, Steven (eds.): Handbook of Law and Economics, Volume 2, Amsterdam: Elsevier, pp. 1073-1225.

Kaplow, Louis/ Shavell, Steven (2001): Fairness versus Welfare. In: Harvard Law Review, Vol. 114, pp. 961-1388.

Kash, Don E./ Kingston, William (2001): Patents in World of Complex Technologies. In: Science and Public Policy, Vol. 28, pp. 11-22.

Katz, Ariel (2007): Making Sense of Nonsense: Intellectual Property, Antitrust, and Market Power. In: Arizona Law Review, Vol. 49, pp. 837-909.

Katz, Michael/ Shapiro, Carl (1994): Systems Competition and Network Effects. In: Journal of Economic Perspectives, Vol. 8, pp. 93-115.

Katz, Michael/ Shapiro, Carl (1985): Network Externalities, Competition, and Compatibility. In: American Economic Review, Vol. 75, pp. 424-440.

Katsoulacos, Yannis (2009: Some Critical Comments on the Commission's Guidance Paper on Art. 82 EC. In: Global Competition Policy, February 2009.

Kerber, Wolfgang (2008): Should Competition Law Promote Efficiency? Some Reflections of an Economist on the Normative Foundations of Competition Law. In: Drexl, Josef/ Idot, Laurence/ Moneger, Joel (eds.): Economic Theory and Competition Law. Cheltenham: Edward Elgar. Online available at http://papers.ssrn.com/sol3/papers.cfm?abstract_id=1075265 (last visit 2008-11-12)

Kerber, Wolfgang (2006): Competition, Knowledge, and Institutions. In: Journal of Economic Issues, Vol. 40, pp. 457-463.

Kerber, Wolfgang (1997): Wettbewerb als Hypothesentest: Ein evolutorisches Konzept wissenschaffenden Wettbewerbs. In: von Delhaes, Karl/ Fehl, Ulrich (eds.): Dimensionen des Wettbewerbs. Stuttgart: Lucius & Lucius, pp. 31-78.

Kerber, Wolfgang (1993): Rights, Innovation and Evolution. The Distributional Effects of Different Rights to Innovate. In: Review of Political Economy, Vol. 5, pp. 427-452.

Kerber, Wolfgang/ Saam, Nicole (2001): Competition as a Test of Hypotheses: Simulation of Knowledge-Generating Market Processes. In: Journal of Artificial Societies and Social Simulation, Vol. 4.

Kerber, Wolfgang/ Schmidt, Claudia (2008): Microsoft, Refusal to License Intellectual Property Rights, and the Incentives Balance Test of the EU Commission. Working Paper. Online available at http://ssrn.com/abstract=1297939 (last visit 2008-11-26).

Kerber, Wolfgang/ Schwalbe, Ulrich (2008): Economic Principles of Competition Law. In: Hirsch, Günther/ Montag, Frank/ Säcker, Franz-Jürgen (eds.): Competition Law: European Community Practice and Procedure - Article-by-article Commentary. London: Sweet & Maxwell 2008, pp. 202-393.

Khan, B. Zorina (2002): Study Paper 1a Intellectual Property and Economic Development: Lessons from American and European History. London: Commission on Intellectual Property Rights.

Killick, James (2004): IMS and Microsoft Judged in the Cold Light of IMS. In: The Competition Law Review, Vol. 1, pp. 23-47.

Killick, James/ Komninos, Assimakis (2009): Schizophrenia in the Commission's Article 82 Guidance Paper: Formalism Alongside Increased Recourse to Economic Analysis. In: Global Competition Policy, February 2009.

Kim, Linsu (1998): Crisis Construction and Organizational Learning: Capability Building in Catching-up at Hyundai Motor. In: Organization Science, Vol. 9, pp. 506-521.

Kim, Linsu (1997a): The Dynamics of Samsung's Technological Learning in Semiconductors. In: California Management Review, Vol. 39, pp. 86-100.

Kim, Linsu (1997b): From Imitation to Innovation: The Dynamics of Korea's Technological Learning. Cambridge, MA: Harvard Business School Press.

Kirkwood, John B./ Lande, Robert H. (2008): The Fundamental Goal of Antitrust: Protecting Consumers, Not Increasing Efficiency. Working Paper, online available at http://ssrn.com/abstract=1113927 (last visit 2008-11-14).

Kitch, Edmund W. (1986): Patents: Monopolies or Property Rights? In: Research in Law and Economics, Vol. 8, pp. 31-49.

Kitch, Edmund W. (1977): The Nature and Function of the Patent System. In: Journal of Law and Economics, Vol. 20, pp. 265-290.

Klemperer, Paul (1990): How Broad Should the Scope of Patent Protection Be? In: The RAND Journal of Economics, Vol. 21, pp. 113-130.

Klump, Rainer/ Reichel, Richard (1994): Institutionelle Unsicherheit und wirtschaftliche Entwicklung. In: Jahrbücher für Nationalökonomie und Statistik – Journal of Economics and Statistics, Vol. 213, pp. 440-455.

Knieps, Günter (2008): Wettbewerbsökonomie. 3rd edition, Berlin: Springer.

Knight, Frank H. (1971): Risk, Uncertainty, and Profit. Boston, Massachusetts: Houghton Mifflin.

Kolasky, William J./ Dick, Andrew R. (2003): The Merger Guidelines and the Integration of Efficiency into Antitrust Review of Horizontal Mergers. In: Antrust Law Journal, Vol. 71, pp. 207-251.

Korah, Valentine (2007): An Introductory Guide to EC Competition Law and Practice. 9th edition, Portland and Oxford, Oregon: Hart Publishing.

Körber, Torsten (2007): Wettbewerb in dynamischen Märkten zwischen Innovationsschutz und Machtmissbrauch. In: Wirtschaft und Wettbewerb, Vol. 2007, pp. 1209-1218.

Kremer, Michael (1998): Patent Buyouts: A Mechanism for Encouraging Innovation. In: Quarterly Journal of Economics, Vol. 113, pp. 1137-1167.

Kroes, Neelie (2005): Preliminary Thoughts on Policy Review of Article 82. Speech at the Fordham Corporate Law Institute, New York, 23rd September 2005. Online available at http://europa.eu/rapid/pressReleasesAction.do?reference=SPEECH/05/53 7 (last visit 2010-01-06).

Krueger, Anne O. (1974): The Political Economy of the Rent-Seeking Society. In: American Economic Review, Vol. 64, pp. 291-303.

Kusonaki, Ken/ Nonaka, Ikujiro/Nagata, Akiya (1998): Organizational capabilities in product development of Japanese firms. In: Organization Science, Vol. 9, pp. 699-718.

Laffont, Jean-Jacques / Rey, Patrick/ Tirole, Jean (1998a): "Network Competition: I. Overview and Nondiscriminatory Pricing. In: The RAND Journal of Economics, Vol. 29, pp. 1-37.

Laffont, Jean-Jacques / Rey, Patrick/ Tirole, Jean (1998b): Network Competition: II. Price Discrimination. In: The RAND Journal of Economics, Vol. 29, pp. 38-56.

Lande, Robert H. (1989): Chicago's False Foundation: Wealth Transfers (Not Just Efficiency) Should Guide Antitrust. In: Antitrust Law Journal, Vol.58, pp. 631-644.

Landes, William M./ Posner, Richard A. (1989): An Economic Analysis of Copyright Law. In: The Journal of Legal Studies, Vol. 18, pp. 325-363.

Landes, William M./ Posner, Richard A. (1987): Trademark Law: An Economic Perspective. In: Journal of Law & Economics, Vol. 30, pp. 265-309.

Lang, Thomas (2008): Immaterialgüterrechtliche Lizenzierung und kartellrechtliche Verfahrenskontrolle: eine Untersuchung der Reichweite gemeinschaftskartellrechtlicher Eingriffsbefugnisse in Immaterialgüterrechtspositionen vor dem Hintergrund der schutzrechtsspezifischen wettbewerblichen Ausschließlichkeit. Frankfurt a.M.: Lang.

Langlois, Richard N. (1984): Internal Organization in a Dynamic Context: Some Theoretical Considerations. In: Jussawalla, Meheroo/ Ebenstein, Helene (eds.): Communication and Information Economics: New Perspectives. Amsterdam: North-Holland, pp. 23-49.

Lao, Marina (2007): Defining Exculsionary Conduct under Section 2: The Case for Non-Universal Standards. In: Hawk, Barry E. (ed.): Annual Proceedings of the Fordham Competition Law Institute: International Antitrust Law & Policy 2006. New York: Juris Publishing, pp. 433-468.

Larouche, Pierre (2008): The European Microsoft Case at the Crossroads of Competition Policy and Innovation. TILEC Discussion Paper No. 2008-021, online available at http://ssrn.com/abstract=1140165 (last call 2010-01-04).

Léger, Andréanne (2007): The Role(s) of Intellectual Property Rights for Innovation: A Review of the Empirical Evidence and Implications for Developing Countries. Working Paper, Berlin, online available at http://www.diw.de/deutsch/produkte/publikationen/diskussionspapiere/akt uell/index.jsp (last visit 2007-08-29)

Leibenstein, Harvey (1966): Allocative Efficiency vs. X-Efficiency. In: American Economic Review, Vol. 56, pp. 392-415.

Lemley, Mark A. (2005): Property, Intellectual Property, and Free Riding. In: Texas Law Review, Vol. 83, pp. 1031-1075.

Lemley, Mark A./ McGowan, David (1998): Legal Implication of Network Economics Effects. In: California Law Review, Vol. 86, pp. 479-611.

Lenard, Thomas M. (2001): Creating Competition in the Market for Operating Systems: A Structural Remedy for Microsoft. In: George Mason Law Review, Vol. 9, pp. 803-841.

Lerner, Josh (2002): Patent Protection and Innovation over 150 Years. Cambridge, Massachusetts: National Bureau of Economic Research.

Lévêque, Francoise (2005): Innovation, Leveraging, and Essential Facilities: Interoperability Licensing in the EU Microsoft Case. In: World Competition, Vol. 28, pp. 71-91.

Lévêque, Francoise (2000): The Controversial Choice of Remedies to Cope with Anti-Competitive Behaviour of Microsoft. U.C. Berkeley Law and Economic Working Paper No. 2000-22. Online available at http://escholarship.org/uc/item/6vb0q3r9 (last visit 2009-11-17).

Levin, Richard C./ Klevorick, Alvin K. / Nelson, Richard R./ Winter, Sydney G. (1987): Appropriating the Returns from Industrial Research and Development. In: Brookings Papers on Economic Activity, Vol. 3, pp. 783-831.

Levinson, Robert J./ Romaine, R. Craig/ Salop, Steven C. (2001): The Flawed Fragmentation Critique of Structural Remedies in the Microsoft Case. In: Antitrust Bulletin, Vol. 46, pp. 135-162.

Lianos, Ioannis (2006): Competition Law and Intellectual Property Rights: Is the Property Rights' Approach Right? In: Bell, John/ Kilpatrick, Claire (eds.): Cambridge Yearbook of European Legal Studies, Oxford: Hart Publishing, pp. 153-186.

Lieberman, Marvin B./ Montgomery, David B. (1998): First-Mover (Dis)Advantages: Retrospective and Link with the Resource-Based View. In: Strategic Management Journal, Vol. 19, pp. 1111-1125.

Lieberman, Marvin B./ Montgomery, David B. (1988): First-Mover Advantages. In: Strategic Management Journal, Vol. 9, pp. 41-58.

Liebowitz, Stan J. (2001): An Expansive Pig in a Poke: Estimating the Cost of the District Court's Proposed Breakup of Microsoft. In: George Mason Law Review, Vol. 9, pp. 727-760.

Liebowitz, Stan, J./ Margolis, Stephen E. (1994): Network Externalities: An Uncommon Tragedy. In: The Journal of Economic Perspectives, Vol. 8, pp. 133-150.

Linge, Gisela (2008): Competition Policy, Innovation, and Diversity. Marburg: Tectum.

Lipsky, Abbot B. Jr./ Sidak, J. Gregory (1999): Essential Facilities. In: Stanford Law Review, Vol. 51, pp. 1187-1248.

Lopatka, John E./ Page, William H. (2001): Devising a Microsoft Remedy that Serves Consumers. In: George Mason Law Review, Vol. 9, pp. 691-726.

Loury, Glenn C. (1979): Market Structure and Innovation. In: The Quarterly Journal of Economics, Vol. 93, pp. 395-410.

Lowe, Philip (2009): The European Commission Formulates its Enforcement Priorities as Regards Exclusionary Conduct by Dominant Undertakings. In: Global Competition Policy, February 2009.

Lueck, Dean/ Micelli, Thomas (2007): Property Law. In: Polinsky, A. Mitchell/ Shavell, Steven (eds.): Handbook of Law and Economics, Vol. 1. Oxford, UK: Elsevier, pp. 183-257.

Lunney, Glynn S. (1996): Reexamining Copyright's Incentives-Access Paradigm. In: Vanderbilt Law Review, Vol. 49, pp. 483-656.

Machlup, Fritz (1958): An Economic Review of the Patent System. Washington: US Government Printing Office.

Machlup, Fritz (1952): The Political Economy of Monopoly: Business, Labour and Government Policies. Baltimore: Hopkins Press.

Machlup, Fritz/ Penrose, Edith (1950): The Patent Controversy in the Nineteenth Century. In: The Journal of Economic History, Vol. 10, pp. 1-29.

Mahoney, Paul G. (2001): The Common Law and Economic Growth: Hayek might be right. In: Journal of Legal Studies, Vol. 30, pp. 503-525

Mansfield, Edwin (1986): Patents and Innovation: An Empirical Study. In: Management Science, Vol. 32, pp. 173-181.

Mansfied, Edwin/ Schwartz, Mark/ Wagner, Samuel (1981): Imitation Costs and Patents: An Empirical Study. In: The Economic Journal, Vol. 91, pp. 907-918.

Mansfield, Edwin/ Rapoport, John/ Romeo, Anthony/ Wagner, Samuel/ Beardsley, George (1977): Social and Private Rates of Return from Industrial Innovation. In: Quarterly Journal of Economics, Vol. 91, pp. 221-240.

Marengo, Luigi/ Vezzoso, Simonetta (2006): Dynamic Inefficiencies of Intellectual Property Rights from an Evolutionary/ Problem-Solving Perspective: Some Insights on Computer Software and Reverse Engineering. In: Proceedings International Schumpeter Conference, Nice, France. Online available at http://eprints.biblio.unitn.it/archive/00001017/ (last visit 2008-06-11).

Matutes, Carmen/ Regibeau, Pierre/ Rockett, Katharine (1996): Optimal Patent Design and the Diffusion of Innovations. In: The RAND Journal of Economics, Vol. 27, pp. 60-83.

Max Planck Institute for Intellectual Property Rights, Competition and Tax Law [MPI] (2006): Comments on the DG Competition Discussion Paper on the Application of Article 82 of the EC Treaty to Exclusionary Abuses. Discussion Paper, Munich, online available at: http://www.ip.mpg.de/shared/data/pdf/comment1.pdf (last visit 2008-11-18).

McCullen, Sharon B. (2001): The Federal Circuit and Ninth Circuit Face-Off: Does a Patent Holder Violate the Sherman Act by Unilateral Excluding Others from a Patented Invention in More than One Relevant Market? In: Temple Law Review, Vol. 74, pp. 469-505.

McGowan, David (2004): Copyright Nonconsequentialism. In: Missouri Law Review, Vol. 69, pp. 1-72.

Melamed, A. Douglas (2009): Afterword: The Purposes of Antitrust Remedies. In: Antitrust Law Journal, Vol. 76, pp. 361-368.

Melamed, A. Douglas (2005): Exclusionary Conduct under the Antitrust Laws: Balancing, Sacrifice, and Refusals to Deal. In: Berkeley Technology Law Journal, Vol. 22, pp. 1247-1267.

Melamed, A. Douglas/ Stoeppelwerth, Ali M. (2002): The CSU Case: Facts, Formalism and the Intersection of Antitrust and Intellectual Property Law. In: George Mason Law Review, Vol. 10, pp. 407-427.

Menell, Peter (2000): Intellectual Property – General Theories. In: Boudewijn, Bouckaert/ de Geest, Gerrit (eds): Encyclopedia of Law & Economics: Volume II, Cheltenham, UK: Edward Elgar, pp. 129-188.

Menell, Peter S. (1987): Tailoring Legal Protection for Computer Software. In: Stanford Law Review, Vol. 39, pp. 1329-1372.

Merges, Robert P./ Nelson, Richard R. (1990): On the Complex Economics of Patent Scope. In: Columbia Law Review, Vol. 90. pp. 839-916.

Metcalfe, J. Stanley (1998): Evolutionary Economics and Creative Destruction. London: Routledge.

Moore, Adam D. (1997): A Lockean Theory of Intellectual Property. In: Hamline Law Review, Vol. 21, pp. 65-108.

Montagani, Maria Lillà (2007): Remedies to Exclusionary Innovation in the High-Tech Sector: Is there a Lesson from the Microsoft Saga? In: World Competition, Vol. 30, pp. 623-643.

Monti, Mario (2001): The Future of Competition Policy in the European Union. Speech at the Merchant Taylor's Hall, 9 July 2001. Online available at http://europa.eu.int/rapid/start/cgi/guesten.ksh?p_action.getfile=gf&doc=S PEECH/01/340/0/AGED&lg=EN&type=PDF (last visit 2008-11-14).

Moser, Petra (2009): Why Don't Inventors Patent? Working Paper, Stanford. Online available at http://ssrn.com/abstract=930241 (last visit 2009-07-21).

Moser, Petra (2005): How Do Patent Laws Influence Innovation? Evidence from the Nineteenth Centuries World Fairs. In: The American Economic Review, Vol. 95, pp. 1214-1236.

Motta, Massimo (2009): The European Commission's Guidance Communication on Article 82. In: European Competition Law Review, Vol. 30, pp. 593-599.

Motta, Massimo (2004): Competition Policy: Theory and Practice. Cambridge, MA: University Press.

Mowery, David C./ Oxley, Joanne E. (1995): Inward Technology Transfer and Competitiveness: The Role of National Innovation Systems. In: Cambridge Journal of Economics, Vol. 19, pp. 67-93.

Müller, Ulf/ Rodenhausen, Anselm (2008): The Rise and Fall of the Essential Facility Doctrine. In: European Competition Law Review, Vol. 29, pp. 310-329.

Nelson, Richard R./ Winter, Sidney G. (1982): An Evolutionary Theory of Economic Change. Cambridge.

Neumann, Manfred (2001): Competition Policy. Cheltenham, UK: Edward Elgar.

Nicita, Antonio/ Ramello, Giovanni B. (2007): Property, Liability, and Market Power: The Antitrust Side of Market Power. In: Review of Law and Economics, Vol. 3, Article 7. Available at: http://www.bepress.com/rle/vol3/iss3/art7 (last visit 2008-11-24).

Niels, Gunnar (2009): Abuse and Monopolization: Unilateral Conduct by Two Competition Authorities? In: Global Competition Policy, February 2009.

Nordhaus, William D. (1972): The Optimal Life of the Patent: Reply. In: American Economic Review, Vol. 62, pp. 428-431.

Nordhaus, William D. (1969): Invention, Growth and Welfare: A Theoretical Treatment of Technological Change. Cambridge, Massachusetts: MIT Press.

North, Douglas C. (2005): Understanding the Process of Economic Change. Princeton: Princeton University Press.

Novos, Ian E./ Waldman, Michael (1984): The Effects of Increased Copyright Protection: An Analytic Approach. In: Journal of Political Economy, Vol. 92, pp. 236-246.

Oddi, A. Sammuel (1996): Un-Unified Economic Theories of Patents - the Not-Quite-Holy Grail. In: Notre Dame Law Review, Vol. 71, pp. 267-327.

O'Donoghue, Ted/ Scotchmer, Suzanne/ Thisse, Jacques-Francois(1998): Patent Breadth, Patent Life, and the Pace of Technological Progress. In: Journal of Economics and Management, Vol. 7, pp. 1-32.

Ohly, Ansgar (2007): Geistiges Eigentum und Wettbewerbsrecht – Konflikt oder Symbiose? In: Oberender, Peter (ed.): Wettbewerb und Geistiges Eigentum. Berlin, pp. 47-68.

Organization for Economic Co-operation and Development [OECD] (1996): Competition Policy and Efficiency Claims in Horizontal Agreements. In: OECD/GD (96) 65, Paris.

Padilla, A. Jorge (2005): Efficiencies in Horizontal Mergers: Williamson Revisited. Working Paper, online available at http://ssrn.com/abstract=812989 (last visit 2009-10-22).

Page, William H./ Childers, Seldon J. (2009): Measuring Compliance with Compulsory Licensing Remedies in the American *Microsoft* Case. In: Antitrust Law Journal, Vol. 76, pp. 239-269.

Palmer, Tom G. (1989): Intellectual Property: A Non-Posnerian Law and Economic Approach. In: Hamline Law Review, Vol. 12, pp. 261-304.

Pate, R. Hewitt (2002): Refusals to Deal and Intellectual Property Rights. In: George Mason Law Review, Vol. 10, pp. 429-442.

Patel, Pari/ Pavitt, Keith (1995): Patterns of Technological Activity: their Measurement and Interpretation. In: Stoneman, Paul (ed.): Handbook of the Economics of Innovation and Technological Change. Oxford, UK: Blackwell, pp. 15-51.

Penrose, Edith (1959): The Theory of the Growth of the Firm. London: Basil Blackwell.

Peritz, Rudolph (2004): Re-Thinking U.S. v. Microsoft in Light of the E.C. Case. New York Law School Research Paper No. 04/05-4. Online available at http://ssrn.com/abstract=571803 (last visit 2009-10-22).

Picker, Randal C. (2002): Pursuing a Remedy in Microsoft: The Declining Need for Centralized Coordination in a Networked World. In: Journal of Institutional and Theoretical Economics, Vol. 158, pp. 113-154.

Pierson, Mattthias/ Ahrens, Thomas/ Fischer, Karsten (2007): Recht des geistigen Eigentums: Patente, Marken, Urheberrechte, Design. München: Vahlen.

Pigou, Arthur C. (1924): The Economics of Welfare. 2nd edition, London: Macimillan and Co.

Plant, Arnold (1934): The Economic Aspects of Copyright in Books. In: Economica, Vol. 1, pp. 167-195.

Png, Ivan P.L. (2006): Copyright: A Plea for Empirical Research. In: Review of Economic Research on Copyright Issues, Vol. 3, pp. 3-13.

Png, Ivan P.L./ Wang, Qiu-hong (2006): Copyright Duration and the Supply of Creative Work: Evidence from the Movies. Working Paper. Online available at http://www.comp.nus.edu.sg/~ipng/research/ (last visit 2009-10-27).

Pollock, Rufus (2009): Forever Minus a Day? Calculating Optimal Copyright Term. In: Review of Economic Research on Copyright Issues, Vol. 6, pp. 35-60.

Pollock, Rufus (2007): Optimal Copyright Term over Time: Technological Change and the Stock of Works. In: Review of Economic Research on Copyright Issues, Vol. 4, pp. 51-64.

Porter, Michael E. (1985): Competitive Advantage. New York: Free Press.

Porter, Michael E. (1981): The Contributions of Industrial Organization to Strategic Management. In: Academy of Management Review, Vol. 6, pp. 609-620.

Porter, Michael (1980): Competitive Strategy. New York: Free Press.

Posner, Richard A. (2002): The Law & Economics of Intellectual Property. In: Daedalus, Vol. 131, pp. 5-12.

Posner, Richard A. (2001): Antitrust law. 2nd edition (of Antitrust Law: An Economic Perspective), Chicago: University of Chicago Press.

Posner, Richard A. (1976): Antitrust Law: An Economic Perspective. Chicago: University of Chicago Press.

Pyndick, Robert S./ Rubinfeld, Daniel L. (2005): Microeconomics. 6th edition, London: Prentice Hall.

Radin, Margaret Jane (1982): Property and Personhood. In: Stanford Law Review, Vol. 34, pp. 957-1015.

Reed, Richard/DeFillipi, Robert J. (1990): Causal Ambiguity, Barriers to Imitation and Sustaibable Competitive Advantage. In: Academy of Management Review, Vol. 15, pp. 88-102.

Régibeau, Pierre/ Rockett, Katharine (2004): The Relationship Between Intellectual Property Law and Competition Law: An Economic Approach. In: Anderman, Steven D. (ed.): Intellectual Property Rights and Competition Policy. Cambridge, pp. 505-552.

Reinganum, Jennifer F. (1983): Uncertain Innovation and the Persistence of Monopoly. In: The American Economic Review, Vol. 73, pp. 741-748.

Richardson, Megan/ Gans, Joshua/ Hanks, Frances/ Williams, Philip (2000): The Benefits and Costs of Copyright: An Economic Perspective. Redfern: Centre for Copyright Studies Ltd.

Rocket, Katharine (2008): Property Rights and Invention. Working Paper. Essex, UK. Forthcoming in Hall, Bronwyn/ Rosenberg, Nathan (eds.): Handbook for Economics and Technical Change.

Röller, Lars-H. (2005): Der ökonomische Ansatz in der europäischen Wettbewerbspolitik. In: Monopolkommission (ed.): Zukunftsperspektiven der Wettbewerbspolitik: Colloquium anlässlich des 30-jährigen Bestehens der Monopolkommission am 5. November 2004 in der Humboldt-Universität zu Berlin, Baden-Baden, pp. 37-47.

Röpke, Jochen (1977): Die Strategie der Innovation. Tübingen: J.C.B. Mohr (Paul Siebeck).

Rosenberg, Nathan (1982): Inside the Black Box: Technology and Economics. Cambridge, MA: Cambridge University Press.

Rothaermel, Frank T./ Hill, Charles W.L. (2005): Technological Discontinuities and Complementary Assets: A Longitudinal Study of Industry and Firm Performance. In: Organization Science, Vol. 16, pp. 52-70.

Rubin, Jonathan L. (2005): The Truth about Trinko. In: Antitrust Bulletin, Vol. 20, pp. 1-13.

Rubinfeld, Daniel L./ Maness, Robert (2005): The Strategic Use of Patents: Implications for Antitrust. In: Leveque, Francois/ Shelanski, Howard (eds.): Antitrust, Patents and Copyright: EU and US Perspectives, Cheltenham: Edward Elgar Publishing Ltd., pp.85-102.

Rule, Charles F./ Meyer, David L. (1988): An Antitrust Enforcement Policy to Maximize the Economic Wealth of All Consumers. In: Antitrust Bulletin, Vol. 33, pp. 677-712.

Rumelt, Richard P. (1984): Towards a strategic theory of the firm. In: Lamb, Robert B. (ed.): Competitive Strategic Management. Englewood-Cliffs, NJ: Prentice-Hall, pp. 556-570.

Ruttan, Vernon M. (1997): Induced Innovation, Evolutionary Theory and Path Dependence: Sources of Technological Change. In: The Economic Journal, Vol. 107, pp. 1520-1529.

Saloner, Garth (1990): Economic Issues in Computer Interface Standardization. In: Economics of Innovation and New Technology, Vol. 1, pp. 135-156.

Salop, Steven C. (2006): Exclusionary Conduct, Effect on Consumers, and the Flawed Profit-Sacrifice Test. In: Antitrust Law Journal, Vol. 73, pp. 311-374.

Salop, Steven C. (2005): Question: What is the Real and Proper Antitrust Welfare Standard? Answer: The True Consumer Welfare Standard. Presentation before the Antitrust Modernization Commission, 4.11.2005. Online available at http://govinfo.library.unt.edu/amc/public_studies_fr28902/exclus_conduct_pdf/051104_Salop_Mergers.pdf (last visit 2009-10-22).

Samuelson, Paul A./ Nordhaus, William d. (2005): Microeconomics. 18th edition, Boston, Massachusetts: McGraw-Hill/ Irwin.

Samuelson, Pamela/ Scotchmer, Suzanne (2002): The Law and Economics of Reverse Engineering. In: The Yale Law Journal, Vol. 111, pp. 1575-1663.

Saviotti, Pier Paolo (1998): On the dynamics of appropriability, of tacit and of codified knowledge. In: Research Policy, Vol. 26, pp. 843-856.

Scherer, Frederic M. (1980): Industrial Market Structure and Economic Performance. 2nd edition, Chicago : McNally.

Scherer, Frederic M. (1972): Nordhaus' Theory of Optimal Patent Life: A Geometric Reinterpretation. In: The American Economic Review, Vol. 62, pp. 422-427.

Scherer, Frederic M./ Ross, David (1990): Industrial Market Structure and Economic Performance. 3rd edition, Boston, Massachusetts et al.: Houghton Mifflin.

Schmalensee, Richard (1982): Product Differentiation Advantages of Pioneering Brands. In: American Economic Review, Vol. 72, pp. 349-365.

Schmalensee, Richard (1974): Brand Loyalty and Barriers to Entry. In: Southern Economic Journal, Vol. 40, pp. 579-588.

Schmidt, André/ Voigt, Stephan (2006): Der "more economic approach" in der Missbrauchsaufsicht: Einige kritische Anmerkungen zu den Vorschlägen der General-direktion Wettbewerb. In: Wirtschaft und Wettbewerb, Vol. 56, pp. 1097-1106.

Schmidtchen, Dieter (2007): Die Beziehung zwischen dem Wettbewerbsrecht und dem Recht des geistigen Eigentums – Konflikt, Harmonie oder Arbeitsteilung? In: Oberender, Peter (ed.): Wettbewerb und geistiges Eigentum. Berlin: Duncker & Humblot, pp. 9-46.

Schumpeter, Joseph (1942): Capitalism, Socialism, and Democracy. 3rd edition, London : Allen & Unwin.

Schumpeter, Joseph (1934): The Theory of Economic Development: An Inquiry into Profits, Capital, Credit, Interest, and the Business Cycle. Cambridge, Massachusetts: Harvard University Press.

Schwalbe, Ulrich/ Zimmer, Daniel (2006): Kartellrecht und Ökonomie: Moderne ökonomische Ansätze in der europäischen und deutschen Zusammenschlusskontrolle. Frankfurt a.M.: Verlag Recht und Wirtschaft.

Schweitzer, Heike (2007): Controlling the Unilateral Exercise of Intellectual Property Rights: A Multitude of Approaches but No Way Ahead? The Transatlantic Search for a New Approach. EUI Law Working Paper No. 2007/31, online available at http://ssrn.com/abstract=1093243 (last visit 09/09/2008).

Scopelliti, Alessandro Diego (2010): The Interaction between Antitrust and Intellectual Property : the Interoperability Issue in the Microsoft Europe Case. Warwick Economic Research Paper No. 924, online available at http://d.repec.org/n?u=RePEc:wrk:warwec:924&r=com (last visit 2010-01-22)

Scotchmer, Suzanne (2004): Innovation and Incentives. Cambridge, MA: MIT Press.

Scotchmer, Suzanne (1999): On the Optimality of the Patent Renewal System. In: RAND Journal of Economics, Vol. 30, pp. 181-196.

Scotchmer, Suzanne (1991): Standing on the Shoulders of Giants: Cumulative Research and the Patent Law. In: The Journal of Economic Perspectives, Vol. 5, pp. 29-41.

Scully, Gerald W. (1997). Rule and Policy Spaces and Economic Progress: Lessons for Third World Countries. In: Public Choice, Vol. 90, pp. 311-324.

Shapiro, Carl (2001): Navigating the Patent Thicket: Cross Licenses, Patent Pools, and Standard Setting. In: Jaffe, Adam B./ Lerner, Josh/ Stern, Scott (eds.): Innovation Policy and the Economy No. 1, Cambridge, Massachusetts, pp. 119 -150

Shapiro, Carl (1999): Exclusivity in Network Industries. In: George Mason Law Review, Vol. 7, pp. 673-683

Shapiro, Carl/Varian, Hal (1999): Information Rules: A Strategic Guide to the Network Economy. Boston, Massachusetts: Harvard Business School Press.

Shelanski, Howard A./ Sidak, J. Gregory (2001): Antitrust Divestiture in Network Industries. In: The University of Chicago Law Review, Vol. 68, pp. 1-99.

Sher, Brian (2009: Leveraging Non-Contestability: Exclusive Dealing and Rebates under the Commission's Article 82 Guidance. In: Global Competition Policy, February 2009.

Solow, Robert M. (1957): Technical Change and the Aggregate Production Function. In: The Review of Economics and Statistics, Vol. 39, pp. 312-320.

Spence, A. Michael (1984):Cost Reduction, Competition and Industry Performance. In: Econometrica, Vol. 52, pp. 368-402.

Spulber, Daniel F. (2008): Competition Policy and the Incentive to Innovate: The Dynamic Effects of Microsoft v. Commission. In: Yale Journal on Regulation, Vol. 25, pp. 247-301.

Stephan, Michael (2003): Technologische Diversifikation von Unternehmen: Resourcentheoretische Untersuchung der Determinanten. Wiesbaden: Deutscher Universitäts-Verlag.

Sterk, Stewart E. (1996): Rhetoric and Reality in Copyright Law. In: Michigan Law Review, Vol. 94, pp. 1197-1249.

Stigler, George (1968): The Organization of Industry. Chicago: The University of Chicago Press.

Stigler, George (1952): The Case Against Big Business. In: Fortune, Vol. 45, May, pp. 123-167.

Stratakis, Alexandros (2006): Comparative Analysis of the US and EU Approach and Enforcement of the Essential Facilities Doctrine. In: European Competition Law Review, Vol. 27, pp. 434-442.

Sullivan, E. Thomas (2002): The Jurisprudence of Antitrust Divestiture: The Pass Less Travelled. In: Minnesota Law Review, Vol. 86, pp. 565-642.

Sullivan, Lawrence A./ Grimes, Warren S. (2006): The Law of Antitrust: An Integrated Handbook. 2nd edition, St. Paul, MN: Thomson West.

Summers, Lawrence (2001): Competition Policy in the New Economy. In: Antitrust Law Journal, Vol. 69, pp. 353-359.

Swann, G. M. Peter (2009): The Economics of Innovation: An Introduction. Cheltenham, UK and Northampton, Massachusetts: Edward Elgar.

Takalo, Tuomas (2001): On the Optimal Patent Policy. In Finnish Economic Papers, Vol. 14, pp. 33-40.

Takalo, Tuomas (1998): Innovation and Imitation under Imperfect Patent Protection. In: Journal of Economics, Vol. 67, pp. 229-241.

Taylor, Christopher T./ Silberston, Z. Aubrey (1973): The Economic Impact of the Patent System: A Study of the British Experience. Cambridge, UK: Cambridge University Press.

Teece, David J. (2006): Reflections on „Profiting from Innovation." In: Research Policy, Vol. 35, pp. 1131-1146.

Teece, David J. (1986): Profiting from technological innovation: Implications for integration, collaboration, licensing and public policy. In: Research Policy, Vol. 15. pp. 285-305.

Teece, David J. (1984): Economic Analysis and Strategic Management. In: California Management Review, Vol. 26, pp. 87-110.

Teece, David J. (1982): Towards and Economic Theory of the Multiproduct Firm. In: Journal of Economic Behavior and Organization, Vol. 3, pp. 39-63.

Teece, David J./ Pisano, Gary (1994): The Dynamic Capabilities of Firms: an Introduction. In: Industrial and Corporate Change, Vol. 3, pp. 537-556.

Teece, David J./ Pisano, Gary/ Shuen, Amy (1997): Dynamic Capabilities and Strategic Management. In: Strategic Management Journal, Vol. 18, pp. 509-533.

Thyri, Peter (2005): Immaterialgüterrechte und Zugang zur wesentlichen Einrichtung: Der Fall Microsoft im Lichte von IMS-Health. In: Wirtschaft und Wettbewerb 2005, pp. 388-399.

Tirole, Jean (1997): The Theory of Industrial Organization. Cambrigde, MA: MIT Press.

Towse, Ruth/ Handke, Christian/ Stepan, Paul (2008): The Economics of Copyright Law: A Stocktake of the Literature. In: Review of Economic Research on Copyright Issues, Vol. 5, pp. 1-22.

Towse, Ruth/ Holzhauer, Rudi (2002): Introduction. In: Towse, Ruth/ Holzhauer, Rudi (eds.): The Economics of Intellectual Property, Vol. I, Cheltenham/ Northampton, pp. ix-xxxii.

Tyerman, Barry W. (1971): The Economic Rational for Coypright Protection for Published Books: A Reply to Professor Breyer. In: UCLA Law Review, Vol. 18, pp. 1100-1125.

Ullrich, Hanns (1996): Lizenzkartellrecht auf dem Weg zur Mitte. In: GRUR Int 1996, pp. 555-568.

Van den Berg, Roger J./ Camesasca, Peter D. (2001): European Competition Law and Economics: A Comparative Perspective.

Varian, Hal R. (1992): Microeconomics Analysis. 3rd ed., New York: Norton.

Verheyden, Alexandre/ Desmedt, Yvan (2009): Article 82 Guidelines – Missed Opportunities in the Telecoms Sector. In: Global Competition Policy, February 2009.

Vezzoso, Simonetta (2006): The Incentives Balance Test in the EU Microsoft Case: A Pro-Innovation „Economics-Based" Approach? In: European Competition Law Review, Vol. 27, pp. 382-390.

Viscusi, W. Kip/ Harrington, Joseph E. Jr./ Vernon, John M. (2005): Economics of Regulation and Antitrust. 4th edition, Cambridge, Massachusetts: MIT Press.

Watt, Richard (2004): The Past and the Future of the Economics of Copyright. In: Review of Economic Research on Copyright Issues, Vol. 1, pp. 151-171.

Weber Waller, Spencer (2009): The Past, Present, and Future of Monopolization Remedies. In: Antitrust Law Journal, Vol. 76, pp 13-29.

Weber Waller, Spencer/ Tasch, William (2009): Harmonizing Essential Facilities and Refusals to Deal. Working Paper, Chicago. Online available at http://ssrn.com/abstract=1418081 (last visit 2009-09-16).

Weinreb, Lloyd L. (1998): Copyright for Functional Expression. In: Harvard Law Review, Vol. 111, pp. 1150-1254.

Weiser, Philip J. (2009): Regulating Interoperability: Lessons from AT&T, Microsoft, and Beyond. In: Antitrust Law Journal, Vol. 76, pp. 271-305.

Weitzman, Martin L. (1983): Contestable Markets: An Uprising in the Theory of Industry Structure: Comment. In: The American Economic Review, Vol. 73, pp. 486-487.

Werden, Gregory J. (2009): Remedies for Exclusionary Conduct Should Protect and Preserve the Competitive Process. In: Antitrust Law Journals, Vol. 76, pp. 65-78.

Werden, Gregory J. (2006): Identifying Exclusionary Conduct under Section 2: The "No Economic Sense" Test. In: Antitrust Law Journal, Vol. 73, pp. 413-433.

Werden, Gregory J. (1996): A Robust Test for Consumer Welfare Enhancing Mergers among Sellers of Differentiated Products. In: Journal of Industrial Economics, Vol. 44, pp. 409-413.

Wernerfelt, Birger (1984): A resourced-based view of the firm. In: Strategic Management Journal, Vol. 5, pp. 171-180.

Whinston, Michael D. (1990): Tying, Foreclosure and Exclusion. In: The American Economic Review, Vol. 80, pp. 837-859.

Williamson, Oliver (1968): Economies as an Antitrust Defense: The Welfare Tradeoffs. In: The American Economic Review, Vol. 58, pp. 18-36.

Witt, Ulrich (1987): Indiviudalistische Grundlagen der evolutorischen Ökonomik, Tübingen.

Wright, Donald J. (1999): Optimal Patent Breadth and Length with Costly Imitation. In: International Journal of Industrial Organization, Vol. 17, pp. 419-436.

Yen, Alfred C. (1990): Restoring the Natural Law: Copyright as Labor and Possession. Research Paper 1990-04, Boston, Massachusetts. Online available at http://ssrn.com/abstract=916110 (last visit 2008-11-21).

Zahra, Shaker A. / George, Gerhard (2002): Absorptive Capacity: A Review, Reconceptualization, and Extension, in: Academy of Management Review, Vol. 27, pp. 185-203.

Zohios, Georgios (2009): Commission Guidance Paper on the Application of Art. 82: A Step towards Modernization or a Step Away? In: Global Competition Policy, February 2009.

Schriften zur Politischen Ökonomik
Evolutorische und ökologische Aspekte

Political Economics, Competition and Regulation

Herausgegeben von / Edited by Udo Müller, Oliver Budzinski, Yücel Calbay,
Jörg Jasper und Torsten Sundmacher

Band   1   Jörg Jasper / Torsten Sundmacher (Hrsg.): Ökologische Kompatibilität und technologischer Wandel. 2000.

Band   2   Torsten Sundmacher: Das Umweltinformationsinstrument Ökobilanz (LCA). Anwendungsbezug und instrumentelle Ausgestaltungsmöglichkeiten. 2002.

Band   3   Oliver Budzinski / Jörg Jasper (Hrsg.): Wettbewerb, Wirtschaftsordnung und Umwelt. Festschrift für Udo Müller. 2004.

Band   4   Robert König: Die Elementarschadenversicherung in der Bundesrepublik Deutschland als Element der finanziellen Risikovorsorge gegen Naturereignisse. Diskussion staatlicher Regulierungsoptionen am Fallbeispiel der Hochwasser 2002 unter Berücksichtigung versicherungswirtschaftlicher Präferenzen. 2006.

Band   5   Sven Twelemann: Stromwirtschaft im Spannungsfeld zwischen Wettbewerb und Klimapolitik. Eine Untersuchung am Beispiel des deutschen Strommarktes. 2006.

Band   6   Shin-Yuan Tsai: Globalization Effects on China's Influence on Taiwan Economy. 2007.

Vol.   7   Marina Gruševaja / Christoph Wonke / Ulrike Hösel / Malcolm H. Dunn (Hrsg.): Quo vadis Wirtschaftspolitik? Ausgewählte Aspekte der aktuellen Diskussion. Festschrift für Norbert Eickhof. 2008.

Band   8   Ann Kathrin Buchs: Schutz der Biodiversität durch Benefit-sharing? Das Beispiel pharmazeutischer Bioprospektierung. 2009.

Band   9   Susanna Hübner: Wettbewerbsanalyse des Fernsehsektors. Anforderungen an eine neue Rundfunkordnung aus ordnungspolitischer Sicht. 2009.

Band   10   Arndt Christiansen: Der "More Economic Approach" in der EU-Fusionskontrolle. Entwicklung, konzeptionelle Grundlagen und kritische Analyse. 2010.

Vol.   11   Claudia Schmidt: Refusal to License Intellectual Property Rights as Abuse of Dominance. 2010.

www.peterlang.de

Arndt Christiansen

Der „More Economic Approach" in der EU-Fusionskontrolle

Entwicklung, konzeptionelle Grundlagen und kritische Analyse

Frankfurt am Main, Berlin, Bern, Bruxelles, New York, Oxford, Wien, 2010.
697 S. zahlr. Tab. und Graf.
Evolutorische und ökologische Aspekte.
Verantwortlicher Herausgeber: Oliver Budzinski. Bd. 10
ISBN 978-3-631-59609-8 · geb. € 98,– *

Das Hauptergebnis des Reformprozesses in der EU-Fusionskontrolle stellt der „More Economic Approach" (MEA) dar. In dieser Arbeit werden die wettbewerbsökonomischen Grundlagen des neuen Ansatzes intensiv rezipiert und kritisch gewürdigt. Den oftmals unterbelichteten normativen Implikationen wird ebenfalls breiter Raum eingeräumt. Die damit einhergehende zunehmende Einzelfallanalyse wird aus einer institutionen- und ordnungsökonomischen Perspektive grundsätzlich hinterfragt. Abschließend werden die Wirkungen auf die Entscheidungspraxis untersucht. Im Ergebnis wird gezeigt, dass der MEA in der bisherigen Form zu kurz greift. Geboten erscheint daher eine Weiterentwicklung des Ansatzes mit dem Ziel einer umfassenderen Anwendung von ökonomischer Analyse.

Aus dem Inhalt: Der Reformprozess in der EU-Fusionskontrolle · Die wettbewerbsökonomischen Grundlagen des „More Economic Approach" · Die normativen Implikationen des „More Economic Approach" · Die institutionen- und ordnungsökonomische Perspektive: Einzelfallanalyse versus Regelorientierung · Zusammenfassende Bewertung des MEA und Skizze seiner wünschenswerten Weiterentwicklung

Peter Lang · Internationaler Verlag der Wissenschaften

Frankfurt am Main · Berlin · Bern · Bruxelles · New York · Oxford · Wien
Auslieferung: Verlag Peter Lang AG
Moosstr. 1, CH-2542 Pieterlen
Telefax 00 41 (0)32 / 376 17 27

*inklusive der in Deutschland gültigen Mehrwertsteuer
Preisänderungen vorbehalten
Homepage http://www.peterlang.de